# SON, BUILD ME AN ARMY!

## MY LIFE STORY

# MORRIS CERULLO

Published by
Morris Cerullo World Evangelism
Copyright © 1999
San Diego, California
Printed in the United States of America

Morris Cerullo World Evangelism
P.O. Box 85277
San Diego, CA 92186-5277

Morris Cerullo World Evangelism of Canada
P.O. Box 3600
Concord, Ontario L4K1B6

Morris Cerullo World Evangelism
P.O. Box 277, Hemel Hempstead,
HERTS HP2 7DH

Tel: (858) 277-2200
Web: www.morriscerullo.com
E-mail: morris cerullo@mcwe.com

# TABLE OF CONTENTS

# PREFACE

You hold in your hands the story of the life of a little Jewish orphan boy who found that it doesn't matter who you are, but what matters is what God can make of you.

In the course of writing this book, I have found myself spending many hours making decisions, not on what to include, but what to leave out. The reality is, if I included every detail of my more-than fifty-three years of ministry, I would have to write dozens of books, not just one.

I have seen so many faces, so many salvations, so many healings in the course of my ministry that I literally can't physically commit it all to paper.

What I have written in this book is the most thorough overview of the ministry God has allowed me to participate in for more than fifty-three years. In these pages, I have tried to give you a clear, unobstructed view into my personal life, my thoughts and meditations, and prayers as I have partaken in victories and overcome hurdles.

But most of all, I have tried to paint a clear picture of the incredible power of God – the overriding providence of a Creator Who is so loving, so passionate and so merciful that He would reach into the world and pluck a rebellious boy up into heaven to commission him to use for His own purposes.

My entire life and ministry has been focused around one goal: training people to realize that the ministry God does through me is possible for everyone. God's anointing is not prejudiced; He will use anyone who is willing to be used. God will minister the Gospel through anyone who will surrender themselves to Him and allow Him to operate through them.

As you read this book, keep that in mind; keep in your consciousness that God wants to use this book to inspire you to minister in the arena to which He has called you. God wants you not to look at this book and put me on a pedestal, but to put Him in the center of your heart, the center of your life.

One of the overriding principles of my life has been this:

*"What shall we do, that we might work the works of God?"* (John 6:28)

I'll give you the key right here, in the foreword, before you ever get into the tremendous story of God's power in my life:

*"Also I heard the voice of the Lord, saying, Whom shall I send, and who will go for us? Then said I, Here am I; send me"* (Isaiah 6:8).

Surrender.

Commit yourself to giving yourself to Christ, fully and completely. There is no secret to being used by God. All you have to do is obey Him. All you have to do is what God tells you to do, no matter who tells you you're crazy, no matter who laughs at you, no matter what obstacles seem to be in your way, if you have a single-minded devotion to fulfilling God's will.

If you look at the life of any outstanding character in the Bible, you will find that same dynamic in operation in their life. They all had an intense focus on only one thing: glorifying God through fulfilling His will.

So as you read the story of my life, receive the anointing that God wants to impart into your life – surrender your heart and your life to Him, and let Him make you what He wants you to be.

God bless you.

# Chapter 1

# THE GREATEST MIRACLE

When I heard the bones cracking, I knew this wasn't just another meeting.

Moments earlier, a crippled man had caught my eye. I was on the platform, and, as I preached, I noticed the man lying on the ground, horribly twisted and deformed. He was curled up into a tiny little ball.

This little man's arms were gnarled in toward his stomach. His legs were wrapped up like a pretzel and he looked as if he couldn't move at all. I have never, before that time or, since, seen anyone as horribly deformed as this man. But the reason he had caught my eye was that he indeed had started moving, despite all his deformities.

He was in the front of a crowd of several hundred crippled people and many blind, maimed and deaf people, all who were expecting God to perform a miracle on them.

Some were hideously crippled, bent over canes, and hunched up in wheelchairs, some were unable to even sit upright. Arms were gnarled, legs were shriveled. Eyes were whited out and unseeing. Ears were deformed and unhearing. Fingers were bent painfully over by arthritis that had built up calcium deposits on top of the knuckles, leaving them with huge humps where knuckles should have been.

Tiny children had braces on their legs, their sad parents sitting with eyes that seemed to be pleading for help.

This crowd of needy people was unlike anything I had ever experienced. I was only twenty-seven years old and I had seen many miracles, but the magnitude of so many hundreds of people needing a touch from God took me aback.

I was preaching in Manila, Philippines, the year was 1959, and here I was in front of a crowd of thirty-thousand people, preaching the Gospel, telling the people to expect God to move on their behalf.

I had never expected so many people, though. I had no idea how I could possibly minister to so many.

"God," I had said, "You are going to have to do something, because I'm just a Jew from New Jersey. I can't help these people."

The man who had been lying in front of the platform began to move even more. His legs began to unfurl from their previously twisted positions. His arms began straightening out. And his hideously deformed bones were cracking audibly as God began reconstructing them.

All around this precious man, people began experiencing miracles.

I saw mothers take the braces off their children's legs. I didn't just see one or two, I saw a whole crowd of mothers doing that, shouting to their children to "Walk, in Jesus' Name!"

It was the most amazing thing I had ever seen.

These tiny children would fall as their little crippled legs gave out under the weight of their bodies. Their mothers, undeterred, would lift them up and shout again: "Walk in Jesus' Name!"

The scene was repeated over and over...until one child no longer had to be picked up. His legs straightened themselves up right before our very eyes. He began walking, leaping and spinning as his mother's eyes filled with tears, as she wept and worshipped God.

Then another child was healed. Then another. Then it seemed they all were getting healed.

Crutches began to fly all over the place.

Canes flew through the air as former cripples, who no longer needed them, cast them as far away as they could.

Crutches began to pile up at the front of the platform as people, who once could not walk without leaning on them carried their crutches up to the front and began dumping them.

# The Greatest Miracle

There was a tremendous shriek from the crowd of people. Then a scream.

A man with a shriveled leg looked down in amazement as bones grew, turning his useless leg into an identical match of his good leg.

A woman who was hunched over dropped her mouth open as, for the first time in decades, she stood up to her full height. The twisted bones of her back were healed and the hump that had pushed her over was gone.

The blind began to look around in wonderment, many seeing for the first time ever...

The place had gone into a complete frenzy.

I could barely believe my eyes.

Before my very eyes, the living God, the Creator of the entire universe, the King of all creation had reached through the heavens into the Philippines and had begun divine surgery on hundreds of people all at the same time.

God's sovereign hand was fixing the ills of so many people, I was overwhelmed. It was such a tremendous move of God, tears burst from my eyes involuntarily. I began weeping like a little child. I was awestruck to be in the Presence of such a holy God Who so easily could perform such incredible, tremendous miracles for so many people.

I didn't know what to do. What does the preacher do when God has stepped in personally and taken over a service so completely?

I did the only thing I thought I could do.

I ran.

I ran off the platform. There was a huge post behind the platform. I ran behind that post and hid.

It seemed I was there for some time when a very large Assembly of God missionary named Alford Cawston came over to me. He looked just as awestruck as I felt. No one in that place could possibly have not been impressed with the power of God that was in action there.

The missionary put his arm across my back.

"Brother Cerullo, you'd better get back to the rostrum or we are going to have a riot on our hands," he said to me. I could see the concern in his face was real. He looked as if he could think of no other solution. "You are the only person who can hold this meeting in order."

I didn't want to go.

When the power of God is being manifested so sovereignly, there is a feeling in the air that everyone knows God is moving – no man in his right mind would want to undermine so powerful a move of God.

I almost told the missionary that, I wouldn't go out, and that he would have to do without me. But just as I was about to protest, God reminded me of the story in the second chapter of Acts, where the power of God was moving similarly on the day of Pentecost.

The apostles had all just received the Holy Ghost, and they were all speaking with other tongues and causing a commotion among the people. That group of people also had a near-riot situation on their hands, but in Acts 2:14, "Peter, standing up with the eleven, lifted up his voice..."

God had used Peter to direct the service, to be a vessel through which God ministered to all the people, not just the ones who had received a miracle...

Gathering all the courage I had in my young, inexperienced body, I stepped back on the platform, and the scene was no different. Canes were still flying. Crutches also were flying. Babies were falling, babies were walking. And I was still weeping in the Presence of the Lord.

"God, no one should ever see this much of Your glory and be allowed to live," I said to God in the midst of being

10

overwhelmed by His incredible power. "God, take me home. I want to die."

I wasn't kidding. I did not know what could happen that could compare to what I was witnessing. It was as if a river of power had washed over a beach full of people, crumpled and broken, and, as the tide hit them, they were all straightened and healed.

I truly did not see how I could go on living after seeing such an incredible move of God.

And I fully expected God to take me home right then.

But God did something I didn't expect, and something I will never forget.

God said to me, "Son, you haven't seen anything yet."

The magnitude of that statement didn't hit me just then.

For everything I had seen this night in Roxas Park in Manila, God was promising I would see more in the future. I thought I had seen all anyone could see and still live, but God said I would see more.

Throughout the fifty-three years of my ministry, God has indeed allowed me to see more.

I have had the privilege of ministering on every inhabited continent on the face of this earth, preaching the Gospel of Jesus Christ, face-to-face, to literally uncountable millions of people.

By the grace of God, I have witnessed more miracles than I can count, with every conceivable kind of illness or deformity healed by the power of God. I have seen literally millions of people turn from the darkness of the devil that had enslaved them and turn to the light of Jesus Christ, receiving forgiveness for a lifetime of sins.

But when I was a little boy in a Jewish orphanage, I could have never imagined living such a life.

Instead, my goal as a rebellious young, hurtful boy was to cause trouble and rebel against every kind of authority figure.

My very first memory is of tragedy, though I didn't know it was a tragedy at the time.

Most little boys are all the same; they cling to their mothers. They run to them when they've banged up their knees, or when they hear a scary sound. They ask their mothers to read a bedtime story to them as they drift off to sleep at night.

Many of us forget how central mothers are to the lives of tiny children. Their entire lives are wrapped around their mothers.

I was no different. My mother was very kind and loving, and as a little boy, I was very attached to her, I am told, because I have no memory of her.

The earliest thing I can remember is sitting in the back seat of a car, wondering where my mother was. I knew something was going on, but I didn't know exactly what it was.

I didn't know where my father was, either. All I knew was that something bad had happened, and I wanted my mother.

My brother and three sisters were in the car with me. They were all older than I. They all seemed to be upset about something. I didn't know where the car was taking us.

It was the 1930s. Cars were much larger than they are now. To a very small boy, however, the car seemed even larger – cavernous. I couldn't see out of the windows through the pouring rain. All I could see was my brother and sisters.

The car finally stopped at an orphanage. I don't remember very much about my experience there, because I was too young. I do remember learning that my mother had died, but I didn't understand what that meant. All I knew was that she was no longer around to bandage my scraped knees. She was no longer around to read bedtime stories to me.

When I was four, my brother, my sisters and I were all moved to a foster home in Teaneck, New Jersey, with an Orthodox Jewish family, because my mother, Bertha Rosenblatt, was a Jew.

# The Greatest Miracle

Although I was only four or five years old, I was already rebellious. I hated authority and did not like being told what to do.

When I entered school, I was already known as a problem child by the authorities.

I had run away a few times, and I withstood my teachers and elders when they would tell me to do something. There was a strong bitterness and resentment building up in me. Who stole my mother? Why did she have to die? Where was my father? I was told he was an alcoholic, but I didn't know what that meant.

God has a plan for everyone's life. He had a plan for my life, and even from an early age, the enemy was trying to divert my attentions; he was trying to get me to rebel not only against the authority figures in my life, but also against the plan God had for my life. I was a young boy, and I was all too happy to oblige.

When I was six, I was sent to the principal's office – as I had been many times before – for misbehaving.

The principal had bought a paddle just for me – a little six-year-old boy – because I misbehaved that badly.

The paddling was no different from any other time. She bent me over her lap and paddled me particularly hard.

But I was determined not to give her the satisfaction of knowing her spanking had hurt me. Afterward I looked at her defiantly and gave her the meanest scowl I could form on my little face.

Then, cursing under my breath, I turned and left her office.

I heard a voice, which said, "You don't have to take this. Why don't you run away?"

It seemed like a good idea.

My life was not fun anyway. I had to sleep in an attic bedroom with my four siblings, and we had to eat our meals in the cellar. I wasn't too keen on being in that situation any longer, and I was mad at the principal. So instead of going back to class, I walked out the door of the school and ran down the sidewalk into the street.

I knew that the railroad tracks that were nearby led to some swamps, and I thought I could hide for quite a while there.

I was a very unhappy little boy.

When the other boys would play games of kickball or football, they all smiled and laughed, tumbling and roughhousing. But I couldn't have fun like they did, because I was bitter and sullen.

I was constantly in trouble at school, and I felt like the foster home in which I lived was a prison.

I knew that if I were to be caught running away, the punishment would be severe. So I hurried to make my getaway as quickly and completely as I could. I was upset and angry, and I didn't want to be around any of the people I was around.

It was very cold, but I also didn't care about that. I made my way to the swamps and marshes, more worried about the prospect of getting caught than the dangers that were doubtlessly all around me, a little boy alone in Teaneck, New Jersey.

Not very long after I left the school, the principal called the police and informed them that I was missing.

The police found me, wandering around the marshes, and put me in the back of one of their cars.

In the back seat of the car, I was lonely and hungry. The policemen seemed to be very nice, but I knew they were taking me back to my prison, back to what I knew would be an awful punishment.

As we rounded the corner and I saw the house I lived in, my heart leapt into my throat. I knew what was coming.

The lady of the house thanked the police for finding me and returning me safely. No sooner had they left than her shoe came off and she began beating me with it. She hit me so hard and so many times that my little body gave out. I could no longer kneel upright; my legs gave way and I crumpled to the floor, in too much pain to move, or do anything else but sob silently.

But inside me, fury raged. There was a violence there that I cannot fully explain. After the beating, I was sent to our little attic room without supper. Still stinging and angry, curses and thoughts of revenge raced through my mind and filled me up where food wouldn't.

It seemed that the enemy was infesting my little six-year-old mind with the most angry and vindictive thoughts anyone could imagine. When we read today's newspapers and watch television newscasts, or hear of killings and shootings by young children, I understand the forces that are driving them.

Soon, our family was broken up.

Abraham, my brother, joined the army. My oldest sister, Frances, got married. My sister Pauline went to live with friends. Only Bernice, the youngest next to me, and I were left together, as we were transferred to a Gentile-run orphanage in Passaic, New Jersey.

We were slated to be at the orphanage only until the state could find an Orthodox Jewish orphanage to raise us.

Though we were at the Gentile orphanage only for a short time, I learned more bad habits there. I was eight years old, and I learned by watching the other boys at the orphanage. They would scour the streets, looking for discarded cigarette butts. The boys would then light the butts and smoke them.

I began going with the boys on their cigarette-gathering expeditions, and I joined them in smoking the cigarettes in the basement of the orphanage.

I was already a scrappy little boy. I would fight at the drop of a hat. I was very hard, very tough. If another boy looked at me funny, I would hit him until he dropped. And while he was on the floor, I would ask him, "why did you look at me like that?" It was the late thirties and early forties and Anti-Semitism was engulfing the country. Hitler was stirring up hatred of the Jews in Europe, and the sentiment had crossed the ocean and was very prevalent in the U.S. Other boys would call me derogatory names they had for "dirty Jews," and they gave me a very hard time about being Jewish. I learned very quickly that the only way to silence their racist banter was to shove a fist in their mouths, so that's how I conducted myself. I hit first and asked questions later.

A few months after Bernice and I arrived at the orphanage, the state was able to locate an Orthodox Jewish orphanage in Clifton, New Jersey, called the Daughters of Miriam.

The Daughters of Miriam was not only an orphanage, it was also a home for the aged. It was a very strict place.

Rabbi and Mrs. Gold were in charge, and when they met me, they already had the scoop.

"I understand you can be quite a problem," Mrs. Gold said, looking down at me as she led me down the hall. "To help you stop getting into so many fights, I've decided to put you in with the older boys; I don't think you'll give them quite the guff you're used to dishing out."

I wasn't scared. It didn't matter to me who it was, if someone bothered me, I was going to silence them any way I could.

The orphanage was a very tough place for a little boy. Our beds had to be made just right; if they weren't, they were ripped apart and we had to start over. I picked tomatoes and ran the potato-peeling machine, along with other duties like scrubbing floors, cleaning bathrooms and washing windows and dishes.

We attended public school, but we didn't participate in many of the activities because we were Jewish.

## The Greatest Miracle

One day, a boy at school called me a "kike," a derogatory name for Jew. Immediately, I lashed out at him and began punching and kicking him.

Other boys joined in the fray and, though I gave as good as I got, I came away bloody.

Rabbi Gold was accustomed to seeing me come home bruised or with a busted lip. I frequently fought with other boys after school.

The rabbi told me to put a piece of ice on my nose and get ready to attend Torah class, which started in ten minutes.

As I was walking down the hall, another boy in the orphanage named Joey quipped, "Well, Morris, it looks like they got the best of you in school today."

My vision went red. I jumped and began swinging my fists as hard as I could, knocking Joey to the floor. I followed him there and continued punching him. Finally, his head slammed into the floor and bounced back up, chipping my tooth. I felt nothing. I kept pummeling and pounding until Rabbi Gold physically picked me up and held my arms so I couldn't swing them anymore.

My razor-thin temper had erupted again. I was ready at all times to erupt into violence; the enemy was doing his best to turn me into what he had designed for my life so he could keep me from what God had designed for my life.

The orphanage authorities had to restrain me for quite a while before I calmed down. A fury was boiling just below the surface at all times, and when it was released, it took a while to calm down.

Once I had settled down, I was rushed to the hospital so doctors could look at my mouth and my tooth.

That night, while I was lying in bed, I was just a little boy again. My tough facade was gone; I was just a little boy whose tooth was throbbing, whose mouth ached and throbbed with every heartbeat. I hated life in the orphanage. I hated going to school. I hated being a Jew. I hated everything.

I began to cry silently in the darkness of the orphanage dormitory. I would never have let any of the other boys see me cry, but in the darkness, I was alone and I didn't want to live any more.

I was only eight years old, but I had already decided that I wanted to die.

It was two o'clock in the morning. I quit crying and slipped out of bed.

I silently made my way to the bathroom. Once inside, I craned my neck around the corner to make sure I hadn't awakened any of the other boys. I looked all around the bathroom to make sure no one else was there.

I opened the second-story window and climbed out onto the ledge there. The concrete below beckoned to me, "Jump; it will all be over."

It seemed everyone had either deserted me or, the ones who had remained, hated me. My mother was dead. I had only seen my dad twice since I left what was home, and my brother and two sisters were gone. My classmates at school hated me because I was Jewish. I felt unloved and unwanted.

I squatted down on the ledge and tried to prepare myself to leap. I breathed in very deeply, then let the breath out. This would be just like diving off the diving board at a pool. I closed my eyes and tilted my little head upward, taking another deep breath and holding it inside. It seemed my heart stopped beating for just a moment.

I started to jump, but no sooner had my brain sent the signal to my legs to begin moving, I felt someone was in the bathroom behind me.

Startled, I whispered, "Who's that?"

No one answered. But I knew someone was there.

I slowly turned around, grabbing the ledge with my hands so I wouldn't lose my balance. As I turned, it became clear to me that the bathroom was empty. But I still sensed the presence of someone other than myself.

I turned around, and the sheer beauty of the night struck me as it never had before. The stars were twinkling; there seemed to be millions of them.

The air smelled fresher, more crisp, cleaner than it ever had before.

The moon glowed brilliantly, hung in the nighttime sky of Clifton, New Jersey, beaming down on me with what seemed to be a brand-new clarity. I had never seen such a beautiful sight.

I felt a warmth coarse over my entire body, from the tip of my head to the soles of my feet. I had never felt anything like it before. I didn't understand what was happening, but the anger was gone. My tooth and nose stopped hurting, but I didn't notice that until later.

I was overwhelmed by a Presence all around me. I knew I was experiencing something supernatural. I knew I was not alone. I climbed back in the window and made my way back into the dorm room. As I passed, I looked at the clock on the wall and saw it was 2:45a.m. It seemed impossible. The experience had seemed as if it had happened in a few seconds, but apparently it had taken three quarters of an hour!

Though God had supernaturally intervened to stop me from committing suicide, I was still rebellious, still disobedient, and still always looking for a way to escape from the orphanage.

By the time I was thirteen, I was ready to get my Bar Mitzvah. Bar Mitzvah means "son of the commandment," and it denotes that the recipient is an adult, according to Jewish tradition.

When a Jewish boy attains Bar Mitzvah, he is legally obligated to keep the commandments. His vows are considered valid. He can perform acts having legal implications, such as buying and selling property.

The calling up to the reading of the Torah is a symbol of a boy's attaining maturity. He is called up on the first occasion that the Torah is read following his 13th birthday. To a Jewish boy, it's a very big deal.

The boy is required to put on tefillin (which the English Bible translates as "phylacteries") for the morning prayer. The tefillin are two black leather boxes containing scriptural passages that are bound by leather strips on the left arm and on the head.

The boy is required to deliver a *derashah* "talmudic discourse", which he has been well-coached to give in Hebrew, though he may not understand what he is saying.

Since children are not allowed to carry the Torah, a boy is recognized as having reached maturity when he is allowed to finally carry the Torah at his Bar Mitzvah.

All the boys in the orphanage looked forward to their Bar Mitzvahs, and I was no different. It was a very big accomplishment, and a very exciting time.

I didn't understand the spiritual significance of Bar Mitzvah, only of the historical tradition that I would be considered an adult – at least in religious matters – by everyone in the orphanage and the synagogue, which was a part of the orphanage.

When I was fourteen, I and another boy decided to sneak out of the orphanage one night.

The orphanage had a crude alarm system that would sound if the door was opened, but I had been in the orphanage for years and I knew I could get out without alerting anyone.

I beckoned the other boy to follow me, and I stooped down to the baseboard, removing the wood, exposing two wires. I knew if I disconnected the wires, the alarm system would be disabled, allowing us to exit with impunity.

We quickly rushed out of the building, down the fire escape. We were free (if only for a few hours), and we could do whatever we wanted without any of the orphanage's strict rules or regulations.

## The Greatest Miracle

By the time the sun started to peek over the horizon, we realized we had to quickly sneak back home to the orphanage. We slipped into the front door and ran to the dormitory, slipping back into our beds, ready to pretend that we had just enjoyed a good night's sleep.

That very same day, the orphanage hired a new nurse, Mrs. Ethel Kerr. Since the Daughters of Miriam was also a facility for the elderly, most of Mrs. Kerr's time would be taken up with helping aged people live their lives.

Mrs. Kerr was a Gentile, and a Christian, no less, who somehow had gotten a job at a Jewish Orthodox orphanage.

Most of my experiences with Gentiles had been painful. They had called me names and abused me, and I really had no interest in spending time with anyone who was not Jewish.

My only Gentile friend was a boy whose father owned one of the largest trucking companies in New Jersey, Odstdyk Motors. We hung out together at school, but he had never tried to tell me about Christ, so I didn't think about the fact that he called himself a Christian.

The first time that Mrs. Kerr, this new Gentile nurse, spoke to me, she called me aside.

"I have something special for you, Morris," she said to me, holding out a candy bar.

What kind of game was this?

I immediately became angry. I grabbed the candy bar and threw it on the floor as hard as I could, shouting, "I don't want any of your stupid candy! Just leave me alone!"

I stomped away.

What did she think she was doing? I was unaccustomed to anyone being kind to me, and I was extremely suspicious of Mrs. Kerr's unsolicited offer of a candy bar to me, a boy she didn't know. I had even cursed at her, but she seemed unflapped.

Every time I saw Mrs. Kerr, she was smiling. She always said the same thing, in the same cheerful voice: "Hello, Morris."

It seemed she had forgotten about the candy bar episode altogether. She was never once unkind to me.

My initial fury at her offer had turned to curiosity. What was making this woman so kind to a boy who obviously did not want to give her the time of day?

I made up my mind that I was going to find out what this woman was thinking and why she was being so nice to me. I was very suspicious. In the past, everyone who had been kind to me had some sort of secret agenda or ulterior motive, something they wanted from me. What was her angle? I was going to find out.

Late one night, after I had assured myself that no one would do a surprise room inspection and catch me, I sneaked out of my room and down the fire escape. I loitered around the back court a while to make sure I had not been detected while making my exit. Once I was sure the coast was clear, I crept over to the quarters where the hired help were housed.

I walked up and tried to open the door to that wing of the building, but to my chagrin, it was locked.

I muttered a quiet curse and began to think of a way to get to Mrs. Kerr's room. I was determined to find out tonight exactly what she had up her sleeve.

As I was trying to think of a solution to my problem, I noticed that the wall under Mrs. Kerr's window looked as if it wouldn't be too hard to climb.

I ran over to the wall, and, placing my fingers gingerly in its' crevices, I pulled on the wall to see if I could climb up. It worked. I was able to slowly work my way up the wall, sliding my fingers into the crevices and my feet into crevices below, inching my way toward Mrs. Kerr's window.

When I got to her window sill, I grabbed hold of it with one hand, and with the other, I knocked on her window.

Nothing.

Where could she be? It was too late for her to be out; surely she was there. Maybe she just hadn't heard my knock. I knocked again.

Still nothing.

I knocked again.

Still nothing. I was getting frustrated. Surely my knocking had awakened her. Why wasn't she coming to the window?

Little did I know that Mrs. Kerr was inside her room, panicking. She didn't know what to make of the knocks on her window so high off the ground.

On my fifth knock, Mrs. Kerr gathered her courage and peeked out the window at me. Relief washed over her face when she saw my little head popping up over the window sill.

She threw the window wide open and grabbed my hand, helping me climb into her room.

"What are you doing here?" she asked. "What brings you out here at this time of night?"

I hadn't expected to have to answer that question. I had expected to be the one asking questions.

"Because," I stammered. "Because I want to know what you are up to. Why are you bugging me?"

I was unprepared for her answer. I had half-expected to hear her list of demands. After all, no one would be so nice without wanting something.

But her answer caught me completely off guard.

"God sent me here for you."

WHAT?

I couldn't believe my ears. I had been to Hebrew school nearly every day since coming to the Daughters of Miriam orphanage, and I had never heard such a thing.

God had spoken to Abraham, Moses and the patriarchs, but Rabbi Gold had never claimed to have heard from God. Yet, here was this Gentile claiming to have heard from God,

23

and not only to have heard from God, but to have been "sent" for me.

Incredulous, I asked, "What do you mean you were sent here for me?"

She opened up her Bible and read from Isaiah:

> *"Take counsel, execute judgment; make thy shadow as the night in the midst of the noonday; hide the outcasts; betray not him that wandereth. Let mine outcasts dwell with thee..." (Isaiah 16:3-4)*

"God has sent me to tell you about the Messiah," she continued.

My mind began to race. Why had I come here? It seemed this woman was saying things I just couldn't believe. How could a Gentile expect to tell me, a Jew, about the Jewish Messiah?

I knew all about the Messiah, I thought. In Hebrew school, we had learned all about it. We were waiting for the Messiah to come and be the King of Israel. What could she possibly know about the Messiah that I had not already learned from the rabbis?

"You've got to be kidding," I snapped at her. "What can you tell me about the Messiah?"

She began to explain that the Messiah had come already.

"Stop," I said. "We're still waiting for the Messiah. Why are you saying He already came?"

"Because He has," she explained patiently, that now-familiar smile still on her face. She began to explain to me that the Messiah had come to Israel nearly 2,000 years ago, and that He had died for my sins.

"This is too much," I said. "I'm going back to my room."

Abruptly, I climbed back out of the window and down the wall.

My mind was racing. This Gentile nurse obviously didn't know what she was talking about I thought in my young mind. But she seemed so sure, so peaceful and so kind. I couldn't stop thinking about what she had said about God sending her to tell me about the Messiah.

I stayed awake for many hours, lying in bed, going over the conversation I had just had with this peculiar woman.

The next night, I couldn't contain my curiosity any longer. I climbed back out of my window, sneaked down the fire escape and climbed the wall to Mrs. Kerr's room again.

We continued that pattern for many nights. I would come to Mrs. Kerr's room, and we would debate and discuss the Old Testament heroes of faith: Abraham, Moses, Isaac, Jacob, David, Samuel, Gideon and others.

I questioned Mrs. Kerr on every point she made.

Already, my ambitions had turned toward the future. I wanted to be a lawyer, and I was already honing my skills at debating. Mrs. Kerr would make a statement, and I would challenge her on it.

But over time, I began to listen more. I enjoyed being in Mrs. Kerr's room. It was the most peaceful place I had ever been in.

Slowly, though I didn't realize that my heart was changing. I was spending so much time learning in Mrs. Kerr's room that I didn't even think about running away any more, or about stealing.

One night, Mrs. Kerr handed me a small, folded piece of paper. On the outside was a simple title: "Questions."

The tract was written by a Christian lawyer named James Bennett, which immediately piqued my interest.

I read the tract once, and then I read it again and again.

The tract's title was prophetic: all sorts of questions began popping into my mind.

The next night, I poured out all my questions to poor Mrs. Kerr. I had what seemed to be an unending stream of questions, and with each answer, more questions came to mind!

Mrs. Kerr finally put her foot down. "Morris, it is too dangerous for you to be coming to my room all the time. Eventually someone is going to see you."

She took a little black book from her pocket and handed it to me.

"This is a gift for you," she said. "You don't have to take it if you don't want to. It's a New Testament. Do you want to read it for yourself?"

Did I!

Finally, we were getting somewhere. I couldn't wait to get the book back to my room and begin reading it, looking for the answers to my questions.

As I was about to leave, Mrs. Kerr stopped me.

"You'll need this," she said, holding out a tiny little flashlight. "You'll need to be very careful reading that New Testament. You'll have to read it at night when everyone else is sleeping or in some secret place."

As soon as I got back to my bed, I pulled the covers over my head and flicked on the tiny little flashlight.

This little New Testament was unlike anything I had ever read. Its pages were whisper-thin, and the ink smelled cheap. I eagerly read the first book, Matthew. Before I knew it, I was done with Matthew, so I began reading Mark. I finished Mark, but I was still hungry so I read Luke. I was not yet sated so I read on through to John.

What an incredible person this Jesus was!

His demeanor was loving and caring, but when the rabbis of His day tried to trick Him and trip Him up in His words, He always knew just how to answer them!

And I was fascinated by His teachings. How could a man be born again? His words spoke directly to my soul.

The New Testament revealed a man much different than I had imagined the Messiah would be. Jesus was misunderstood, beaten, laughed at, scourged, ridiculed, persecuted, mocked and reviled. Yet He had a zeal for God that was unmatched by any of the Old Testament prophets I had spent years learning about in Hebrew school.

Jesus had come to earth and had taken upon Himself the life of a lowly carpenter. He taught that we were to love our neighbors, to bless people who cursed us.

When I read about Jesus' sufferings on the cross, how He endured the bitter words and the beatings of those who reviled Him, I remembered my own life, how instead of "turning the other cheek," as Jesus advised, I had been the first to strike, to lash out at those who had hurled hateful words at me.

Jesus, however, had only kindness for those who mistreated Him. He had only love for those who hated Him.

I wanted to be like Him. I wanted to be strong enough to love those who hated me. I wanted to be strong, like Jesus, who feared no man, but feared God alone. I wanted to be compassionate like Him and to be wise like Him.

I eagerly and ravenously read and read. I couldn't get enough. But after I had read the four Gospels, I could no longer keep my eyes open.

Ever mindful that being caught with a New Testament would mean a more severe punishment than I cared to think about, I carefully pulled up the mattress of my bed and hid the New Testament and the pen light between the springs and the mattress.

When I woke up in the morning, I was careful to make my bed discreetly, working to avoid exposing the treasure I had hidden under my mattress.

I went about my chores, picking tomatoes, cleaning and running the potato peeler, but my mind wasn't in my work.

I was in awe, thinking about Jesus.

He had done more miracles than Elisha, and His words were filled with such wisdom, I could hardly contain my hunger to know more about Him.

Time seemed to slow to a crawl.

I eagerly awaited bedtime.

When bedtime came, I listened carefully for signs that everyone had fallen asleep. It was a skill I had perfected during my many jaunts of escape and crime.

I listened to hear the deepening sighs of bodies that had fallen asleep.

It seemed to take forever.

Finally, everyone, but me, was asleep.

I pulled the covers over my head so fast, I almost pulled them completely off the bed.

I got out my little flashlight and the New Testament and began reading where I had left off.

I began reading about people who had lived my new dream to be like Jesus. Here were Jews, just like me, who had been laughed at because they were born in Galilee, just as I had been laughed at because I was born a Jew. They had been beaten, but just like Jesus, they were kind to those who beat them.

I read about New Testament heroes like Peter, John, Paul and Barnabas. I read how Paul and Silas worshiped God and the prison doors flew open.

Again, longing was sparked in my heart. I was in my own little prison. I knew how they felt.

Up to this point, Mrs. Kerr had been attending a church that was not very keen on loud displays of worship or operating in the gifts of the Spirit.

One day, Mrs. Kerr went to an Assembly of God church in Patterson, New Jersey. After attending the service, Mrs. Kerr came back to the orphanage very excited, and immediately told me about how the people praised the Lord aloud in the service, and how they worshiped God with such feeling!

She handed me a magazine she apparently had gotten at the service.

# The Greatest Miracle

The magazine was called the *Pentecostal Evangel*. I knew what Pentecost was; it was a feast that took place fifty days after Passover. And I also knew from reading the New Testament that during the Feast of Pentecost, the apostles had started their ministry in Jerusalem.

I was eager to read anything I could about Jesus, so I gladly took the magazine from Mrs. Kerr and began reading it as soon as I got to my room.

Once I read the magazine, however, I discovered that it was not what I had expected. I was expecting the magazine to tell me about what Mrs. Kerr had just described to me; I wanted to read about worshiping God aloud and about the feelings she was describing. Instead, what I read was about missions reports and other things that I was not interested in at the time.

I didn't think about hiding the magazine at all. Instead, I stuck it in the back pocket of my robe and hung the robe up on my locker.

The very next morning, the orphanage decided to do a locker inspection. I didn't think anything about it. My locker was nice and neat, my shoes lined up just so, my clothes neatly arranged and my school books stacked just right. I had no worries until I heard the horrified gasp of the nurse who was inspecting my locker.

The nurse grabbed the magazine and ran, full-speed, down the corridor, yelling, "Look at this! Look at this! A *Pentecostal Evangel*!"

In a matter of a few minutes Mrs. Kerr had been called into the rabbi's office. The rabbi immediately knew Mrs. Kerr was responsible for bringing the *Pentecostal Evangel* into the orphanage.

Rabbi Gold fired Mrs. Kerr, and then immediately called me into his office. "Morris! Morris! Come into my office this second. I want to talk to you!"

I hadn't even completely closed the door when Rabbi Gold thrust the magazine in my face and shouted, "What is this?"

Was this a trick question? I didn't know what he wanted to hear. I began to think of how I could explain what the magazine was, when my thoughts were interrupted by the rabbi speaking again.

"Morris, this is absolute trash," he told me. "I don't know for sure what Mrs. Kerr has been telling you, but I do know it is all wrong. I don't ever want you to see that woman or talk to her again; is that understood?"

My heart sank.

I had never had a person to whom I could talk. I had never been able to really discuss things with anyone. Now he was telling me to no longer talk to Mrs. Kerr.

I began to cry. That in itself was a tremendous change for me. Whenever I had been confronted about things in the past, or when I had been scolded, my first reaction was to rebel, to lash out, or to simply ignore whoever it was scolding me.

But my heart had changed, and I was upset. I didn't know, but Mrs. Kerr was out in the corridor, praying, "Oh my God, what is going to happen?"

Her prayers must have helped, because when I spoke to answer the rabbi, it was with confidence.

"Listen, Rabbi Gold," I said. "I don't know much about what I read in that magazine. I don't even understand it. Even what Mrs. Kerr has been telling me is not completely clear. It's so different from anything I have ever heard, but I know it's real. It's real."

I began sobbing.

"It's real, and you can't take it away from me!"

It was to become a quote I would repeat many times, both to the rabbis who tried to convince me to give up my belief in Jesus, and to my friends in the orphanage who asked me what was going on.

I became accustomed to punishment again, as I began receiving punishment, not for the crimes I formerly had committed, but for my unwillingness to waver from my newfound belief in Jeshua, the Messiah.

Finally, one day when I was in the basement receiving punishment, I stood up and said, "I have not fought back all this time, but if you lay your hands on me once more, I am going up to that front door and I am going to walk out and you are not going to stop me."

The rabbi laughed at me.

He knew that I didn't have any money, extra clothes. or a place to sleep.

I turned and walked away from the rabbi. I didn't look left or right. I focused only on the front doors to the orphanage. I slowly walked toward the doors. I didn't run, I didn't speed up my pace at all. I fully expected Rabbi Gold to grab me from behind and stop me from leaving, but he didn't.

When I got to the doors, I pushed them open and walked outside.

Freezing sleet and snow pelted me in the face on this cold, snowy, mid-December night.

But I couldn't turn back now.

I walked out into the midst of what must have been a blizzard.

I had nowhere to go. I was completely alone.

After Mrs. Kerr had been fired from the orphanage, she would meet me in the school yard so that we could continue our discussions about Jesus. She had given me the phone number of her new job as a registered nurse.

I decided I would call Mrs. Kerr. I walked to the house of my Gentile friend from school. After I knocked, my friend's father opened the door and looked quite surprised to see me standing outside.

"Sir," I asked, "can I use your telephone?"

He agreed and I went inside. I then used his phone to call Mrs. Kerr. Miraculously, she was home and answered the phone. I told her what had happened, and we agreed that I would meet her at the Montauk Theatre in Passic, which was four miles away.

I thanked my friend's father and went back into the freezing cold.

Suddenly I remembered, I had no idea how I was going to get to the theatre. I had no money...

I looked up into the forbidding sky, and fear began to rack my body. I had no idea where to go, or how to get to the theatre.

Finally, I thought, "I'll head down to Main Street where there's a lot going on. Maybe I'll know what to do when I get there."

I was terrified. It was snowing and sleeting, and I was wandering along a very busy street. At one point, an angry driver had honked at me and shouted, "Watch where you're going, kid!"

I was in desperation. I was not even fifteen years old, and yet I was on my own with no friends, no food, no house to sleep in and I was very cold.

Right there on that street corner, I cried out to God: "Dear God, if there be such a person as Jesus up there in the heavens, please let Him be with me now!"

Almost immediately, a burst of warm air surrounded me. I did not understand what was happening, but I knew one thing: God had answered my prayer.

I began to weep again. "Thank you, God," I said. "Thank you so much."

I felt a nudge on my right side, just as if someone had walked up to me and elbowed me. I looked, but nobody was there.

Then I felt another nudge, this one on my left side. It was as if God stood right beside me on both sides, protecting me from the elements and the loneliness that had threatened to send me into despair.

My countenance was immediately changed. I instantly forgot about the fear and trepidation I had felt up to that point. I began to sing.

I also began to walk while I sang, for two-and-a-half miles, with God's presence surrounding me.

I can't explain the joy I felt. I can't explain the peace I felt.

All I knew was that I was not alone. God was with me, just as He had been with me six years earlier when I had thought about jumping from the orphanage ledge. I knew that everything would be all right, because God was there.

I was in complete joy. I paid absolutely no attention to where I was going. I had no regard for streets or the cars that were zipping by perilously close to where I was.

My right hand opened, and the Presence of God left my right hand. My left hand opened, and the Presence of God exited my left hand.

Suddenly, just as quickly as it had appeared, the warming Presence of God had disappeared. I closed my eyes and prayed. "Oh, God, please don't leave me now."

Before I could despair, however, I opened my eyes and discovered that I was standing in front of the Montauk Theatre, and there, less than two feet away, under an umbrella beneath the theater's lights, was Mrs. Kerr, looking more shocked than I had ever seen her.

We both burst into joyful tears!

Mrs. Kerr had been waiting at the theater for a long time, not knowing how or when I would get there.

Little did she know God Himself was guiding me!

Her next question was very welcome: "Are you hungry?"

I was hungry, but I was also still in amazement of the supernatural manifestation we had just witnessed. I could hardly believe what God had just done, protecting and directing me to just the spot where Mrs. Kerr had been patiently waiting for me.

But as God would tell me in the Philippines more than thirteen years later that, if I thought He had worked His most impressive miracles by getting me this far, I hadn't seen anything yet.

## Chapter 2

# HEAVEN AND HELL

All of my short life, I had lived very firmly in what I could see, feel, hear, taste and smell.

My life was very physical. I mopped floors, made beds, got into fights, smoked cigarettes and did pretty much whatever I wanted to do.

But now I had changed. I didn't know much about this Jesus; but I knew that He was real and I could already feel the change that He had made in my life. The violent anger that had always boiled just beneath the surface was gone. The hard veneer and rebellious spirit were gone.

After I left the Daughters of Miriam Orphanage and miraculously found Mrs. Kerr, I needed a place to live.

Up until this time, I had never had to find a place to sleep. I would fend for myself in other ways, but I had never been without a place to go home to.

I discovered that I was not the only soul Mrs. Kerr had reached with the Gospel. She had taken the message of the Gospel to her very own brother, Mr. Maurer, and his family. Mrs. Kerr took me to their house and they generously offered to take me in. As soon as I arrived at their big and inviting house, their first order of business was to warm me up.

I had been walking through a tremendous winter storm. My clothes were soaked. My hair was dripping wet. I was incredibly hungry; I had left the orphanage without eating.

When Mrs. Maurer saw me, her face dropped. She rushed into the kitchen and began moving pots and pans around. I couldn't see her; I could only hear the commotion in the kitchen. While Mrs. Kerr explained to Mr. Maurer what had happened with me leaving the orphanage, I listened intently to the goings-on in the kitchen. I heard water running and what sounded like fire from a stove. But my attention was drawn to the home I saw around me. Pretty pictures hung unobtrusively on the walls. The living room furniture, that consisted of a couch, a coffee table, an easy chair and a rocking chair, all went together nicely, and formed what seemed to me to be a perfect family of furniture.

The dining room table at which I was sitting appeared to be the most used piece of furniture in the house, as if the family spent a lot of time here, talking, praying and visiting together.

Very quickly, Mrs. Maurer appeared with a bowl of liquid in her hands, steam rising from the bowl through the air.

"Now, eat this slowly, Morris," Mrs. Maurer admonished as she placed the steaming bowl of chicken soup in front of me.

At that moment, I didn't think I had ever seen a more beautiful thing than that bowl of soup. I was suddenly ravenously hungry – I wanted to pick the bowl up and drain it in a few gulps. But I listened to Mrs. Maurer and slowly ate the delicious soup, spoonful by spoonful, savoring the succulent flavor of the broth as it rolled around in my mouth.

The whole time I was eating, Mr. and Mrs. Maurer and Mrs. Kerr went about the business of discussing what to do with this fourteen-year-old boy who had been placed in their care by the hand of God.

I couldn't pay very close attention to them, though. I was exhausted. After I was finished with my soup, I tried to listen closely to their discussion; but it seemed my eyelids betrayed my interest as they kept trying to close. Periodically, I would notice that my eyes were closing and I would snap them open in a hurry, but I was fighting a losing battle.

I had been in an emotional war all day long. First, the beating at the orphanage, then the argument and threat to leave. Then actually leaving, fearing every second that the rabbi would grab me by the shoulder and jerk me into his office. And finally making my way through what amounted to a blizzard in a miraculous experience of which I was still in awe.

My body was just too tired to continue any more. I wanted nothing more than a good night's sleep.

Sometime during their intense conversation, Mrs. Maurer glanced over and noticed that the object of their concern was trying his very best to keep from nodding off.

Smiling, she directed me to the room where I would stay. It, too, looked perfect. The bed was neatly made. Beside it there was a night stand and a lamp. On the night stand, prominently placed, was a Bible. The last thing I remember from that eventful day was climbing in between two of the softest sheets I had ever felt in my life. "She must iron these sheets," I thought. Then, I fell asleep.

The next few days, I read the Bible every chance I could find.

I no longer had to hide my New Testament under the sheets and wait until after all the boys had fallen asleep to read it. Instead of the little pen flashlight that Mrs. Kerr had given me, I now could simply turn on the lamp beside my bed, or read in the living room by the light of the winter sun.

I began to understand a little bit of how the Israelites must have felt when they were delivered from the bondage in Egypt.

Where before I had to be careful of my every move, making sure the rabbi didn't find out about my new interest in the Messiah; now I could read, pray and meditate on the goodness of Jesus Christ with impunity. I was free! It was as if an incredible weight had fallen off my shoulders. Even the air was easier to breathe, it seemed.

It was an experience that I would never forget. Years later, as I struggled with every bit of my being, to take the Gospel of Jesus Christ into countries where the people were forbidden to even speak His Name, I remembered vividly the struggle of my own exodus from the oppression of not being able to worship Him. My compassion for these precious souls was forged through the restrictions I myself had suffered; though in many cases, they could not compare to the oppression many of the world's Christians face daily in their attempts to worship the one true God.

Those who never know bondage can never truly appreciate freedom when they have it.

But I had been oppressed. I had been restrained from worshiping Jesus. I understood the precious value of the freedom that Jesus had brought me to through my exodus from the orphanage. Though, as a fouteen-year-old boy I couldn't yet articulate the value of my deliverance, I somehow had a powerful understanding of just what Jesus had done for me.

Every sight held new meaning for me. Every experience had a new perspective. My small little world had just expanded beyond my wildest imaginations.

The thankfulness I had in my heart has never left.

When Sunday came around, I had no way of knowing, but my life was about to undergo yet another radical change, another transformation deeper into the reality of the New Covenant of which I had been made a partaker.

It started simply enough.

Brother Maurer came up to me and explained to me that it was his family's practice to attend church every Sunday morning and Sunday night.

"Do you want to go with us, Morris?"

He didn't know it, but he didn't even need to ask. I was hungry for knowledge. I was anxious to do anything that would help me to learn more about Jesus and my newfound relationship with Him. My answer was an immediate yes.

I had left the orphanage with only the clothes on my back and they were nothing to brag about. I had to depend on the Maurers, who generously provided me with clothes to wear;

a suit nicer than I had ever worn, with a nice pair of freshly polished shoes.

I was so excited to experience anything I could that had to do with Jesus. I could hardly wait to get in the church – though I had never attended one before. My previous experience was centered on the synagogue which was nothing like a church, I was soon to find out.

As we approached the Bethany Assembly of God on Broadway in Patterson, New Jersey, I could hardly believe my eyes.

The building was enormous.

Bethany Assembly had been built to seat a thousand people. In those days, that was a huge church. I was awestruck.

The church had recently been bought by the Assemblies of God from a Presbyterian congregation at a cost of one million dollars. This was in about 1946, when a car sold for only a few hundred dollars. One stained glass window in this enormous church was worth more than $30,000. Everything about the church spoke of fine workmanship and great care taken in craftsmanship.

I was very impressed.

But that impression was not to last long.

Mr. Maurer led the way into the church through the oak doors in the front. As we passed through the foyer, it seemed like a busy day at Grand Central Station. People were everywhere. Mr. Maurer began to head down toward the front of the church in the main auditorium.

I couldn't believe my eyes. Even the rows of pews impressed me. It seemed they stretched on forever, row after row after row of pews. Where would they find enough people to sit in so many seats?

I began to get nervous as Mr. Maurer continued toward the front of the church. He kept going and going.

"Is he going to get up on the platform?" I wondered to myself.

My heart was pounding. I was ready to go to church, but I had not been prepared to be on a platform in front of so many people.

Each time we passed a row of pews, I would secretly wish, "Let this be the one we sit in." But it seemed every time, we would keep on walking, closer and closer to the front.

Just as I was about to tug on Mr. Maurer's sleeve and ask him to stop, he stopped and moved into one of the rows of pews.

I don't know if I made an audible noise, but I know I was tremendously relieved. Apparently, Mr. Maurer had a favorite place that he was accustomed to sitting near the front of the church, and we had finally arrived at it. It was so close to the front of the church that I felt I could probably reach out and touch the platform from my seat.

I sat in the pew with the Maurer family and began craning my neck around, watching what seemed to me to be an immense crowd of people as they filed into the building, all dressed in their Sunday best.

Men were wearing suit coats and colorful ties, covered with dark trench coats and topped with hats, which they all promptly removed as they entered the sanctuary. Again, this was different from the synagogue, where it was customary to don a yarmulke upon entrance.

All the women were smartly dressed in long dresses, and most wore gloves. Many of the children were dressed just like their parents, the little boys wearing miniature versions of their dads' suits and the little girls wearing tiny copies of their mothers' dresses.

Another thing I noticed immediately was that everyone seemed to have a Bible tucked under their arm. Even the children had tiny little New Testaments clutched in their chubby little hands.

This, too, was a change from the synagogue in which I had been raised. In the synagogue, the Torah was stored in a special cabinet designed specifically for it. It was usually written on real lambskin, and rolled up as a scroll on two ornate spools.

It was a very solemn occasion when someone would take the Torah out of its cabinet and prepare it to be read.

The person who was to carry the Torah had to pray special prayers and sing special songs; he had to be specially prepared, and he had to be Bar Mitzvah.

But here, every person carried their own Bible. Every person was able to open it at any time and read every word – in English.

It wasn't until several years later that I was able to articulate the significance of the difference I observed that very first time that I went to a church: Jesus had come to give the Word to EVERYONE, who could access it at any time and ponder the truth therein!

My thoughts were interrupted by the vibrato hum of the church's organ as everyone seemed to take their seats at the same time and begin to sing from the church's hymnal.

The pastor was an Englishman, the Rev. David Leigh. He was not prone to displays of emotionalism. By all accounts, he was a very dignified man who preached in measured tones, rarely descending into emotionalism, but this Sunday, he would be different. Only a few minutes after the service had started, a tremendous move of the Spirit of God began to sweep through the sanctuary.

Somewhere toward the back of the congregation, a man lifted his hands and shouted "Hallelujah!"

I just about jumped completely out of my seat.

I whirled around in my seat to see who was causing all the commotion. I thought this might be some kind of isolated outburst. The man hadn't stopped his ruckus, though. In fact, other people began doing the same thing.

"What have I gotten myself into?" I thought. I had never in my wildest dreams thought that something like this was going to happen. Not only had these people begun making noise, but it had begun to spread throughout the sanctuary.

People all over the place were shouting and raising their hands to God.

I nervously glanced over at Mr. Maurer. Beads of sweat were running down his forehead.

The poor man was sweating for more reasons than one.

I found out later that he was praying to God that the church wouldn't be wild that day so that it wouldn't spook me.

But God had other plans.

If I thought the service would calm down after the congregation was done singing, I had another thing coming.

Brother Leigh, normally serene and collected, made his way to the pulpit and the service became wilder.

As he preached, his voice rose and fell like the mountains and valleys of the Himalayas. He paced back and forth on the church's huge platform like a caged tiger eyeing his next meal.

Periodically, he would stop at the pulpit for a few seconds and give it a good whack with the palm of his hand before springing off in another direction, preaching ever louder through the service.

I had never seen a rabbi behave this way. They were always calm and dispassionate, delivering their messages and prayers in a practiced, measured tone.

But this preacher was on fire!

His words weren't just loud, they were laced with the conviction of a man who knows that what he's saying is the absolute truth. The power of his delivery did nothing to diminish the bullseye aim of his message – a message clearly flowing directly from heaven.

I was amazed at his athleticism. A professional athlete couldn't have performed with this much energy for so long, but the preacher continued to pace and speak, as the sweat was pouring down his face and saturating his shirt. The congregation seemed to hang on every word. As if choreographed, they would shout "amen" and "preach it" when the preacher delivered a particularly powerful point.

Though I squirmed a bit at the beginning of this man of God's message, within a few minutes I, too, was hanging on every word. I didn't shout "amen" with the rest of the congregation, but somewhere deep inside, I wanted to. I could understand their enthusiasm.

Finally, the service neared an end.

It was the custom, in that church, that at the end of the service, the congregation would be dismissed with prayer and the pastor would make his way toward the back of the sanctuary, where he would shake hands with everyone as they left.

But this morning, the pastor changed the routine. He called everyone down to the altar at the front of the church for prayer.

It seemed like the ocean at high tide as people from all over the congregation began edging their way out of their pews and heading toward the front of the sanctuary as the organ hummed in the background.

I had no way of knowing it at the time, but my presence in the church was responsible for some of the excitement. Apparently, the church had been praying corporately for God to save my soul and bring me out of the orphanage. When the congregation saw me walk into the church with

Mrs. Kerr and Mr. Maurer, they began rejoicing at the answer to their prayers.

I looked at Mr. Maurer, sweat still beading on his face a little more heavily now.

"Do you want to go to the altar, Morris?" Mr. Maurer asked me.

"Go to the altar?" I thought. I looked at the altar, and then I looked back at Mr. Maurer. We couldn't have been more than 15 feet from it anyway. "I've come this far, a few more rows surely cannot hurt me."

I timidly stepped forward, made my way through the people who already were at the front of the church and knelt down at the altar to pray.

To tell the truth, I did more looking around than praying.

I had placed my hands over my eyes, but I had separated my fingers just enough to sneak a glimpse through them.

I would periodically close my eyes and pray; but more often than not, I peeked through my fingers and watched the people around me pray. Just as everything else this Sunday morning, the congregation's prayers were completely new to me.

Many people prayed out loud – VERY loud. I was accustomed to a very quiet volume in prayer. Some rocked back and forth. Some raised their hands.

And many of the people had tears streaming down their cheeks as they made their petitions to God, hands stretched toward heaven, lips rapidly moving in words I could not distinguish because of the noise of so many gathered people all praying at once.

I had never witnessed anything like the service that morning. Mr. Maurer must have been walking on pins and needles, wondering how I was going to take what many people of the day doubtlessly called fanaticism.

But I didn't regard what was happening as fanaticism or as emotionalism. It was unusual to me, but instead of being put off by the commotion, I was made hungrier.

The people in this congregation seemed to be reaching out to a God they knew would answer their petitions. They were praising a God they knew would hear and appreciate their worship. They were speaking prayers of adoration to a God they knew had delivered them from the bondage of sin. I wanted what they had.

After the service, I thought of all the men of God I had learned about in Hebrew school who had spontaneously burst into worship of God: Abraham, Isaac, Moses, Joshua, Gideon, and Samuel. David had even worshiped God so hard that some of his clothes had fallen off by the sheer force of his dancing.

Though it was strange to see in person, I innately understood that the display I had witnessed that morning was simply a manifestation of people who were deeply and fundamentally changed by God, and they were expressing their thanks to Him in the only way they knew how.

I wanted what they had. I wanted to worship God with the freedom they displayed.

Just a few nights earlier, I had been reflecting on the freedom I felt in being delivered from the orphanage, in being able to worship Jesus without worrying about repercussions; but this Sunday morning service demonstrated to me that I could be even more free than I currently was in worshiping Him. There was something deeper that these people had and I wanted it.

I could hardly wait to return to the church Sunday night.

My soul longed to reach closer to Jesus, to dive into whatever He had for me. I wanted to get what the people in the congregation had. I wanted everything my new Lord had for me.

That night, I was no longer worried as Mr. Maurer and I approached the front of the sanctuary.

During the song service, I didn't turn around when people started shouting and praising. During the preaching, I concentrated on the message, not on how the preacher was delivering it. I was focused. I knew within myself that tonight was a turning point in my life; a point where I would leave much different from the way I had come. I didn't understand how, but I knew something was coming.

When the altar call came, no one had to ask me if I wanted to go.

I was the first person to jump out of my seat and make my way to the altar. I immediately knelt down and lifted my hands, tears streaming down my cheeks, praising God for delivering me, for revealing to me that Jesus is the Messiah!

I began to praise and worship God for removing the scales from my eyes, for allowing me to see clearly what so many other Jewish people still could not: that Jesus is the Son of God.

As I worshiped, the entire world seemed to disappear from my attention. My ears no longer heard the music and my eyes were squeezed tightly shut. All my attention and focus were on my Messiah.

I praised God like that for about ten minutes, then my life was changed forever.

In the midst of praising God, I felt something like a hand on my forehead. With that touch, my entire body just gave out from underneath me.

I fell to the floor. No human had touched me; I was touched by the very hand of God.

I knew I was on the floor, but I couldn't do anything about it. I was embarrassed. I had no idea that this sort of thing happened all the time in some churches. All I knew was that I was on the floor, and I had never seen anything like that happen to anyone else.

I tried to get up, but I couldn't. All I could do was praise God. More and more praise flowed from my lips. Bit by bit, I became enveloped again in worshiping God and forgot completely that I was on the floor as the world disappeared once again and my focus returned to the Prince of Peace.

Gradually, I began to see a vision of the sky.

I had never seen the sky look so beautiful, though. The blue was brilliant and resplendent, deeper and more clear than I had ever seen it. The clouds were the purest white I had ever seen – it seemed as if they were tiny puffs of cotton gently floating on the most brilliant blue lake.

Within a short time, beads of water began to form in the sky, and as they gathered more mass of completely transparent water, they would drop. Each drop had a word written across it in a language I had never seen before and that I couldn't understand.

As each drop came closer to me, it engulfed my entire body, my whole being, like being completely immersed in a warm, relaxing pool.

About ten minutes later, I was speaking in unknown heavenly tongues, praising God. God was baptizing me with the Holy Spirit, though I didn't know that terminology at the time.

I didn't understand what was happening to me at the time; all I knew was that God was answering my heart's cry. All I wanted was to know more of God, to wrap myself up in Him. All I wanted was to live my entire life in Him. I knew that whatever this was that was happening to me was God answering my heart's cry. As each drop of water enveloped my being, it seemed I was overtaken with a wave of holiness – with a massive overwhelming tide of the very Presence of God that ebbed and flowed in increasingly intense pulses of power.

Later, I remembered Acts, chapter 2, where the apostles had spoken with unknown tongues after they had been baptized with the Holy Spirit.

I stayed on the floor at the altar a very long time. All I could do – was to praise God. I didn't want to leave. By the time we made our way back to the Maurers' house, it was one o'clock in the morning, and I was still speaking in tongues, magnifying God, still basking in the waves of God's glory that had been enveloping my body for hours at the altar.

When we got to the Maurers' home, we all intuitively knew that God was not done.

The Maurers had not yet been fully committed to the Pentecostal experience. They had not yet decided if it was for them. They had been "dabbling" in Pentecostalism, according to their words, but they had not yet made the commitment to involve themselves in it and receive the Baptism of the Holy Ghost – they were Baptists.

But when we got to their home, they and Mrs. Kerr all realized what a tremendous work God had just done in me, and they all fell to their knees to receive the Baptism in the Holy Spirit as God moved in another tremendous demonstration of power, baptizing each one of them tremendously in the Holy Spirit.

That night, a few hours after we got home, the Spirit of God moved on me again and I began speaking in tongues.

As I spoke in the heavenly language, I began to understand the words that otherwise would have sounded like gibberish. I didn't quite understand what was happening. I knew that I wasn't speaking in English; but just the same, I knew what it was I was saying. After some prompting by the Holy Spirit, I began to offer interpretations in English of the tongues I was speaking.

I was astounded. Nothing like this had ever happened to me before. I had read in I Corinthians where Paul encouraged the Christians to pray for interpretations of tongues, but I had never seen or heard anyone actually do it. I was simply obeying what God led me to do. Judging from the expressions on their faces, Mr. and Mrs. Maurer and Mrs. Kerr were astounded too – their faces literally shone with amazement. But God was not done yet. A few minutes later, following the same prompting by the Holy Spirit, I began to prophesy. God spoke through me that He had called me to do a special work.

I had no idea what God meant by a "special work," but I knew something revolutionary had taken place.

In the course of a few short hours, God had moved in such a tremendous way that I had received the Baptism of the Holy Spirit, spoken with unknown tongues in a heavenly prayer language, interpreted unknown tongues and prophesied in the Spirit of God.

I knew that I had participated in an experience the saints of the Old Testament had dreamed about, had prayed for, and had died awaiting.

I knew that God had bestowed on me a tremendous gift, that could not be ignored or shut up.

I didn't know exactly what God intended, but I had a sense within myself that what I had experienced that night was not ordinary. I knew God had pulled out all the stops for a reason – I didn't yet understand.

Much as my statement to Rabbi Gold that "It's real, and you can't take it away from me," I knew that what I had just experienced would be with me forever, that God had separated me for a special reason. I knew that God had powerfully answered my heart's cry to know Him deeper.

But, as He would tell me thirteen years later on a platform in the Philippines in front of 30,000 people, I hadn't seen anything yet.

## The Vision

Almost immediately, God began to thrust me into the ministry, though I didn't know it at the time. I have often wondered, "Why me, God?"

I was just a Jewish orphan boy who had run away from his orphanage. I had no special training to minister. I had never been interested in ministering. I was the last person anyone would pick if they were choosing someone to share the message of the Gospel of Jesus Christ. But as I questioned why God would use me to deliver the message of the Gospel, a passage of Scripture would always come to mind:

> *"But God hath chosen the foolish things of the world to confound the wise; and God hath chosen the weak things of the world to confound the things which are mighty; And base things of the world, and things which are despised, hath God chosen, yea, and things which are not, to bring to nought things that are, That no flesh should glory in his presence"* (I Corinthians 1:27-29).

I had not been to any Bible school. I had not learned the fundamentals of homiletics or of composing a three-point sermon. I never learned that the preacher should use humorous anecdotes to bring the sermon home to his congregation.

And though those things are all fine, God had chosen another way for me. He had begun with a shapeless lump of clay and started shaping and molding it into a minister – though I didn't know it, and probably would have resisted if I had known that was what was happening.

Nevertheless, by the time I was fifteen, God was using me to preach or witness or testify an average of three to four times a week. I had preached in churches of all denominations and had seen many people saved by the power of God.

I never knew what to say when God would call upon me to minister. I would stand in front of a crowd of people who all seemed older than I and who all had certainly been in church longer than I had; and I knew within myself that if God didn't speak through me, there would be no speaking at all – I had no reserve of predigested sermons, and no years of ministerial experience to fall back on. I was literally an empty vessel waiting for the Lord to flow through me – and if He hadn't, the services simply would have been without preaching.

But God always came through, and His power began leading many people to the Lord through this little Jewish orphan boy who had surrendered his life to the Messiah.

I had stood in front of congregations of hundreds at a time. Me! Only fifteen years of age! A nobody, by my estimation. You can probably imagine my trepidation the first time I got up on a platform and saw several hundred eyes peering out from the congregation at me. In those days, I was what the old-timers would probably call a whippersnapper. What could people who had been in church for fifty years possibly hope to learn from a fifteen-year-old boy? But God knew what He was doing.

My goal was never to be a minister.

I wanted to be a lawyer. I wanted to serve Christ by being an advocate for Christian people, by giving Christians an honest attorney who would honestly represent them as an advocate before the judge.

I had read many stories and had witnessed lawyers firsthand. I was in enough trouble as a youngster to understand that a lawyer could be your best friend or your worst enemy.

When a lawyer is prosecuting you, his attacks know no bounds. Nothing is sacred. He can attack your character, your past, your family, your friends, your actions, even your attitude. There is nothing quite as intimidating as facing a very talented lawyer whose single goal is to see you put behind bars or to see you lose a judgment.

Conversely, though, I also knew that a talented defense lawyer could bring immense relief and provide protection from the barbs of a vicious prosecutor. When the prosecutor's accusations stray out of bounds, a good defense lawyer will stand up and shout, "I object!"

When his grounds are justified (and a good lawyer's grounds almost always are), the judge will agree with him and rein in the prosecutor.

When someone is in court facing the accusations of a zealous prosecutor, he can have no better friend or advocate than a good defense lawyer.

I wanted to be that kind of friend, that kind of advocate. Not only as a defense lawyer, but as a lawyer to represent Christian people in all legal matters. I wanted to be a shield against those who would seek to take advantage of Christians, knowing that Christians by nature wouldn't put up too much of a fight even if they knew they were getting the shaft.

I had always been scrappy, so I figured a career in law would fit my personality just right – I would fight now, however, for the rights of those I represented. Instead of using my fists, I would use the brain that God had given me.

But God continued to stir up a fervor in me, a desire to reach out to those who had not known the Jesus who had set me free – a hunger to lead more souls into the exodus I had experienced.

My goal was to practice law, then to become the governor of my state, New Jersey; but God seemed to be developing other plans in my life.

Each time I preached, the results were tremendous; with God reaching into the souls of the listeners, reaching beyond the day-to-day religion they had become accustomed to and pulling the strings of their very hearts. Salvation and other miracles seemed to flow like a mighty river.

One of my most vivid memories of those early days was when I preached in a Baptist church in Nutley, New Jersey.

I had no way of knowing the spiritual condition of the people at that church. By all appearances, the congregation was just like any other congregation – completely committed to God. In my six short months out of the orphanage, I had met many Baptists who were wholly wrapped up in God and completely committed to serving Him; and I had no reason to think that this congregation was any different.

But as I stood up on the platform (again, I wouldn't have had anything to say if God had not moved) God began moving through me to preach a salvation message.

"Someone must have brought some unsaved loved ones," I thought to myself as I continued to preach the message that God had given to me. As I preached, every eye in the congregation was trained on me. They watched my every movement and seemed to listen intently to every word.

As I began to drive the message home, it seemed most of the people in the church began leaning forward in their seats.

> *"Many will say to me in that day, Lord, Lord, have we not prophesied in thy name? and in thy name have cast out devils? and in thy name done many wonderful works? And then will I profess unto them, I never knew you: depart from me, ye that work iniquity." (Matthew 7:22-23)*

I could see tears welling up in many of the congregation members' eyes. I could see husbands looking at their wives, children looking at their parents as if seeking confirmation for what they were feeling in their hearts.

As I closed the sermon, people began weeping openly. As I called the congregation to come to the front to pray and receive Jesus as their Lord, I expected a few people to come to the front of their own volition. I expected that maybe one or more people would coax a relative nearby to come to the altar to receive Christ.

But what I saw completely amazed me.

By the time God was done in that church, the pastor, his wife and thirty-five of his congregation members had come to the altar to be born again by the power of God.

I was shocked. I knew right then an important truth that would stick by me until this very day: *"...no man can come unto me, except it were given unto him of my Father"* (John 6:65).

If God could use an uneducated, brand-new believer to lead people of this caliber to Himself, it was certain and undebatable that no man could accomplish anything for God on his own.

God revealed to me then (although not in these exact words): "This is not the work of a man, but the work of the Holy Spirit."

Appearances almost never tell the whole story. In almost any church, large numbers of people may not even know Jesus; but oftentimes, preachers assume everyone is saved so they don't reach out to those souls. I was so young and inexperienced that God was able to reach those people through the simplicity of my child-like delivery and willingness to do whatever He said.

It seemed as if every time I preached, when I gave the altar call for people to meet my Messiah, tears would stream down my cheeks as I wept for a tremendous harvest of souls. I couldn't help thinking of Jesus' indictment of the workers:

> *"The harvest truly is plenteous, but the labourers are few." (Matthew 9:37)*

I wept for those souls who weren't being reached. It seemed my singular goal in life was to reach out to lost and dying souls. I would have rather ministered the Gospel than to eat or sleep. It consumed my every thought. Every day, I was thinking of new ways I could spread the good news that had brought me freedom and had introduced me to the Messiah.

But still I resisted the call of God that gently tugged on my heart, calling me to surrender to His will for my life: preaching.

I had only been out of the orphanage for six months; but already, God was dealing with me in a tremendous way.

I was in prayer one day at Bethany Assembly of God, when I felt God's hand on my forehead again. I have only felt that hand twice in my life; once when I was baptized in the Holy Spirit and, again, this time in prayer.

I had never seen a vision up to that point. I had heard about them, and understood that they happened frequently in the Bible, but I didn't even have any idea what a vision would be like.

In today's world of televisions in every room of the house and instant access to the Internet, it's not hard for many people to imagine what a vision from God might be like. They've had years of movies produced with multi-millions of dollars by imaginative and creative Hollywood directors to shape and mold their idea of what visions and dreams should look like.

I had no such background to shape my perception. Sure, I had seen a movie or two, but I had no indication at all of what a vision from God was supposed to look like. I really didn't give it much thought, either, until this day.

As I felt the hand on my forehead, I again was slain in the Spirit, lying prostrate on the floor.

At first, nothing else happened. I was simply lying on the floor before God for what seemed to be quite a long time.

After a while, a vision began to unfold and assemble itself before my very eyes, as pieces of a puzzle that are miraculously putting themselves together to form a whole.

As the vision assembled, from one end of my field of vision to the other, I saw a beautiful blue sky.

This was not a normal-looking sky, however. Normally, as you look to the sky and the horizon, the sky fades from a darker blue at the top to a lighter blue the closer you get to the horizon. It's a natural result of your vision and the angles at which light is hitting the earth's atmosphere.

But the sky I saw was all one shade of blue. It was completely blue and the deepest, most beautiful blue I had ever seen – it immediately had the feel of something supernatural. No natural sky could ever look so incredible.

I became very nervous and confused. I didn't know what to think of what was going on.

Was I in heaven?

Had I died, and was this what happened before I was taken to heaven?

Was this the Second Coming I had been reading about? Would I soon see Christ come through the sky, and rise up to meet with Him in the air?

My heart was pounding.

But as these and a thousand other thoughts raced through my mind, I knew they could not be what was happening. I knew within myself that I was lying on the floor of Bethany Assembly of God, not up in the air or dead.

I was startled out of my wondering by a flash that brought an image of a multitude of people, all seated in concentric rows, radiating outward from my position as far as the eye could see, people upon people. They flashed before my eyes, one at a time in rapid succession.

Even more amazing, right in the front row, I saw myself sitting with the rest of the multitude of people.

When I saw myself, my brain completely lost contact with my body. I no longer was aware that I was lying on the floor at Bethany Assembly. I no longer felt the church's carpet against the back of my neck. I no longer felt the sweat that was beading down my forehead. I no longer felt the gentle pinching of my sock against my calf. I no longer heard my breathing or felt the breath.

My spirit had been lifted from the earth and taken into the heavens.

The sensation was as if I had looked into a mirror, and had been sucked into the mirror to become part of the scene I had just seen.

My entire spirit was vibrating with pulses of excitement and awe.

I could hardly believe my eyes, as before me and the incredible crowd of people, the Godhead was manifested.

I saw a flaming ball of brightness and glory, about as tall as a man and about two feet wide. I don't know how I knew that this flaming ball represented the glory of God – I just knew. There were no human-like features to it at all. It had no mouth, no hands, no legs, no nose and no eyes.

I began to shake and tremble, just as the people around me did, in the Presence of the holiness of God.

To this point, the entire vision had been silent – the tremendous, holy Presence of God commanded reverent silence.

The Presence of God was brighter than anything I had ever seen. It was ten thousand times brighter than the sun in its radiance. But this incredible, resplendent, brilliant light – as bright as it was – did not hurt my eyes at all. I could look directly at it, and understanding that it was so bright it could leave me blind, but I had no worry at all; I knew the light of God would not damage my eyes.

The color was a color I had never seen. It was both a warm and cool color at the same time. It was simply the crystallization of the glory of God. Through the years, I have tried to describe this Presence of God, and I have never been able to – my human words have no way of expressing what I saw. The best I can say is that it was the radiant glory of God, and it illuminated the entire sky and shone everywhere.

While I was sitting in awe of this magnificent glory I was seeing, I lost track of time. I don't know how long I had been there when a tremendous beam of light began to emanate from the right side of the glory of God, much as a person would stretch forth their arm in front of their body.

The light headed toward me as I sat there. I could see that this ray of light was filled with glory. The beam struck my body; and immediately, I was paralyzed by its glory. Every muscle in my entire body seemed to yield. Before I knew what was going on, I was standing.

My mind hadn't told my body to stand up. As far as I know, my leg muscles hadn't moved to lift my body. None of my muscles seemed to be working. I simply found myself standing, without having gone through the action of standing up from my sitting position.

My legs began moving, and I began walking toward the light.

I cannot adequately describe the emotions I felt at that time.

I felt completely humble as one cannot feel until he finds himself in the Presence of Almighty God. Suddenly everything about me was wholly overshadowed by the presence of the One I was approaching. Everything about Him seemed so much higher, so much cleaner, so much holier, that I could do nothing but reflect in myself that God is indeed holy – I had a brand-new understanding of that word, "holy." I understood that even the presence of shoes on top of ground that holiness is standing on is an affront to the holiness.

I suddenly knew how Moses must have felt when God, in the bush that was burning but was not consumed, commanded him to take his shoes off because he was on holy ground.

How could something made by man, like shoes, even dare to appear in the presence of a God whose creative power was so much higher? His holiness demanded that the feet He had created walk the ground in His presence.

My body was still walking me toward the presence of God – the presence of the triunc Godhead; the Father, the Son and the Holy Ghost.

I walked until I stood about an arm's length from the Presence of God – this brilliant light that outshone the sun in its radiance. Everything was still silent.

Every fiber of my being was in complete ecstasy. Every cell, every molecule, every atom seemed to be rejoicing to be standing in the Presence of the holy Creator of all things. I felt completely and utterly full of the glory of God. I could not imagine ever receiving any more and living to tell about it. My entire being was on fire with the glory of the living God. I was completely overwhelmed.

Just then, the Presence of God that had been no more than an arm's length away from me moved about a foot away from Its previous location, a foot further away from me.

I had just been reflecting on the tremendous blessing that God had drawn me so close to His Presence. I was just rejoicing in the nearness I felt to God, but now He had moved away. I could not understand why He would draw me so close to only move away from me.

But I didn't have very much time to dwell on my disappointment that He had moved away.

My eyes were drawn to where the Presence of God had been standing.

Where He had moved away, there were two footprints. It looked just as if someone had cut two footprint-shaped holes in a giant cheesecake upon which I was standing.

I looked through those footprints, and what I saw changed the course of my life forever.

As I looked through those footprints, I saw the very flames of hell licking upward toward where I was. It is surely one of the most unusual things anyone could ever experience to be standing in the holy Presence of the living God and to be looking at the same time into the pit of hell.

I had never imagined that such torment could exist.

The flesh of the people seemed to be on fire, but they were not burned up. They were continually scorched by the red-hot flames, but they were never consumed.

There seemed to be no relief. No matter where the people were, the flames seemed to burn them equally. Every inch of every person's body was engulfed in the flames continually.

The horror in their eyes was uniform in every person I saw. They were the eyes of people who knew there was no escape from the utter damnation they were experiencing; people who knew they would never have relief, never again have a moment's peace from a pain more intense than any they had felt when they were alive.

The pit seemed to go on forever, lined with people who were tormented by the flames.

As they were burned, the multitude – I could see thousands upon thousands of people – were screaming out for mercy. Children were crying out to their parents saying that they would obey now if they could only have a second chance.

Others were crying out, hoping futilely that the prayers of their loved ones would rescue them.

Backsliders were crying out for another chance to serve God.

Adulterers were crying out that they would now be faithful.

Fathers were screaming that they would raise their children right, in the knowledge of the Lord.

Ministers were crying out that they would preach the Gospel now if they could only have a chance.

Some were screaming at others, asking why they had not told them of the Gospel and salvation.

Others were just screaming. Screaming in pain and horror. Screaming in sadness and grief. I had seen people grieving at funerals before, but the people above the ground were not grieving even the tiniest percentage as much as these people who were below it, their flesh constantly torched with undying flame.

Many people were screaming through clenched teeth as they gnashed them together against the pain, to no avail. In this pit, there was no death to end the pain, no morning sunrise to end the nightmare, no water to quench the fire.

Through all the cries, the same voice was heard: anguish. All were reaching their hands upward, seeking someone to come and pull them out of the flames.

But no one answered their cries.

My heart was moved with compassion beyond anything I have ever felt. How would people be saved from such a tremendously hideous fate if no one would tell them of the saving love of Jesus?

It was then that the scripture came to life to me: *"How then shall they call on him in whom they have not believed? and how shall they believe in him of whom they have not heard? and how shall they hear without a preacher?"* (Romans 10:14)

I was presented with a choice.

I could serve as a friend and advocate for people as a Christian lawyer, representing them in temporal matters before earthly judges and eventually as the governor of New Jersey.

Or I could serve as the messenger for the true Advocate, Jesus Christ, Who came to represent them in eternal matters before the Judge of all things.

My reaction was instantaneous. When God had presented me with this tremendous vision of the ultimate end of sinners, I did not hesitate. I knew what I had to do.

I stepped over and put my feet in the footprints that the Presence of God had left when He stepped away.

To my complete astonishment, my feet fit the footprints perfectly.

I realized that God had called me to this vision for a specific purpose, to *"... make up the hedge, and stand in the gap..."* (Ezekiel 22:30).

God had called me to surrender completely to His will, to dedicate my life to fulfilling the purpose for which He had called me. As a result, my life – dedicated to and directed by Him – would make a difference for thousands and thousands of souls who otherwise may never walk through the gates of glory.

But how could I, a fifteen-year-old Jewish orphan boy, hope to reach so many people?

How would I possibly make a difference in their lives? I had no formal training, I didn't understand why God would want me. I began to get nervous and fear that I would be inadequate for the task God had called me to do.

No sooner had I made the decision to surrender than I felt a warmth all over my body. I turned around, and the Presence of God was right next to me, right by my side; I had moved closer when I had stepped in His footprints.

The ray that had emanated from the Presence of God and drawn me to Him was now engulfing me, glowing all around my shoulders.

Immediately, all my fear and nervousness fell away. I felt strength flow into my body. I felt power from God strengthen me completely.

Until this point, the brilliant light that was the Presence of God had spoken nothing.

But now, the voice of a man, kind, gentle, young and full of gentle authority, spoke from the light. It was a voice that sent waves of glory all over my body. It was the richest, most comforting voice I had ever heard. The words were not in English – they were in a language I had never heard, but I understood them in English:

"My son, arise, shine, for thy light is come and the glory of the Lord is risen upon thee. Thou shalt not be afraid, for thou shalt not stand in thine own strength; neither shall thou stand in thine own place, but you shall stand in the place I have made for thee and My strength shall uphold and guard thee."

Then with a tremendously powerful force, the glorious Presence of God began to shoot forth rays of bright light and glory over the heads of the sea of humanity that were gathered.

Once again, He spoke to me: "When you see My Glory in the midst of My people, know then that I am there in the midst to bless you as you minister to My people."

And then, as suddenly as it had started, the vision was over.

I again was lying on the floor of Bethany Assembly of God. I began to praise God for the call He had just demonstrated so powerfully in my life.

From that point forward, my life changed. Though I had been preaching before this vision, I had never preached like I soon would.

From that point forward, my life was dedicated to keeping more souls from entering that fiery, eternal grave.

The vision remained vivid in my memory; and every day, it drove me to reach out more fervently to the souls who were crying for help all over the world.

But I hadn't seen anything yet.

## Chapter 3

# A Family of Miracles

The effect of the miraculous vision I had just experienced was much like the effect of a match lighting the fuse of a bottle rocket.

God had not only given me a mandate, but He had also given me supernatural zeal and wisdom beyond my years to start accomplishing that plan.

I began preaching wherever I could, whenever I could, to whomever I could.

I would minister anywhere, whether it was to ten people in a storefront church or a thousand people in a huge cathedral, I didn't care. All I cared about was ministering the Gospel of Jesus Christ.

My entire life began to be consumed with getting closer to God and with fulfilling the vision He had given me.

I traveled all over the east coast – New York, New Jersey and the New England area, preaching any time I got a chance. During this time, I met Dr. Rev. Nickolas Nikolof, the president of an Assemblies of God Bible college in North Bergen, New Jersey.

Rev. Nikolof became like a spiritual father to me.

I spent as much time with him as I could, like a sponge, soaking up all the knowledge he released.

I would ask him all the questions that came to my mind.

We spoke on subjects ranging from sin to heaven, from dedication to tithing to faithfulness and evangelism. Dr. Nikolof, like me, had a tremendous heart for souls. He originally came from Russia, so he understood the need overseas firsthand, but he also understood the need right in his own neighborhood.

He was a minister of tremendous integrity, and I grew to love and respect him very deeply.

When I was almost seventeen years old, Dr. Nikolof and I were nearly inseparable. Every chance I could, I spent time with him discussing the Bible and the Church. The Bible college moved from North Bergen, New Jersey, to Suffern, in upstate New York.

One day, during one of our long conversations, almost out of the blue, Dr. Nikolof asked me to speak at a chapel service at the Bible college.

I was always glad to minister, but it was a bit intimidating to speak in front of a group of Bible students who were in classes to become ministers day in and day out.

But I loved and respected Dr. Nikolof very much, and so I agreed.

When the day came, I was still a bit nervous, but I spent a very long time in prayer with God before the service, as my practice had become. I remembered vividly God's words to me in the vision I had when I was fifteen: "When you see My glory in the midst of My people, know then that I am there in the midst to bless you as you minister to My people."

It immediately had become my practice to pray and worship God until I saw His glory – until I was sure that it was He, not me, ministering to the people.

This morning was no different.

Once I was sure God's glory was in the place, and that God was there to bless the people, I walked up to the pulpit and delivered my message to the Bible college students.

When the service was over, Dr. Nikolof invited me to eat lunch with him. As we entered the cafeteria, the table was already set up, with plates, knives and forks at each setting.

I sat down, and found myself sitting next to the most beautiful girl I had ever seen.

During the meal, we talked very little, but I did learn that her name was Theresa LePari. I knew right then that this was the girl with whom I would spend the rest of my life.

I've never been shy, so after the meal, I called Theresa into the hallway with me because I had something I wanted to say to her.

There's no telling what was going through her mind at the time. I had never laid eyes on her before; and this was the first time she had met me. Doubtlessly, she was wondering what I could possibly have to say to her in the hallway.

My heart was pounding, but I've never been one to mince words, so I just blurted it out: "I want to tell you something before I leave this Bible college. One day, I'm coming back here, and I just want you to know that I'm going to marry you."

Her reaction was not exactly what I had hoped for or envisioned.

I had hoped she would be swept off her feet and rejoice at the news that I was going to marry her.

Her reaction was a bit less encouraging, though.

Theresa's eyes seemed to get about as big as grapefruits. Her mouth formed a big "O" as her jaw dropped. She threw her hands on top of her head, slammed her eyes shut and screamed.

She whirled around like a spinning top, and still screaming, ran away as fast as her legs could carry her.

You would figure a move like that would discourage the most persistent of suitors, but I was not in the least bit deterred.

I went home to the Maurers' house, and as soon as I opened the door, I told the Maurers, "Today, I saw the young lady I'm going to marry."

They didn't react quite as surprised as Theresa had, but I could tell they were not convinced. I wasn't worried, though. I knew I would marry her, and that was settled.

In fact, Theresa was one of the main reasons I decided to attend Bible college that September. I also wanted to learn more from Dr. Nikolof, but still, Theresa was the reason.

At the time, she was engaged to another boy, who ended up being my roommate at the college.

I didn't see Theresa for the entire summer after I made my surprise announcement to her. I thought of her often, but I didn't pursue her yet; I knew everything would work out in God's timing.

In fact, Theresa, although she was engaged to my roommate, was beginning to have second thoughts about her relationship with him.

As I found out later, Theresa's entire life is wrapped up in pleasing God. She wants everything God has for her, and nothing God doesn't have for her. I have never met a more dedicated woman in my entire life.

Her parents were not crazy about the idea of her marrying this other boy, and their opinions had always mattered a lot to the young Bible school student. But more importantly, Theresa began to feel that she was making a mistake.

Unwilling to do anything out of the will of God, Theresa placed a fleece before God.

"God," she had told the Lord, "If I am not supposed to marry this boy, please have him write a letter telling me we should separate for a while."

Much to her surprise, a few days later, he had called her on the telephone in a panic.

"Theresa," he said to her. "I sent you a letter the other day, I don't even know what I was thinking when I wrote it. I didn't realize what I had done until I had already closed the envelope and put on the stamp and mailed it. Please, when you get the letter, don't read it."

"I can't do that," Theresa told him. "I asked God to have you write that letter. I think we should separate for a while, and see what God does."

After a time, the boy grudgingly agreed, and he left the Bible college Theresa and I were attending, and he began attending Central Bible College in Springfield, Missouri.

By the time six months had passed, the two had grown apart, and Theresa knew he was not the man God wanted her to marry.

I knew some of the story at the time, but I didn't immediately begin courting Theresa. I knew God would work in His time, and I was in no rush.

Those were different days; boys and girls didn't just go out on dates, they spent time together in the worship of God and the reading of His Word.

By the time I was ready to begin courting Theresa, I knew the way to her was through her mother. Theresa loved and respected her mother, and I had a great deal of respect for her, too.

I called one day, and before Theresa could object, her mother had invited me over to the house.

When I arrived, I had a fistful of flowers in one hand and in the other hand a box of candy. But if Theresa thought those goodies were for her, she had another thing coming. I had brought them for her mother, who fixed a large meal of spaghetti. That meal was some of the best food I ate while I was in college.

To this day, every once in awhile, Theresa teases me about how her mother got candy and flowers and she got nothing.

Theresa worked at the kitchen in the college, and one day, I was assigned kitchen duties.

In between washing dishes and cleaning tables, Theresa and I began to talk. Our talking eventually led to courtship.

I studied very hard at the college during the week, and worked odd jobs during the evenings and weekends to earn money for necessities like socks and toothpaste.

I became the pitcher for the college's softball team. But as far as I'm concerned, "softball" is a misnomer. Those balls are anything but soft.

During one game, I delivered a pitch like I always did. The guy I was pitching to was huge – he was 6-foot-2 and looked like he spent a lot of time at the gym.

The ball I pitched apparently was perfect – perfect for him to give it a good whack and drive it right into my face.

I had just turned my head a bit, and the ball slammed into my head like a freight train. All I remember is a burst of light, and then I was out like a light.

Students rushed to me and took me to the hospital.

The doctors didn't like what they saw. My mouth was hanging open, and blood was everywhere.

The ball had broken my jaw in two places, and it had splintered my cheekbone.

The year was 1949, and the doctor told me he would not be able to fix my jaw completely. In these days of modern reconstructive surgery, such a thing is almost unthinkable. It seems like a small thing for doctors to reconstruct a bone, augmenting it with high-tech compounds, molding it with high-tech computers and setting it to perfection.

But this was 1949, not today. The doctor said he was almost certain I would never be able to speak or preach with a normal movement in my jaw.

He had to send to New Jersey for a brace to put on my jaw to hold my mouth shut for six months, while the bones would heal as best they could.

In the meantime, he bandaged up my jaw with an elastic cloth band that he wrapped around my head to hold my jaw into place.

I couldn't move my jaw at all. I couldn't move it to eat and I could barely move it to speak.

All I could eat was whatever I could fit through a straw. I could do no chewing.

The injury was very painful. In fact, even if I had been physically able to chew, I don't think I would have wanted to. The entire side of my face throbbed constantly and ached. It was an ache unlike I had ever felt, hollow and pervasive. Nothing I did would make the pain go away; I could not ignore it by reading a book or listening to people talk. It was always there.

To make matters worse, I was trying desperately to court Theresa. I was so embarrassed to see her with a big, white bandage wrapped around my head. I'm sure I looked like a Civil War vet!

I mumbled to her through the bandages. I'm sure the scene was pretty comical from her perspective – here's a young man trying to mutter amorous words, but he can't move his jaw, so it comes out as gibberish. But comical as it may have looked, Theresa never laughed. She always listened intensely to my mutterings.

Before the softball game, I had been invited to speak at a little Pentecostal church in the area. The pastor was very excited, and he said the congregation was anxiously awaiting the upcoming Sunday when I would minister.

But that was before my jaw was broken, and everyone expected me to cancel, after all what good is a preacher who can do no more than mutter?

I was sorry that I would have to miss this opportunity. The zeal I had gotten during my precious vision with God was still burning brightly in my heart, and I regretted any time I wasn't able to minister the Gospel.

One day, I was deep in prayer in my dorm room at school. I was praying as I always did, thanking God for His workings in my life, and pleading with Him for lost souls. I prayed for those people I knew of personally and those I had yet to meet, when God interrupted my petitions with His wonderful voice: "Son, if you will keep the commitment you have made to minister, I will heal you."

That settled it for me. God had never led me wrong. When He had spoken, He had always done what He said He would do.

This time, I had no reason to doubt Him, even though I had never suffered an injury quite this severe, and I had never had need of such a visible miracle.

I began telling my friends and fellow students that I would not cancel on my commitment to preach. "And God will heal me," I told them, matter-of-factly.

I learned right then a valuable lesson.

People rarely believe a miracle, and especially before it happens. I had never expected to be met with such doubt and nay-saying.

Nearly everyone (with a few exceptions) I told about the healing God was going to perform reacted the same way: "Morris, don't go up there and bring disgrace on this school. What if God doesn't heal you?"

They needn't have wasted words, though. In my mind, what they were saying is, "I don't believe God will heal you."

I learned about going through criticism, especially from those who you normally wouldn't expect it. I understood then why Jesus had told the leper He healed in the eighth chapter of Matthew: *"See thou tell no man; but go thy way, shew thyself to the priest..."* (Matthew 8:4)

The entire school was abuzz by the time the Sunday rolled around when I was to preach. Everyone was talking about this crazy Jewish orphan who was going to preach with a broken jaw, believing that God would heal him.

# A Family of Miracles

The little Pentecostal church wasn't designed to hold very many people. In fact, when I arrived, I looked at the little white building, and I was reminded of the picturesque paintings I had seen of little whitewashed churches in country settings, with trees all around, grass vibrantly green and gravel walkways leading up to wooden steps and a small, white door.

This little church looked like a house in every way except for the steeple. It had two little windows on the front, and the door looked just like a door on any of a number of houses in the area.

There were two small rows of pews on either side of the aisle that led directly from the front door to the platform, which was actually just a space at the back of the building with a small, wooden pulpit and a short pew sitting cockeyed in the corner.

I had expected possibly ten people, maybe fifteen, to show up to hear this Bible school student preach. But when I got to the little church, I was amazed to see a crowd of about one hundred people milling about outside the building.

"They must be waiting to go inside," I thought to myself. But when I reached the church and saw through the doorway, I saw that every pew was packed, with people crammed in as tightly as they could get. I recognized most of the people outside as students from the Bible college.

I will never forget that moment. I had my Bible tucked under my arm, and I had a bandage wrapped around my head, holding my jaw in place.

"All right, God, here we go!" I thought.

I reached up and peeled the top of the bandage until a little piece came loose that I could get my fingers around. When I had a piece sufficient enough, I tore the bandage off.

My jaw dropped open.

The pain was beyond anything I have ever experienced. It was even worse than when the jaw had actually been hit by the softball.

My entire body throbbed with the tremendous pain, and for a moment, I thought I might pass out. But I decided I would not concentrate on my circumstance. I would not look at the natural, I would remember and operate on the promise God had made to me. I was holding up my end by being here and ministering. I knew within myself that God would hold up His end.

So, despite the tremendous pain, I took the first step up the stairs to enter the church. With each step, the pain seemed to increase, as the motion of my body moved the bones around inside my head.

As I walked forward through the church, every eye in the place was on me. I didn't greet anyone – I couldn't! There was no way I could speak at all with my jaw in such excruciating pain.

Each step blurred my vision with pain, but I made my way up to the platform and took my seat.

The man leading the worship service was singing songs of praise, but I could tell by the puzzled look on his face, he was wondering what in the world was going on with this young preacher, his jaw agape, sitting on the platform. If I wasn't in such pain, I would have found the look on his face humorous, and I probably would have burst out in laughter. But the pain kept me from doing something embarrassing like that.

I couldn't sing along with the songs. My jaw continued to hang open.

When the song service ended, the man began to give the church's announcements. As he ticked off each announcement from the list he had in front of him, he

74

periodically glanced over his shoulder at me. I'm sure I looked frightful with my jaw hanging down like that.

When the announcements were made, the man began taking up the offering. As he spoke, his words began to slow down. Was he stalling? He continued to look at me, probably unaware that he was doing it so often.

When the offering was taken up, the man led the congregation in a few more songs. I became certain that he was stalling – he had no idea what to do with this young preacher whose jaw was hanging so obtrusively open.

Finally, when he could stall no more, the man mustered up the courage to introduce me to minister.

I still had experienced no healing. Through the song service, the announcements, the offering, the extra songs, nothing had changed. The pain was still there. My jaw was still hanging open. Nothing had changed at all.

Every eye in the place was fixed on me. There was a tangible silence in the room, with everyone wondering what I would do, and what was going to happen.

I gingerly stood up and made my way to the pulpit. As if nothing was any different from normal, I took my Bible from under my arm, nonchalantly laid it on the pulpit and flipped through it until I found the place I wanted.

I looked out at the congregation. They were looking at my jaw hanging open, fascinated by the story that was unfolding before their very eyes.

I took a deep breath and looked down at the Bible to begin reading the verse I had chosen for my text.

Suddenly, as I prepared to begin reading, my jaw snapped back into place. I'm sure it wasn't as loud to everyone in the congregation, but inside my head, the pop and crack were enormous, as the two breaks in my jaw and the splintering in my cheekbone instantaneously popped back into their normal locations. I was totally, perfectly healed.

I began reading the Scripture as if nothing had happened. When I paused for a second and looked out at the congregation, they all looked like I had looked a few minutes earlier – their jaws were all hanging open! They hadn't broken anything, they were simply shocked at the miracle they had just witnessed.

I never gave it another thought. I preached my entire sermon without any problems whatsoever – the pain and the throbbing were completely gone, and my jaw moved normally, just as it had my entire life.

This was not just a healing, it was an instantaneous miracle of God.

The Holy Spirit descended upon that little, white church, and revival broke out immediately. The service was full of the power of the Holy Spirit, and the revival that began there spread throughout our Bible college.

It was not too long afterwards that Theresa and I were married.

As I stood at the front of Dr. Nikolof's little church in Newberg, New York, Theresa came down the aisle wearing a beautiful white wedding dress. I had never seen anyone look quite so beautiful, so radiant.

Though I had known it from the moment I met her, I still could hardly believe this beautiful vision of a young woman would soon be my wife.

I had thirty-five dollars in my pocket – the extent of my wealth. After we were married, at the reception, generous friends had given us a grand total of $350, which was quite a princely sum in those days.

Some very good friends of ours who were in our wedding party knew we didn't have enough money for a honeymoon, so they invited us to spend a few days with them in North Bergen.

I had just received a pastorate at a small church in Claremont, New Hampshire, and our friends wanted us to have some time to ourselves before we went off to all that work.

We didn't have a car, so Theresa's father was kind enough to loan us his big, bright Chevy to make the drive to North Bergen.

Since we hadn't had a honeymoon, I wanted to treat my new bride to something special, so I did about all we could afford, I took her to a baseball game in North Bergen. It was her first and only baseball game.

I don't remember who was playing or what the score was, but Theresa and I had a wonderful time, new husband and wife, just enjoying each other's company. We really didn't pay too close attention to the game. Instead, we sat and held hands, eating our ballpark hot dogs and drinking our soft drinks, while enjoying the crack of the bat and the roar of the crowd as we caught ourselves gazing into each other's eyes.

It was a perfect moment. We were so happy. Before us lay a tremendous adventure, and behind us lay tremendous victories, such triumphs for people so young.

But this night, we were simply caught up in the moment, enjoying the company of each other and knowing that God had brought us together and would keep us.

That night, we walked out of the ball park, hand in hand, swinging our arms and laughing and giggling together.

We got into Theresa's dad's car and drove to the home of our friends. I parked the car at the top of a big hill, and I guess I was so wrapped up in my new wife that I forgot to put the car in gear and set the parking brake.

I grabbed Theresa's hand and we began walking across the street. We hadn't even made it to the other side of the street when we heard a loud crash, and then tinkling of glass. Then silence.

We both jumped when we heard the crash, and Theresa tightened her grip on my hand.

I spun around and looked toward the source of the noise.

To my horror, the noise had come from Theresa's father's bright, shiny new Chevy, which was now at the bottom of the hill, wrapped around a tree.

I was horrified.

Mr. LePari had been so generous in allowing us to borrow his car. We had driven it so carefully, not wanting even one little scratch or ding to get on the car while we had it. We had even made sure our feet were clean of mud or dirt before we had gotten into the car. We had wanted to return the car to him in pristine condition.

But now, here the car was, not only dirty, but smashed up around a tree where it had jumped the curb and smashed into it.

My heart dropped. How could I possibly return the car to Mr. LePari in such a horrible condition? How could I possibly do such damage to his car and then just return it to him? I couldn't.

There was only one thing we could do.

The next day, I called all around town to all the service shops, asking for estimates on what it would cost to repair the damage the tree had done to Theresa's dad's car.

Eventually, I found the right shop, and I spent all day there as the men from the shop worked to hammer out the dents, replace the parts that weren't repairable and re-paint the rear of the car.

The repairs took every last penny of our wedding money – all $350. We were flat broke, but it was worth it to return the car to Mr. LePari in the same condition he had loaned it to us.

The only money we had was what remained of the $35 that was in my pocket when we got married. It was only enough money to get us back to Newberg, and then on to Claremont, New Hampshire, where we were to begin pastoring.

I had received the pastorate in kind of an unusual way.

I had just graduated from Bible college, and Rev. Smuland was the district superintendent of the Assemblies of God. I was on my way up to conduct a meeting with Rev. Flower, who later became the secretary treasurer of the Assemblies of God. On the way to the meeting, I stopped overnight in Rev. Smuland's house in Framingham, Massechussets, because we were friends.

Rev. Smuland got a call to preach at the Claremont Assembly of God, which was without a pastor, but he was suffering with heart problems and asked me if I would go instead.

I immediately said I would, and I filled in for him at the Claremont Assembly on Sunday with about fifteen people in the service.

The next day, when we arrived back, representatives from the church called Rev. Smuland and said that they had gotten together and taken a vote – and they had selected me as their new pastor.

I got a call from Rev. Smuland, and he informed me that the Claremont Assembly of God had voted me in as their new pastor, and gave me a number where I could contact them.

I broke into laughter when I received the news. At that time, I was scheduled to preach in most of the larger Assembly of God churches on the East Coast. I called the church and told them that pastoring their church was out of the question. I was getting married and then going out on the evangelistic field.

As soon as I had hung up the phone, the Spirit of God spoke to me as cleary as He ever had.

"Son," God said. "Go back, pick that phone back up, call that church and tell them you will be their pastor."

I was shocked.

I was called to the evangelistic fields, to reach out to the world with the Gospel. But God obviously had other plans for me right then. So I turned back and picked up the phone and told the church that even though I didn't fully understand what was happening, God had told me to take the church.

"As soon as I get married, you can expect me to come up and pastor your church," I said.

When we arrived in Claremont, we were exhausted from the trip. We found the little apartment that we had rented and headed that way, stopping only at the grocery store to pick up a few cans of Franco American spaghetti.

Back then, food was much less expensive than it is now, but we still had to scrape together our pennies to even buy those few small cans of food.

We opened the door to our new apartment – where we would begin our new life together – and looked inside at its bare interior.

We had no furniture. All we had was a sewing machine that Theresa's grandmother had given to her. We had no couch, no nightstand, no bookshelves, no bed. Nothing. All we had was ourselves, our clothes, our Bibles and our few cans of food.

We sat on the floor in the kitchen, opened a can of Franco American spaghetti, got two forks, smiled at each other, and dug in.

That first meal will be with me for the rest of my life (and Theresa, too – she says she's never opened up another can of Franco American).

# A Family of Miracles

We were poorer than poor, but we had a child-like faith, and an understanding that it didn't matter how much money we had. God would take care of us, just as He always had.

We were sitting in a tiny apartment in a town we didn't know, eating cold Franco American spaghetti, but we were together, and God had our futures in His hands. Not only were we not worried or sad, we rejoiced that now we were beginning the biggest adventure of our lives. We were married, and we were given a church to pastor. Our lives were good, and we were happy.

We had to sleep on the floor, because we didn't have a bed.

There's a tremendous lesson to be learned from our circumstances. I think sometimes people focus too much on their circumstances. They see the bills they can't pay, they see the empty cupboards, they hear the growl of their stomachs, they feel pain in their bodies, and they get their eyes off God. But God is bigger than our circumstances.

Theresa and I had to sleep on the same floor and eat food that was less than desirable, but we were happy because we knew we were in God's will, doing God's purpose.

In fact, our first Christmas together, I had no money to get anything for Theresa, but I wanted to be able to buy her some kind of gift. So I went out and spent all the money I had – twenty-five cents – and got her a little plastic apron.

We didn't think about our squalid circumstances. We didn't concentrate on the fact that we didn't have nice things like other people. We didn't think about the fact that we didn't eat big meals like everyone else. We had no perception that we were "suffering for the Gospel" or anything like that. We were simply overjoyed to be in the will and the purpose of God.

When we arrived at the little church we had been called to pastor, there were possibly fifteen members.

The church building was small and a bit musty. The building needed repairs, and it needed some cleaning.

But that first Sunday, I spent a few hours before the service praising God, worshipping Him and seeking Him for His presence in our service, as He had promised me after the vision He had shown me.

After a few hours, I saw the glory of God descend into the building, and I knew God was preparing to minister to this tiny group of people who had assembled to hear their new young pastor minister.

We had only a piano, so we sang songs of worship with clapping to help us keep the rhythm.

During the worship service, I could already sense that God was moving mightily through the congregation.

As I approached the pulpit to deliver my first message as a pastor, I knew that God was preparing to do a mighty work in the church; to expand it, not by adding members from other churches or having current members bring their families in, but by creating a new congregation from scratch by turning all of these few current members into evangelists who will fill the church up with brand new Christians.

And that's exactly what I preached, day in and day out, to this congregation.

During the week, I divided my days between mowing the grass at the church, repairing the roof and floors, scrubbing the walls and cleaning the church and studying for sermons. It certainly came in handy that I had been forced to work odd jobs to pay my way through school. Now the skills I had learned at those odd jobs were paying off as I worked to repair the church and make the place presentable.

The congregation was still small in the early weeks, but it began growing very rapidly. First it was one family that came to hear the strange new pastor in town.

That very first service they attended, the entire family gave their lives to Jesus. After that, the growth was exponential.

We prayerfully decided to hold a citywide crusade to reach out to the people of Claremont. In the midst of working to put on this crusade, I came down with a terrible sickness. The doctors told Theresa to keep me in bed at all costs, and that I was not to get up. But when Theresa left, I got up anyway, and went about making arrangements for the crusade, going to the newspapers, printing hand bills and other details.

We were going to have the meeting at City Hall.

Right then, the presidential primary season was heating up, and one of the candidates decided to hold his meeting for Claremont right on the front steps of the City Hall, where I was going to have the citywide crusade.

As he was speaking to the people of Claremont, across the top of his head behind him was a banner that read "Citywide crusade, salvation, healing, miracles. Cerullo crusade."

All of the newsreel cameras (back in those days television was in its infancy, and most people got their news from newsreels at the movie theatres) captured the banner as they were filming the presidential candidate.

Two days later, I got a call from one of my business friends in the city, and he said:

"Reverend, did you know you're in the movies?"

"What?" I asked him, thinking he was kidding.

"Well," he said, "when the senator was here running for the presidency and gave his speech in front of the City Hall, he was underneath your banner, and now you're in all the movie houses."

So God gave our crusade a publicity boost through that experience, and the crusade added many families to the church, who gave their lives to Jesus and stayed to become members.

Within eight months, because of this tremendous influx, the church had grown from just a handful of members to the sixth-largest Spirit-filled, Charismatic church in the six New England states.

Every service, my practice was the same. I would not approach the platform until I knew the glory of God was there – until I knew that He was going to minister to His people.

I didn't see any point in having a church if God wasn't going to do the ministering. After all, who was I but a Jewish orphan boy? Without the glory of God, I could never have hoped to effectively minister to this growing congregation of people.

As the church began to grow more and more, we began to enjoy a sense of security. We were building a solid ministry, and we began to feel comfortable.

That's when God started what was to be a pattern in my life.

His will for me was to never settle for what I had, never settle for the plateaus I reached. Though we had built a comfortable ministry and were feeling secure, God's plans for us were to step out in faith and live, day-to-day, in His provision.

I had only been a pastor for eight months, and the church was booming, but God spoke to me. "Son, your work here is finished. You must go back into full-time evangelism."

Within myself, I had known this day would come. Despite the stability of pastoring, I knew that God had called me to reach out to the corners of the earth. I knew that He had not called me to be a pastor for the rest of my life; He had called me to step out on the edge and forge ahead where nobody had gone.

The vision He had given me when I was fifteen years old was still vivid in my mind: People from all over the world were dying every day, having rejected Jesus – and God had called me to reach them.

I could not forget the screams I had heard from the souls in hell. I could not forget the anguish on their faces, or the pain in their eyes.

I had to fulfill God's call for my life – to reach the souls no one else could.

It was easy for me to tell God I would obey, but telling Theresa would be another matter.

Eight months of pastoring full-time had dried up my invitations to preach. I had no meetings lined up whatsoever, and to make matters worse, Theresa was seven months pregnant.

When it had just been her and me, it was easy to envision living out of a suitcase, carting ourselves and all our belongings from town to town, living in motels and the homes of pastors, but with a new baby on the way, that lifestyle would become more complicated.

Right now, Theresa and I enjoyed some measure of security and stability, which is what any couple craves when a new baby is on the way.

It wasn't easy to break the news to her. When I told Theresa, her eyes dropped. She knew God had called us to minister evangelistically, and she had made a commitment to God to do whatever He asked of her, to go anywhere He asked her to go. But those kinds of things are hard to reconcile when you're carrying a tiny little infant in your womb, when your only instinct is to nest into your home and build a comfortable and warm environment for your soon-coming baby. The last thing she wanted to do was travel, without a home, with a new baby.

But despite the enormity of the struggle, Theresa knew God had called her to this ministry, and she obeyed.

Stepping out on faith, we resigned a growing church, packed up our belongings, and moved back to Theresa's mother's house in Newburgh, New York.

We again had no money. I began to get meetings, and I would travel alone, sometimes with only enough money to get to the meeting. Theresa stayed with her mother until the baby was born, and then we began traveling together, mother, father and our son, David.

Most of the time, we had no money for motel rooms, so we would stay with generous pastors, who would let us sleep in their homes while we were ministering in their churches.

Two months into this renewed evangelistic ministry, our first son, David, was born.

I had never seen anything so beautiful, I was convinced. I had seen many miracles already in my young life – I had seen people healed, I had seen deliverances, and of course, I had been healed myself. But I didn't think I had ever seen any miracle quite as great as this pink little person who peered at me from beyond his infant blankets, his brilliant blue eyes twinkling at his dad.

Even his cries sounded like music to my ears. Everything about him was perfect. I counted – ten fingers on his tiny little hands and ten toes on his tiny little feet. There was just a tuft of black hair on top of his tiny little head.

I long had been in awe of the biblical David's unabashed love for God, and his unrelenting faith in the God who had delivered him from a lion, a bear and the champion of the Philistines, Goliath.

In the face of all opposition, the biblical David stood for fidelity to God and believing that God is Who He says He is. Through all of life's trials and tribulations, he stood fast and furious for God and consistently admonished the people to worship God with all their hearts.

I could think of no better namesake for my little miracle. Theresa and I agreed that David would be his name; we believed our son would be just such a person as the biblical David, standing fast for God no matter what happened.

Just ten short days after he was born, we bundled little David up, packed him in the car and headed toward the city where we would be conducting our next meeting.

Stop and imagine for a second what a sacrifice that was for Theresa. Today, a woman will oftentimes walk out of the hospital a few days after she's given birth because of modern methods of healing that make her recovery much easier.

But in those days women stayed in hospitals much longer after they had given birth during their long recovery.

Yet, here it was, scarcely a week after she had given birth to her first son, and Theresa was with me in the car, her baby in her arms, headed to the next meeting.

Already, this new mother was exhibiting the qualities that would later endear her as "Mama" to many nations of the world.

They were hard times.

There never seemed to be enough money. We often only had enough to get from one meeting to the next, and many times, we didn't even have enough money to eat.

We had no laundromats, no plastic diapers, so everything had to be washed by hand. Theresa worked day and night to take care of her growing family. There were no refrigerators to cool down the milk – none of the things we take for granted, so Theresa had her hands full. But she never complained.

On one occasion, we were en route from one meeting to the next. It was getting late and we needed gas, so I pulled over into a truck stop to fill up the tank on our car.

After I had finished pumping the gas and paying for it, I realized that we barely had any money left.

We knew that God always provided for our needs, so Theresa and I decided we would go into the restaurant that was attached to the truck stop anyway.

As we sat down at the counter and looked at the menu, we sipped at the glasses of water the waitress placed in front of us.

So many of the items on the menu sounded delicious to us.

The restaurant offered steaks, hamburgers, chicken, salads, baked potatoes, meat loaf and other goodies we knew we couldn't afford. Each item had a price that was quite a bit more money than we had.

Finally, we found an item we could afford – a bowl of soup.

We couldn't afford two bowls of soup, so we ordered one and shared it.

The restaurant supplied as many crackers as you wanted with soup, so I think we ate far more crackers than we ate soup!

Four months after David was born, I had the scare of my young life.

Theresa, David and I were in Wisconsin holding a crusade. We had run advertisements in the local newspaper that said a Spirit-filled Jew would be ministering the Gospel of Jesus Christ.

Little did we know it at the time, but our advertisement stirred up quite a bit of ruckus. The owner of the newspaper was a well-known stern Communist and avowed atheist named John C. Chappel.

When Chappel saw my advertisement in his newspaper, he was furious. The principles of Communism developed by Karl Marx state that religion is the "opiate of the masses." In other words, a good Communist believes that religion is no better than a drug, deceiving and enslaving people who are not smart enough to free themselves from its bondage.

John Chappel was a good Communist, and so he was infuriated that this Jew was coming to his town to infest the people with the "opiate of the masses."

He was so mad, in fact, that he showed up at the meeting with clenched fists so he could tell me a thing or two – and I'm not sure he wanted to tell me something by talking about it.

During the meeting, however, the Spirit of God began speaking to this atheist and Communist.

He knew in an instant that he had been mistaken. He knew he was lost, knew he was in trouble, and so, in front of six hundred people, he began running up and down the aisles, screaming at the top of his voice, "Lord Jesus, have mercy on my soul!"

When John Chappel, the famous atheist and Communist, was won to the Lord, it made newspaper headlines all over the state, and people were incredulous, unable to believe that so stolid an atheist had been won to Christ.

Theresa and I were staying in a little rented room inside a vacation house about a block from the home of the pastor who was hosting the crusade.

There was a narrow staircase leading up to the little house from the sidewalk.

One day, while I was preaching at a ministers' fellowship, Theresa became violently ill. She was in so much pain that she couldn't even hold four-month-old David. Her pain was so intense, she couldn't even stand up.

She knew she needed to get some help.

Theresa laid little David down, crawled out the door, closed the door, crawled down the narrow little staircase and crawled down the street the entire block to the pastor's house.

The minister's wife, horrified at the look of pain on Theresa's face, immediately called the doctor and then ran to our room to get little David.

The doctor told the minister's wife that it sounded as if Theresa was having a gall bladder attack.

He advised the minister's wife to get Theresa to a hospital immediately.

She was doubled over in pain. She was in the middle of her third attack, and the pain simply would not subside. She was throwing up green bile as she was doubled over.

The minister's wife told Theresa that the doctor had recommended she get to a hospital immediately, but Theresa would have none of it.

"Just pray," Theresa told her. "The Lord knows I am having a problem. He will take care of me. Let's just wait for Morris."

When I got back after preaching, I was shocked to find my wife doubled over in such pain. The minister's wife was clearly distressed, and she told me all that had happened.

It was hard for me to believe Theresa had resisted going to the hospital in the face of all that had happened.

I prayed for her and took her back to our room. I was very concerned for my wife. She was in intense pain, and her condition did not seem to change at all.

I wanted to take her to the hospital so doctors could have a look at her.

I believe in a God Who heals us, and I also believe God uses doctors to heal. Theresa would not go to the doctor, though. "No, darling," she told me. "I'm believing God. God will heal me. I am not going to the hospital. I'm not going to be operated on. God is going to take care of me."

So we could continue the meetings, which were reaping great rewards, I took care of David during the day, put him to sleep and went to minister to the needs of the increasingly large crowds. I never told them the problem that was going on at the little vacation house.

After we closed the meeting, I was scheduled to go to another crusade in Wisconsin. I packed up our clothes and put them in the car. After I had loaded everything in the car, I went back up the narrow little staircase, gingerly picked up my ailing wife, who winced with pain, and carried her down to the car and laid her in the back seat as we left for our next crusade.

For weeks, her condition remained the same. In the meetings I was preaching, God performed miracle after miracle. I felt completely helpless to address Theresa's situation.

## A Family of Miracles

In the meetings, God was clearly working miracles, but there seemed to be no change in Theresa's condition at all.

One night stuck out in particular, because during the service, a little girl who was blind came up to the front of the church for prayer.

As I laid my hands on her, I felt the virtue of God flow through me like liquid fire, and through my hands into the little girl. Immediately, her formerly useless eyes received sight, and she jumped around the auditorium, praising God with her family. I was so happy for the little girl, but when I went home, I still could not get a breakthrough for my dying wife, who was in almost constant pain and suffering.

Finally, Theresa was nearly comatose for three days and three nights. She faded in and out of consciousness, never fully coherent.

I continued as before, taking care of David during the day and ministering at night, never losing my faith in God or my confidence that He would heal her.

One day, between meetings, I was pouring out my heart to God in prayer. I wasn't just seeking for Theresa's healing, but I was praying for His glory to descend in the upcoming service as well. God spoke to my heart, just as clearly as He has ever spoken to me: "Son, fast and pray for three days. On the third day, I will heal your wife."

I had no idea why God wanted me to fast and pray for three days. I didn't understand what my fasting and praying had to do at all with Theresa's healing. But I did not question God. Instead, I immediately began fasting and praying. I knew God's providence was bigger than my purposes or understanding. Though I didn't understand why He wanted me to do what He asked me to do, I obeyed Him, because His works go beyond theology or head knowledge – there comes a time when we must simply obey, not negotiate.

"Theresa," I whispered to my barely-conscious wife. "God will heal you in three days."

I could see no sign on her face that she had even heard me, much less understood. All I knew was God always had done what He said He would do in the past, and I had no reason to doubt that He would again do what He said.

I obeyed God's command to me. I fasted and prayed each of the three days, beginning when I woke up and ending when I went to sleep, prayers all day long.

The fourth day, when I woke up, I reached over to Theresa next to me in the bed. She was not there!

Startled, I jumped out of bed and ran into the bathroom

There Theresa was, brushing her teeth and washing her face.

"What are you doing up?" I asked her, still a little groggy from just waking up. I had forgotten that this was the fourth day; all I knew was she was too sick to be up and about.

"Darling, didn't you tell me God said if you fasted and prayed three days He would heal me?" she asked, nonchalantly. " Well, three days are up. I am healed."

A few months later, Theresa, David and I were driving down the road again, on the way to another meeting, this one in Ohio.

I was driving, and it was just like any of the hundreds of trips we had made on our way to meetings. The countryside in Ohio was beautiful, with very nattily trimmed grass lining the highway, and tall, thin trees set back about fifty feet from the roadway. The scenery was really picturesque, with a completely blue sky framed by the trees, which seemed to form a living wall of brown and green. The ground underneath the trees was a rich, dark brown, with pine needles and fallen oak leaves lining the trunks of the trees, and doubtlessly providing shelter for any number of creatures and an entire community of insect life we're not normally aware of.

As I was driving, I was thinking of the diversity of God's creation; the many ways and forms of life He created on this earth. But in the midst of my musing, the Holy Spirit spoke to me, "Stop and go into the woods, I want to talk to you."

I knew how this would look when I told Theresa that I had to go into the woods to talk to God, but I knew I had married a wife who was committed to God, and she would understand.

When I found a spot that looked like I could safely pull the car over and park it on the shoulder of the road without subjecting it to danger from passing drivers, I gently pulled the car over on the side of the road, with the left tires parked on the road's asphalt shoulder, and the right tires gently resting on the lush green grass that lined the highway.

I made my way into the woods, gingerly stepping over mounds of leaves and grass that I thought might contain little critters who might not appreciate my foot ruining their homes – and I wasn't anxious for their teeth to bite my ankle, either!

Once I had made it a little way into the trees, I began walking with God, no longer paying much attention to my surroundings, when a bright red bird flew right in front of me. I had never seen a bird so vibrantly red.

Immediately, God spoke: "Son, this red bird is a sign. Tonight, there will be a lady in the back of the auditorium. She'll be wearing a red coat. She is in a wheelchair. Tell her to rise, and that I am the Lord thy God that healeth thee."

I stayed a little while longer in the woods, praising and worshiping God, and then I made my way back through the woods to the car I had parked beside the road. It's probably a good thing I didn't go too deep into the woods; I hadn't left any bread crumbs to help me find my way back out!

I got back in the car, and continued driving along the scenic highway to my destination. When we arrived at the auditorium where I was scheduled to preach, I followed my custom of spending a few hours with the Lord in dedication before the service.

That night, toward the very rear of the room, the first thing that caught my eye as I looked over the crowd from my vantage on the platform, was a woman in a wheelchair wearing a red coat, just as God had said there would be.

I mustered my courage and spoke to the woman, "Rise and be healed!"

The woman, looking shocked, stood up from her chair! She was completely healed of her malady. She ran all over the auditorium, shouting for joy. The entire crowd was electrified, and revival swept through the auditorium.

Two years after David was born, we had our second child, Susan.

She was a joy as well, and as our little family grew, we had to make new arrangements on the road.

We were now a family of four who sometimes had to cram into one tiny hotel room to sleep. When the children were still tiny, we would pull drawers out of the bureau and make little beds for them.

Theresa became a master scheduler during these years. She understood that I had to spend time with God before I could minister. During the days, she would masterfully schedule the children's sleep time and play time so they would either be asleep or somewhere else eating while I was waiting on God to prepare for the evening services.

Almost every week, we were in a different town, at a different church, preaching every night and sometimes every morning.

Between meetings, when we had a few days, we would go back to Theresa's mother's house to rest.

Money was always tight.

But God always provided. Many times, He would provide through a church offering, or through individuals in the church to whom He would speak directly, and they would bless us with a special gift.

God also used Theresa's precious grandmother to bless us many times. Oftentimes when we would make it back to Theresa's mother's house, her grandmother would pull her aside and whisper in Theresa's ear, "You don't have any money, do you?"

Theresa would just look at her grandmother lovingly and smile.

Her grandmother always would reach down into her pocket and pull out five or ten dollars and slip it into Theresa's hands, just enough to help us get to the next meeting.

Word had begun to spread about the meetings, and about the miracles God was working through His servant.

Soon, most towns no longer had auditoriums with rooms big enough to host a meeting – the crowds were swelling to huge sizes.

God led us to purchase a tent that would hold three thousand people, and a truck to haul it around in, because a tent was simply the most efficient way to get enough people into a meeting as the crowds grew.

In 1958, David was four and Susan was two. We were staying in a tiny little motel room in Plainview, Texas, and I was holding a crusade in a nearby church. Theresa was pregnant with our third baby, but we didn't know it yet.

As Theresa was behind the motel room hanging newly washed diapers to dry on a Sunday morning, one of the ladies at the church had come out and berated Theresa for hanging diapers on a Sunday morning and had terribly upset Theresa. Suddenly, a pain shot across Theresa's belly, she doubled over in pain and let out a scream.

I was in the hotel room, preparing for the service later that night, the last night of the crusade.

I ran outside and saw Theresa doubled up in pain on the ground, bleeding.

I picked her up and carried her into our room, gingerly lying her down on the bed, praying the whole way. Then I ran to the phone and called a doctor, who dropped everything and rushed to our motel room when I described what Theresa was going through.

After he examined Theresa, the doctor's face was grim.

"She's probably having a miscarriage, Mr. Cerullo," he told me. We hadn't even known that she was pregnant. "It would be extremely dangerous for her to continue in this condition without going to a hospital."

There was a small hospital directly across the street from the motel. I took Theresa to the hospital, where the doctors there examined her.

After he had examined her, the doctor told me the best course of action was to allow them to scrape Theresa's womb, because in all probability she had lost the baby already.

"If there's any life left," the doctor told me, "it will be extremely deformed in its body and possibly its mind."

Not only was the unborn baby's life in danger, the doctor told me, Theresa's life also was in danger.

The doctor offered us no hope. In his estimation, we did not have a choice but to do what he had suggested.

In the natural, it was an impossible situation. We had a choice to make, to listen to the doctor, give up hope and allow them to go through this procedure that would certainly end the baby's life, or to believe God for a miracle.

I went to Theresa's bedside and related to her what the doctor had said.

As I discussed it with her, Theresa's face showed she understood the gravity of the situation. She understood the implications of what the doctor was telling us.

"Morris, if we are having another baby, then the Lord is going to either take care of this baby or take the baby,"

Theresa said, looking into my eyes. "I am not letting the doctor touch me."

When I informed the doctor what we had decided, he was incredulous.

He could not believe that we would risk everything and go against his advice.

Finally, he agreed, but he told me, "I must tell you the facts. You may not get down the road very far before your wife starts hemorrhaging again. It is possible that she might bleed to death before you could get her to the hospital. That's your alternative."

Theresa just looked at the doctor for a second.

"Well," she said. "I am willing to see if the Lord can't take care of me."

Her tone of voice produced a change in the doctor's attitude. His countenance changed, as he saw Theresa's determination. He gave Theresa a pillow and a blanket, and with tears in his eyes, he wished us well as we drove off to our next meeting.

We headed east, but I could see the road was very hard on Theresa. She toughed it out, putting on the best face possible, but by the time we got to Memphis, Tennessee, she could handle no more, and we had to stop.

I was scheduled to preach in a crusade in another city, and I knew that God had called me to minister there to the needs of others. But I did not want to leave my hurting wife in a strange city with two small children when she was in critical condition.

But the call of God was strong. I had to go. I left my associate minister, Ralph Bender, with Theresa to take care of her and the children until Theresa's mother could arrive. I called her mother in New York, and she took a train to Memphis.

When her mother arrived, she took Theresa to another doctor.

The Tennessee doctor confirmed what the Texas doctor had said.

There was no way she would ever be able to carry this baby to full maturity, the doctor informed her. Most likely, he said, she would begin experiencing more complications. The best course of action, he said, was to follow the Texas doctor's advice, admit her to the hospital and scrape her womb.

But Theresa still would not budge.

She believed in her heart that God had given her this baby, and that to take the baby or let it be born was God's decision, not Theresa's or mine or some doctor's.

She stayed in Memphis for a few weeks until she was able to fly back to New York with her mother, where she stayed until it was time for her to deliver the baby.

When Theresa was five and a half months pregnant, she still had felt no signs of life. The baby had not kicked, and the doctor was not able to find a heartbeat for the fetus.

The doctor told my wife that she was being foolish, and she should let him perform the procedure the other doctors had suggested.

But Theresa and I stood fast, despite the negative reports. This baby was God's responsibility. It was up to Him to decide what to do with this baby.

During Theresa's pregnancy, I still had to travel all over, preaching in crusades and meetings. My schedule seemed to be getting busier all the time, with invitations coming from all over. And God's call was still so strong – when the people invited me, I had to go.

After one of my crusades, I was slated to fly into New York City, about a sixty mile drive from Theresa's mother's home.

## A Family of Miracles

Theresa wanted to come pick me up at the airport, so I agreed that we would get a hotel room in New York so she wouldn't have to make two sixty-mile trips in one day.

She was seven months pregnant, and had been feeling fine, with no more problems, so Theresa packed up a car with a few things and drove into New York City to meet me at the airport. When I saw her as I deplaned, I was reminded of the beauty I had immediately fallen in love with that day at the Bible school when we ate lunch sitting next to each other. She was radiant, and more beautiful at seven months pregnant than I had ever seen her.

But when we got to the room in New York City, as soon as I had put the key into the room door, Theresa screamed and doubled over in pain, once again hemorrhaging.

"What shall I do?" I asked Theresa as she was doubled over in pain. "Shall I call the hospital?"

No sooner had I asked the question than I felt God strengthening us.

Theresa looked up at me and said, "No, take me home."

With the bellboy at the hotel helping, I got Theresa into our car. She lay down in the back seat. As we drove through New York City, Theresa periodically groaned from the back seat. When we got to the outskirts of the city, God directed me to pull the car over. As soon as I found a hole in the traffic, I pulled the car over, leaned over the seat, placed my hand on her belly and began to pray a very simple prayer.

Theresa fell asleep immediately, and she did not wake up until the car pulled up in front of her mother's house.

When we got to her mother's house, the car stopping woke her up, and I saw in the rear-view mirror as she poked her head up over the seat. Her face was no longer contorted with pain. She was no longer hemorrhaging.

Everything was fine.

Two months later, on New Year's Eve, Theresa and I were in the grocery store, shopping for a few items.

I saw a particularly scrumptious-looking steak at the butcher's counter, and I was reaching out for it when Theresa's voice stopped me.

"Honey, you'd better not get that," she said. "I'll be going to the hospital tonight, and you won't have anyone to fix it for you."

I was startled. Her due date wasn't up yet, according to the doctors. How could she possibly know tonight was when she would be delivering the baby.

Still a bit stunned by her prediction, I said, "You will?"

But she was right.

That night, we went to the hospital. And New Year's day, at three a.m., Theresa delivered our third child – our special little miracle baby, Mark Stephen.

He was seven pounds and an ounce, and perfectly normal. Just like I had when his older brother and sister were born, I counted each little finger and toe. Mark, like the others, had ten of each.

## Chapter 4

# My Wife, Another Barnabas

In 1955, I had been ministering for eight years. It seemed that nearly every night for eight years, God had done a tremendous miracle, sometimes more.

I never had a lot of money, but God had always provided for my needs, and later, when I married Theresa, He had provided for our needs together.

From the very beginning, when God had taken me into heaven and I had seen the tormented souls of hell through the footprints of God, my ministry was aimed at an eventual goal of going overseas to preach to the multitudes there. I knew I was also to minister in North America, but I knew God's call on my life was to the nations of the world.

My heart, and Theresa's too, ached for the day when we could fulfill that vision and reach out to the hurting souls in the world.

By 1955, we had managed to scrape together a little nest egg of savings. Just enough to put a down payment on a home that was being built in Newburgh, New York. The house was not very big, but to us, it was a mansion. It was selling for $11,500, which was very reasonable in those days.

We were very excited that God had put in our hands the opportunity to have a home in which we could raise our children (at that time only David and Susan).

We watched over the construction of that home with eagle eyes.

Everything from the foundation to the roof was built under our watchful observation – $11,500 may have been reasonable to most people, but it was a king's ransom to us, and we wanted to make sure the house was built just right, with every detail taken care of!

We had placed a small deposit of six-hundred dollars to hold the house for us until the escrow closed. We put the remaining part of the down payment in a bank account until construction on the house was completed.

We could hardly wait. I believe Theresa had already decorated that house in her mind before the walls were even built.

While we were waiting for the house to be built, we continued conducting meetings and crusades all over the United States and Canada.

While we were in Pennsylvania, God spoke something to my heart that sent shock waves all over my entire body.

"Son, get ready to go to Athens, Greece."

My heart leapt for joy! Finally, the vision God had given me was coming to pass – our worldwide ministry was to begin!

Many people, who hear a call from God, or get a direction from Him, step out immediately and try to make the call come to pass, working and working, but never seeming to get anywhere.

I had sat under rabbis long enough to know patience, and my long hours with the Rev. Nikolof had taught me that, as the Psalmist says, *"Except the LORD build the house, they labour in vain that build it: except the LORD keep the city, the watchman waketh but in vain. It is vain for you to rise up early, to sit up late, to eat the bread of sorrows: for so he giveth his beloved sleep."* (Psalms 127:1-2)

I knew that He would begin the international phase of my ministry when His time came around; no sooner, no later.

So when I heard His voice speaking to me to prepare to go to Athens, Greece, I could hardly contain my excitement.

I ran to Theresa to tell her the good news.

"Honey, I think this is it," I blurted out to her.

Theresa got a puzzled look on her face.

"What do you mean?" she asked.

"Do you remember hearing about the vision I had when I was fifteen?" I asked her. She nodded her head that she did remember the vision. "I think the vision is beginning to take place! I heard God tell me to get ready to go to Greece."

I didn't really even know where Greece was at the time. All I knew was it was overseas.

Theresa seemed to be just as excited as I was. Though all we had was God's voice telling me to get ready, we knew that God had never spoken in vain before; we knew that whatever He said would come to pass.

So we weren't too surprised two weeks later when we got a letter in the mail with a foreign-looking stamp on it.

I excitedly opened the envelope, and sure enough, it was from Rev. Koustis, the superintendent of the Church of God in Greece.

According to the letter, the Rev. Koustis had been praying, and God had spoken to him, telling him to get in contact with me to ask me to come to Greece to conduct a meeting. Isn't it strange that, just as in Bible days, God would send another Jew to minister to the Greeks?

No sooner had I read the letter than I sat down to reply that I would come and minister. I explained in my reply that God had spoken to me two weeks before I had received the letter, directing me to prepare to go to Greece.

We began to feverishly make preparations for my overseas trip.

Theresa and I were both excited – this was my first overseas crusade.

We had no idea, though, of the magnitude of the preparations that had to be made.

I had to get a passport from the United States government, which I found out was a frustrating and slow process.

In addition, I had to get shots and other peripherals out of the way before I could travel overseas.

As we were making preparations, I looked up Greece on a globe and saw it bordered the Mediterranean. On the globe, it looked very close to Israel, the homeland of my people, the Jews.

Only seven years earlier, in 1948, Israel had become a nation again, after nearly 2,000 years of dispersal. I already knew in my heart that part of my destiny in God was to reach out to my brethren after the flesh, the Jews, and I thought, with Israel so close, it would be a perfect time for me to stop by after the meeting in Greece and get a view of the lay of the land, so to speak, spend a few days in Israel and return home to my wife, my children and our new home.

But my bubble was about to burst.

When Theresa and I went to the travel agent to book a flight to Greece and then to Tel Aviv (Jerusalem was still part of Jordan at that time), we were shocked to learn that the least expensive price we could get for a round-trip ticket was $961.80.

Today, such a ticket price would be an unbelievable bargain.

But in 1955, the travel agent might as well have asked me to pay $8 million – either way, I couldn't pay it.

But God had brought Theresa and me through a lot. We didn't lose hope, we didn't doubt God. We knew that His call to us was real, that He had spoken and confirmed it to us, first by speaking to me, then by having Rev. Koustis send the letter of invitation. We believed that no matter how high the obstacle seemed, God would meet this need, just as He had met every need we had ever had.

We continued with our crusades, preaching in city after city.

We kept making plans, even though we couldn't yet afford a ticket, and set August as the date for the crusade.

I was ministering in a series of tent meetings in Pennsylvania. They, like all the meetings we had held up to this point, were filled with God's Presence and power, working miracle after miracle, night after night.

One night, the Presence of God seemed to permeate the tent more heavily than normal. Outside the tent, a crowd two to three times larger than the crowd inside the tent had gathered. Inside the tent, dozens of people were streaming forward to receive Jesus Christ as their Lord.

In the midst of this most tremendous miracle of salvation, God led me to step off the platform and pray for a farmer woman who was hunched over. Her backbone was so twisted that she couldn't have stood up no matter how hard she tried.

I approached the woman and touched her hand. As soon as I did, God healed her instantly. The woman stood up as straight as any child in the room. Her bones had been racked with arthritis, but when her back was healed, her arthritis also left her. The miracle was only one of many throughout the crusade. Many people were healed every single night.

God's power was so present in the meetings that the crowds just kept getting bigger and bigger each night. The tent overflowed, with row upon row of people standing all around.

About a week later, the same lady came walking up the aisle toward the platform.

When she got to the platform, she got my attention and motioned for me to come forward to where she was standing.

I was a bit self-conscious, because service was going on, but I felt compelled to see what she wanted.

As I approached this precious lady, she shoved something into my hand that felt like paper.

I didn't look at whatever it was. I wanted to cause as little disruption to the service as I could, so I quickly placed whatever it was into my Bible and began heading back to my seat.

But the lady, who had begun walking away from the platform, looked over her shoulder to see what I was doing.

When she saw me, she frowned a little bit, turned around and made her way back up to the platform. When she got to the platform, she pointed her finger at me and ordered me to read what she had given me.

I took the envelope out of my Bible and opened it up.

This lady, with her beautiful penmanship, had written a very touching letter. In the letter, she glorified God for her healing. She spoke about how long she had been afflicted, and about how she had suffered, while praying to God that He would heal her. The letter was very poignant.

She ended the letter like this: "In memorial to the Lord for the healing of my body, I enclose this gift. I sold my farm a little while before you arrived and this is some of the money I received from the sale. I want you to have it for your ministry."

Already, I was touched by this woman's act of selflessness. I was impressed with the powerful letter she had written explaining what God had done for her. But my surprise at her letter was nothing compared to my surprise when I saw the check that was tucked inside the envelope.

The check was made out for the amount of $961.80 – exactly the amount I needed to buy the round trip ticket to Athens and Tel Aviv.

Immediately after the crusade closed, Theresa and I went to the travel agent and booked the ticket to go to Athens, Greece, for my first overseas crusade.

As the day approached, I was feeling a mixture of excitement and apprehension. I knew God had called me to reach out to the nations of the world. There were few things of which I was more sure in my spirit. I could never stop thinking about those souls screaming in hell for very long.

## My Wife Another Barnabas

The drive in my spirit to minister to the nations of the world was intense – extremely intense.

But that drive and that knowledge were no replacement for experience. I was only a young man; I had never left the United States. I had no idea what to expect overseas. I was a relatively new husband and a young father. I would have to leave my family here in the United States as I flew an ocean away to minister to people who couldn't even understand my language.

But God would not allow me to dwell on my anxiety. He knew that it would only be by His strength that I would be able to travel half a world away and minister to people in a foreign country.

When the day came, it seemed my heart was in my throat all day long.

Theresa looked more beautiful to me that morning than she had looked my entire life. Her hair was perfect, her trembling smile betraying the heartache she felt, and her beautiful eyes locked with mine.

Little David was just old enough to understand that his daddy had to travel a lot to minister, but he had no way of understanding that Daddy would now be traveling halfway around the world.

Nevertheless, he clung to me the entire morning before I had to go. No matter where I went, David never wanted me to go. He wanted his daddy to stay with the family. But I had made a commitment to God long before, and as much as my heart wanted to stay and be with my family, I could not ignore the thousands of souls who needed what God had given me.

As we traveled to the airport, the trip was mostly silent. Only the loud hum of the car's motor filled our ears as we approached the airport, where it seemed a host of planes were all taking off and landing at the same time.

107

I had ridden on airplanes plenty of times before, but these had always been domestic flights, going from one state to another. This would be my first flight out of the country – the first time I would be on an airplane for so long.

I boarded the plane and looked longingly back at my family. I did not want to be separated from them for so long, but this was my destiny. Theresa understood that, as she kept a strong appearance for the children, but I could see the pain in her eyes.

A stewardess ushered me to my seat, and I buckled myself in. There's never quite any feeling like the feeling of inevitability that comes with strapping yourself into the seat of an airplane. At that moment you know that, no matter what you do, this airplane will take off, and there's nothing you can do about it. Your life is completely released from your control and given over to the control of someone else. If the pilot who's in charge is skilled, your life is in good hands, and before long you'll be on the ground again, back in charge of your life. But if the pilot is less skilled, you may never again regain control of your life. The worst part is, you don't know what kind of pilot you have until you're already in the air.

As I sat in my seat by the window, the pilot revved up the plane's four huge engines. Through the window, I could see Theresa, David and Susan still where I had left them, although I was almost certain they did not know which window I was looking through.

As the airplane began to taxi down the runway, the reality of my upcoming adventure finally sank in. I was in this now, for better or worse. There was no way I could intervene one way or another now to keep myself from exiting this plane to Greece.

Silently I began to worship God and pray for the upcoming meeting. I was finally fulfilling His plan for my life, and I was extremely aware of the awesome providence He had exhibited to get me to this point.

As the plane took off, the sense of finality was reinforced as I saw the ocean appear below the airplane as it climbed to cruising altitude.

The gentle hum of the plane's huge engines had become an ear-rattling roar.

I had always assumed that flying over the ocean would be a smooth ride, but I was wrong. The ride was extremely bumpy. In fact, at some points, the plane would suddenly drop, possibly hundreds of feet at a time, and then climb back up to its original altitude. It's a bit unnerving to be over the middle of nowhere in the ocean and to be awakened by the plane making a precipitous drop of a few hundred feet.

But the pilot knew what he was doing, and after a long plane ride, we began to circle the airport in Athens, Greece.

My excitement began to build. Here, I would set foot on foreign soil for the first time. I was like a caged tiger, ready to pounce out and preach the Gospel at the first person I saw.

But the first person I saw was already familiar with the Gospel. As I deplaned, I saw the face of Rev. Koustis, who looked extremely tired and a bit dejected.

I didn't understand the look on his face. I was very excited to be finally fulfilling the calling on my life, finally overseas preaching to foreign crowds as God had called me to do.

But Rev. Koustis didn't seem excited at all. "Why couldn't he be a little more enthusiastic about my being here?" I wondered to myself, but I didn't say anything to him. He seemed to have enough trouble without me adding to his worries.

As we walked through the airport, Rev. Koustis said very little. In fact, he said nothing other than to welcome me and to introduce himself. When we exited the airport and began to walk to the bus, I was struck with how Athens was different from towns in America.

Athens had been around literally for thousands of years. In some places, that age was clearly evident in cobblestone streets and ancient buildings made of the rocks that were abundant in the Grecian hillsides. But in other places, all around, modern construction was springing up, with modern-looking glass and steel buildings being built for the bustling city.

Open markets that were essentially unchanged in the last thousand years contrasted sharply with modern automobiles putting by on streets that had been in use since the time of Alexander the Great.

I was shaken out of my musings on the state of Athens and the sensation of being in a foreign country by my curiosity.

"How's everything going?" I asked Rev. Koustis, meaning how was everything going with preparations for the meetings. "Do you have a copy of the handbill you printed for the meeting? I'd like to see it."

Rev. Koustis looked over at me exhaustedly. "We have a little problem there," he said.

I thought a second on just what he could mean by "a problem." Did he mean that the ink had smudged, that they had spelled something wrong? Did he mean that vandals were tearing down the fliers from where they were posted? I wasn't sure "a problem" was a complete enough answer to satisfy my curiosity.

I decided to try another question.

"When will I be able to meet the committee?" I asked. "I'd like to meet all the other preachers and missionaries who will be cooperating in the meeting."

Again, Rev. Koustis shot me the exhausted – almost defeated – look. "We have a little problem there," he repeated.

110

"A little problem?" I asked.

"Yes," he replied. "I didn't tell anybody you were coming."

This was something I hadn't expected to hear. It was common procedure in the United States to advertise a crusade before it was held, both to bring the Christians in and to encourage them to bring their unsaved friends to hear the Word of God.

I pondered a minute on what Rev. Koustis had told me, letting the weight of it sink in. Perhaps, I thought, things were different here. Perhaps the practice was not like it was in the United States. I decided to try another question.

"Where are we holding the meeting?" I asked. "What's the name of the auditorium?" I was almost afraid to hear the answer, but I've never been one to sit back and wait for circumstances to present themselves in untimely ways. I needed to know exactly what the situation was so I would know how to proceed, and how to pray.

"We have a little problem there," Rev. Koustis replied again.

By this time, I was becoming exasperated. "What's the problem," I asked.

"We haven't rented one yet," he replied.

The effect of those five words was like a good punch to my stomach. I had left my wife and children, flown more than four thousand miles, only to find that when I arrived, nothing had been done to arrange the crusade.

Nothing was done. No handbills had been printed. No advertising had been done. No other ministers were coming. No auditorium had been rented. No one knew I was coming. It was as if I had walked off the plane and onto another planet – a completely hostile planet.

But before I could concentrate on what was going on, Rev. Koustis explained what had happened, and I understood why he looked tired.

Apparently, in Greece, the only church allowed to operate openly without strict controls was the Greek Orthodox Church, and it was against the law to print or distribute any literature, advertise in the newspaper, rent an auditorium for a meeting or to openly witness. Each of these offenses was punishable by being thrown in jail for years at a time.

"I bear on my body the marks for preaching the Gospel in this country," Rev. Koustis explained. "I've been in prison. I've been thrown off the mainland onto islands, and I've been put in dungeons for weeks and months at a time because I violated the law."

I knew I was in a foreign country, but the concept of a state religion that is so powerful it can exclude all others was completely foreign to me. I had no concept of this kind of restriction on religious freedom, on preaching the Gospel to countries who did not want it preached.

I had read stories in the Bible about how great men of God like Paul, Peter and John had been imprisoned for preaching the Gospel, but I had no concept that religious persecution on this kind of scale even happened any more in the twentieth century.

Pondering this lack of religious freedom that all but guaranteed we wouldn't be able to hold our meeting, I looked at Rev. Koustis and asked, "Sir, if you knew all this, why did you let me come?"

His eyes lit up a little.

"When I wrote to you and asked you to come, you wrote back and told me that God told you to come to Greece," he replied. "I didn't want to say anything to you that would keep you away."

He was right. Despite appearances, despite the apparent lack of freedom to conduct our meetings, God had indeed called me to come to Greece. As in the past, I had never known God to call me to do something that He didn't provide a way for me to accomplish His will.

I didn't understand how God planned to make this meeting a reality, but I knew God would make sure I hadn't traveled here in vain.

I did my best to make Rev. Koustis feel comfortable about the problems we faced as he took me to the hotel room where he had arranged for me to stay.

As we approached the hotel, I could tell this, too, would not be what I had expected. The room was barely that.

The entire place was smelly. The room they had arranged for me to stay in was at the top of several flights of stairs. When I finally got to the top of the stairs and opened the door to the room, I could hardly believe my eyes.

There was one chair and a bed. The walls were dingy and dirty. The floor looked as if it hadn't been swept in years. The bed didn't even have sheets or pillow cases. It was just a very dirty, smelly, old mattress on an iron bed that looked like it wouldn't even support a child, much less a full-grown man.

I took down Rev. Koustis' address and telephone number so I could reach him and then I told him to wait until I got in touch with him.

I understood what was happening in this country that had been closed to anything but one church for so long. The enemy didn't want our meeting to take place.

That first night overseas was difficult. I was in a strange land where I didn't know anyone. I was in what was quite possibly the worst room I had ever stayed in. I had planned for months for this crusade, and when I arrived over four thousand miles of ocean, the meeting looked like it wasn't going to happen. I had no one to talk to, no one to counsel with.

I understood immediately what God wanted me to do. I began praying fervently, and worshiping God.

Theresa and I had been through many trials of faith in our short marriage, and I had seen God work many miracles in my short Christian life. I had never seen God fall short.

I knew one thing: God had called me to come to Greece.

With that knowledge, I began crying out to God:

"God, You called me to come here. You put it in my heart to reach out to the nations of the world. You supernaturally provided the funds for me to come. You spoke to Rev. Koustis to ask me to come. I know You have me here for a purpose, and I don't believe that purpose is sleeping in a dirty room and fretting over laws that won't allow me to preach. When You called me to preach in that little church in upstate New York, You told me to obey and You would heal my jaw. I obeyed and You healed my jaw. You told me to pray and fast for three days and you would heal my wife, and you healed Theresa. Now, I believe You have a divine purpose for having me here, and I won't give up until Your purpose here is accomplished."

I remembered then a story from the Old Testament, where Gideon was facing what seemed to be insurmountable odds. God had called him to fight for Israel, and Gideon had eventually agreed, but when he assembled his men, God told him he had too many men. Through a process of elimination, God pared down Gideon's force to a paltry three hundred men to face an army numbering in the hundreds of thousands. In God's words, this paring down of Gideon's army was because "...*The people that are with thee are too many for me to give the Midianites into their hands, lest Israel vaunt themselves against me, saying, Mine own hand hath saved me.*" (Judges 7:2)

I knew that God had a plan, and that Morris couldn't make God's plan come to pass. I knew that I was just a Jewish boy in a strange land with no friends and no support, and with laws against what I was trying to do.

In the natural, it would have been a depressing situation, but I remembered what Paul had told the Romans: *"And we know that all things work together for good to them that love God, to them who are the called according to his purpose."* (Romans 8:28)

This was no time to get dejected and upset. It was no time to cry in my cereal and wonder why God had called me to a land that didn't want me.

Instead, I knew it was time to rely ever more intensely on Him, trusting Him to win the battle that I could not hope to win in the natural.

One thing I did know in the natural, however, was that I didn't want to stay in that room any longer.

I stayed up all night, praying to God. The next morning, I took the little money that Theresa and I had scrimped and saved up for this trip and, a suitcase in each hand, I walked through the streets of a strange city in an unfamiliar foreign land, looking for a suitable place to stay.

In the streets, my impressions and the dichotomy of old and new Greece struck me once again. Some people appeared to live in chateaus with no windows, only curtains hanging in holes in the wall. Other people lived in modern houses, complete with porch lights and other amenities.

Taken together, the scenery was beautiful and picturesque. The history of thousands of years of peace, prosperity, conquest, arts, poetry and architecture all met in this great city, and all were here on display, with the centuries all converging in the here-and-now.

But I could not dwell on the beauty of the scenery. I had a problem that only God could solve, and I was anxious to find a room to seek Him in.

After quite a while, I finally found a room in a little hotel on Constitution Square. Once I had paid for the room, I went in the room and contacted Rev. Koustis to let him know where he could contact me. This room was much nicer than the other room, but it was still no five-star hotel by any stretch of the imagination. But at least it had clean sheets.

I locked the door to the room and fell on my face before God.

"Oh, Lord, what am I going to do?"

I had no lofty theological prayers honed in seminary to offer up to God. I had no "thees" and "thous" to pray with flowing words and complicated phrases.

I was a desperate man in a desperate situation, and I didn't have time to offer pretty prayers up to God. I needed God to move in this situation – I needed a miracle, and I prayed the only way I knew how: from the depths of my soul!

I prayed for ten days, on my face in the room. I didn't eat a morsel of food as I was praying. I knew I needed God to move supernaturally in this situation, and I had to get an answer from Him.

One day, quite unexpectedly, there was a knock on my door.

Only Rev. Koustis knew I was there, so I assumed it was him at the door. But when I opened the door, I saw a woman dressed in expensive clothes and wearing expensive jewelry standing in the hallway.

"Can I help you?" was my startled question to the lady.

She explained that she was the wife of the vice president of the Bank of Athens, and that she had come to help me.

Intrigued, I apologized that I could not invite her in because integrity demanded I *abstain from all appearance of evil* (I Thessalonians 5:22), and asked her to please tell me what she meant.

She explained that her adventure had begun two weeks before I came to Athens.

She had been walking down a street, when she heard music and a commotion coming from a room on the second floor of one of the buildings that faced the street. In Athens, the buildings are built quite close to the street, and only a little walkway separates the building walls from the street below. If something loud is going on in one of the rooms, it's pretty hard to miss it.

The lady had ventured up the building's stairway into a small room where a group of Foursquare Church members had assembled for a mid-week service. Every evangelical church had to have a special police permit to meet and hold services. During that little service, this woman's heart had been moved, and she had surrendered her life to Jesus and become a born-again Christian.

She was extremely hungry to have more of Christianity, so she had begun spending most of her time with members of the Foursquare Church to learn everything she could. Her story reminded me of my own hunger to know more about Christ after I had first begun reading the New Testament in the Daughters of Miriam orphanage in New Jersey.

As she had talked to her new Foursquare friends, this lady had learned that I had come all the way from America to hold evangelistic miracle meetings, but was unable to get permits to hold the meetings.

The woman looked me in the eye and said, "I am here to tell you we will get the permits you need to hold the services." She assured me she would ask her husband to use all his influence to make it possible to conduct our meetings.

I thanked the woman for her efforts and, as she left, I praised God for saving her soul, and for giving her a willingness to work for our cause.

But I did not stop praying when the apparent answer to my prayers had presented itself. Once again, I fell to the floor and began crying out to God to move and make a way for the meetings to take place.

Less than two days later, through the intervention of the vice president of the Bank of Athens, the prime minister of Greece had personally approved all the arrangements so that our meeting could take place.

This was an unprecedented miracle in the history of Greece since the days of the Early Church, when Paul and Silas ministered there!

All the walls that formerly had been insurmountable were now coming crashing down so fast the dust barely had time to clear before the next wall came crashing down.

Rev. Koustis and I began to work feverishly to get ready for the meetings.

We went through all the necessary red tape and paperwork to secure a permit for the meetings to take place.

We found a building, the Kentragon Theatre, in central Athens, and paid the rent.

We created handbills, printed them up and worked as quickly as we could to distribute them all over the city. "The blind will see," the handbills proclaimed. "The deaf will hear. The lame will walk."

We bought space in the local newspapers advertising God's miracle-working salvation and healing power; advertising that the citizens of this city would never be the same after they attended the meetings in the Kentragon Theatre.

Greece had never seen such a flurry of evangelistic activity. Laws had been on the books so long banning evangelistic activity (passing out handbills, advertising any kind of evangelistic meeting) that this strategy of media saturation made many in the city curious as to what exactly was going on.

## My Wife Another Barnabas

As the night of the meeting came, we faced only one remaining problem. We had cleared so many hurdles to get to this point: the permits, the rent, printing the fliers, distributing the fliers, advertising the meetings in local media. Our sole remaining problem was we didn't have an interpreter!

If someone couldn't be found to translate what I was saying, all my preaching would be – forgive the expression – Greek to the people of this historic city.

But God had taught me a lesson through my short ministry. No matter what hurdle seemed to be in my way, if God had said something was going to happen, I didn't have to worry myself with the details of how exactly that thing would happen.

If a broken and hanging jaw unable to move was not an obstacle to preaching in New York, the lack of an interpreter also wasn't an obstacle in Greece.

As I was preparing for the meeting that night – as always, seeking God until His glory came into the room – the phone rang at six p.m., one hour before the meeting was scheduled to begin.

People had already packed the Kentragon Theatre, anxious to see what all the hoopla about this American preacher and his miracle meetings was.

I picked up the phone and said hello.

A man's voice spoke on the other end of the line.

"Is this Morris Cerullo?" the voice wanted to know.

"Yes it is," I answered. "Who is this?"

"You don't know me," the voice said, matter-of-factly. "But I am your interpreter."

I was taken aback a bit by this statement. I had expected God to move and provide an interpreter, but somehow I hadn't expected the miracle to call me up on the phone.

"Who are you?" I asked, still a bit surprised by the news that an interpreter had arrived.

119

"I am Rev. Frangus, General Superintendent of the Assemblies of God in Greece," he said. "No one expected me. I'm here just by accident."

It was no accident, I knew. This precious man of God had been on a field missionary trip, and had called the Assemblies of God missionary in Athens. The woman had told Rev. Frangus about our meetings and our need for an interpreter.

"I just want you to know I am rushing to the auditorium right now," Rev. Frangus said. "Don't worry, I will stay here with you through the meetings."

We said good-bye, and I began praising God again as I placed the telephone's receiver back.

Just as He always had in the past, God had come through just in time. He had provided an interpreter just before the beginning of the first service, which was packed.

That night, when I saw the Glory of God come down and prepare to move amongst the people, I knew it was time to begin the ministry of preaching to the huge crowd of people who had assembled in this theatre in the center of Athens.

I knew that they had come because the fliers we had distributed and the advertisements we had taken out in the newspapers had promised healing for their bodies.

And the sick had come en masse to see if this healing from God was really true.

But I knew a greater miracle waited for these Greek people who had come to see what the minister from America was all about.

I had never worked with an interpreter before. It was a bit strange, something I had not really thought about until I came up on the platform.

"I greet you tonight..." I began, and Rev. Frangus broke in, translating what I had said into Greek. "...in the Name that is above every name..." again, Brother Frangus began to speak in Greek. "...Jesus Christ, Son of the living God!" Once again, Brother Frangus spoke in Greek. The only words he said that I understood were "Jesus Christ."

Apparently, Brother Frangus was quite an accomplished translator. He mimicked my every movement, even the intonation of my voice. We developed an anointed rhythm, with me saying a few phrases and him repeating them in Greek.

As I would move to the left on the platform, Rev. Frangus would follow me, repeating my words after I had said them. As I moved to the right, Rev. Frangus moved to the right. As I lifted my hands, Rev. Frangus lifted his hands.

It was as if we were one preacher, preaching in two languages. The best way I can describe the experience was that it was like a symphony orchestra – we were in complete synchronization. After a very short time, I almost completely forgot that I was preaching with a translator, and the style of preaching I had used in the United States quickly adjusted to this new style, pausing between words to give the interpreter time to interpret.

It was an effortless transition. As I found out in later years, when the translator is operating in the power of God, the preacher doesn't even know he's there.

That night, I preached a powerful message on salvation. I knew the crowd was there for healing, but I also understood that healing was only a tiny part of why God had drawn them to that theatre in Athens.

"The greatest miracle is not the healing of blind eyes," I told the crowd as Rev. Frangus translated. "It is not the fixing of crippled legs. It is not the opening of deaf ears." As Rev. Frangus relayed this in Greek, I watched the faces of the crowd. They listened intently, and when they heard the last sentence, they all seemed to lean forward in their chairs. They clearly wanted to know what I thought the greatest miracle was, if healing a blind eye or deaf ear or crippled leg wasn't. "And those miracles will happen tonight. But the greatest miracle," I told them, " is when God saves a sinner's soul from hell. It's called the miracle of salvation."

At this, tears began running down the faces of some of the men and women in the audience.

I preached for at least forty-five minutes that night. No one walked around in the theatre. No one was chatting, no one was falling asleep. There was not a whisper of a noise. Every eye was on me and Rev. Frangus.

That night, when I finished my message, I called for anyone in the congregation who wanted to make Jesus Christ their Lord to stand up.

To my great surprise, ninety percent of the huge audience stood up.

It was by far the largest percentage of an audience I had ever seen answer a call to salvation in one meeting.

That night, in addition to the multitude of salvations, many cripples were healed, blind people saw for the first time, and deaf people heard for the first time. God moved mightily in the miraculous through the entire congregation. The service went on for quite a while after the call for salvation was made, as these precious Greek souls were praying, crying and praising God, packed into the altars.

After the service, I immediately returned to my room, praising God and worshiping Him nearly all night long. He had not only cleared our way to hold the meetings and provided an interpreter at the last minute, but He had moved in the most miraculous way I had ever witnessed with all the salvations He had performed that night.

Late into the night, I finally fell asleep. The next morning, the entire city of Athens was abuzz. Reports were everywhere of the miraculous workings of God. I didn't know what we would do; the auditorium had been packed the first night of the meeting already, and word-of-mouth was spreading all over the city. Surely we would have too many people to fit in the building at the meeting that night.

I was right. That night, as we approached the Kentragon Theatre, people had lined the streets with walkers, canes, wheelchairs and stretchers. The blind and sick people were packing the sidewalks, sick people were sitting on the curbs coughing.

> *"Insomuch that they brought forth the sick into the streets, and laid them on beds and couches, that at the least the shadow of Peter passing by might overshadow some of them."* (Acts 5:15)

It was literally a re-enactment of the Book of Acts. As I walked from the car and into the theatre, people from the crowd reached out to touch me.

I was amazed as a crippled man touched me and dropped his cane, his legs were completely healed by the power of God. A woman who had been coughing violently touched the sleeve of my coat, and she was instantly healed.

I was in awe of God's power, and in awe of the fact that these people were so thirsty for a touch from God right on the street in the entrance to the theatre.

"Lord, this country is so thirsty," I prayed silently to God as tears began to well up in my eyes. "There is so much to do, so many people who need You, and so little time to reach them!"

Each night, the story was the same. As I walked up the walkway toward the theatre, the crowd would press in to touch me, and by the power of God, many would be instantly healed, rejoicing and praising God.

The second night of the crusade, I again preached a powerful salvation message. To my astonishment, again ninety percent of the audience came forward to receive salvation. I could not withhold my tears as I wept for joy over the tremendous miracle God was doing in the lives of so many people.

Every night, the crowds got bigger – there was no place for people even to stand. Every night, sick people lined the streets, trying to get into the meetings.

Every night, ninety percent of the audience came forward to receive Jesus as their Lord.

As the time approached to close the meetings, I found myself being saddened by what I considered a premature end of what God was doing here.

But the financial reality was that I was flat broke.

We were prohibited from taking any offerings in the meetings. I had to sponsor everything, rent the hall, print the handbillls – everything. This was my first overseas meeting; I was not prepared.

I had spent every penny of the little bit of money I had brought with me printing handbills, paying rent on the building, buying advertisements in the newspapers and renting the room I was staying in. In fact, I had even spent the money I had intended to tide me over for my trip to Israel after the end of the meetings. I knew this meant I would not be able to go on that trip, but I considered it to be worth it for the salvations of the Greek people that God had wrought.

As I was thinking about not wanting to close the meetings, Rev. Frangus approached me.

"Brother Cerullo," he said, with concern in his eyes. "You can't close this meeting."

But we had not been given permission by the government to take offerings at the meetings. We simply had no money to continue after my money had run out. I knew how Brother Frangus felt, but I simply had no solution for him.

"I'm sorry, Brother Frangus," I said. "Tomorrow night, I must close the meeting."

I suggested to Brother Frangus that he might try calling the Assemblies of God headquarters to get a few thousand dollars to keep the meeting going.

"Brother Cerullo," he explained to me, "there is too much red tape. By the time the money got here, it would be too late."

I did not want to close the meetings. I did not want to tell these precious, hungry people "no," simply because I didn't have the money to continue.

I knew God had answered my needs before; He had never let me down before, and I had no reason to believe He would let me down now.

That night, in the privacy of my little hotel room, I sought the Lord in prayer, weeping and lying on my face.

"Lord, You hear what these ministers are asking me," I said to God. "They have told me of the stripes on their backs that they have received for the sake of the Gospel. Now the freedom is here. Lord, they don't want this meeting to close. I don't want it to close, but I don't know what to do!"

These ministers had suffered so much for the Gospel. I just didn't see how God would now let money stand in the way where laws, persecution and beatings hadn't stood in the way before.

God spoke to me in the midst of my prayer to Him: "Son, you've got the money."

That was a shock.

"Oh, boy, this is wonderful," I replied to God. "I've got the money!" I was so excited. I was wondering what miraculous providence God had done to get the money we needed. I couldn't even imagine in my head how He would accomplish getting enough money to keep the meetings going. I had seen God do so many miraculous things, I couldn't begin to guess how He had done this one.

"Lord, do You mind telling me where I've got the money?" I asked Him. "If You tell me where it is, I'll go get it."

I didn't know what to expect, but I certainly didn't expect what happened.

"You've got the money at home," God said.

I thought to myself, "No, You wouldn't ask that. Surely You are not asking me to give the money Theresa and I have in the bank for our little dream house."

"Lord," I said, "I can't do that. I can do a lot of things, but I can't do that. That has to be Theresa's decision."

Theresa had waited so long for that little house. She had never complained that we had to live with her mother. She had never complained that we seemed to live out of our car more than we lived inside four walls.

Theresa had never complained about some of the ratty hotel rooms we stayed in. She never once complained about having to pack up our young children and cart them along to town after town, night after night.

Now, when she finally had a place she could call home in her sights, I couldn't imagine telling her that she couldn't have it.

I also couldn't deny God. I knew I had to call Theresa and let her know the situation. I would let her make the decision, though. I would not force her to give up her dream house.

When I heard the phone ringing at Theresa's mother's house back in the United States, I missed her more at that moment than I had allowed myself to think about the past few weeks. I wished Theresa could be with me here, witnessing the tremendous miracles God was doing in the lives of these precious Greek people.

When Theresa answered the phone, her voice, crackly and very quiet over the thousands of miles of telephone wire, made me miss her even more.

I explained to my precious wife what God was doing in the meetings in Greece, how He was saving hundreds of people, healing the sick and working all kinds of wondrous miracles.

Theresa sounded as excited as I was, praising God as I told her of His miracles.

I swallowed a lump in my throat. Here was the big moment.

"Darling," I said, "I can't go on with the meeting. I don't have any more money."

I had expected that announcement to be met with silence, or a gasp or something. But I was shocked as Theresa immediately answered my statement.

"Sweetheart, I know why you're calling," she said. "You want me to take the money for our new house and send it to you."

Wow, I thought. I didn't know if God had revealed it to her, or if my wife just knew me better than I gave her credit for. Regardless, I was caught flat-footed. The only thing I could think of to say was, "I didn't ask."

"You didn't have to ask," she said. I could almost hear her smiling on the other end of the line. "I'll send the money to you."

That day, I learned something about my wife I will never forget. Theresa had silently stood with me, day and night, through the toughest trials we had faced up to this point in the ministry. When we were comfortable in our pastorate, she had given up that security for a life of uncertainty on the road while she was pregnant with our first child. She had always been willing to do whatever God asked to ensure the Gospel was taken all over the world.

They say that behind every successful man, there is a great woman.

That statement has never been truer than of Theresa Cerullo. Many people can talk about the great battles that have been won by this ministry, the tremendous salvations that have taken place all over the world, the incredible breakthroughs that have come as a result of this ministry, and when they talk about those things, they are also talking about the faithfulness of my precious wife, who to this very day has always been willing to give up anything and everything when God asked.

I remembered the story of Barnabas in the book of Acts:

> *"And Joses, who by the apostles was surnamed Barnabas, (which is, being interpreted, The son of consolation,) a Levite, and of the country of Cyprus, Having land, sold it, and brought the money, and laid it at the apostles' feet." (Acts 4:36-37)*

My wife, just as Barnabas, had taken her dream home and laid it at the feet of the ministry so more souls would be won to the Lord!

Theresa withdrew our savings from the bank where we had placed it, waiting for the house to be completed.

She immediately took the money and wired it to me.

It was just enough to enable us to continue the meetings in Greece.

After we had obtained permission from the authorities, we continued the meetings.

Night after night, again, God continued to bless the meetings, healing the sick and leading the lost to Jesus.

The miracles and crowds only got larger every night.

I was very sad when I had to leave Greece, but I knew when I left, the work that had been established there would continue and grow. Even though when I ran out of money, I thought I would have to sacrifice my next trip to Israel, I now had enough money from what Theresa had wired to continue to Israel.

I knew in my heart that God had called me to eventually reach out to the Jews, and I felt a sense of destiny as the airplane flew over the Mediterranean Sea westward toward Israel.

## My Wife Another Barnabas

As the airplane approached the promised land, I gazed out the tiny window by my seat at the land of Israel for the first time in my life.

Israel back then was nothing like it is today. Today, it is bustling with life nearly everywhere, with green fields, and with fig trees and flowers everywhere. Many times, people who visit Israel today are shocked to find a modern, first-world country, when they expected to find it as it was in Bible times, with stone houses and dirt roads.

There is still some of that in Israel, but it's impossible to go almost anywhere without seeing modern life.

But in 1955, Israel was still in the beginning stages of growth into a modern nation. Many roads were still made of dirt, and many houses were still made of stone.

It indeed resembled the Israel of Bible times in 1955. I stood on the mountaintops of Israel and rejoiced in God as I knew I would be back some day to reach out to my brethren after the flesh – the Jews.

But I knew that 1955 was not God's timing. I realized that we must do all things when God gets ready for us, not when we get ready.

I remembered the story in the Bible when Jesus began teaching in the temple:

> *"The Spirit of the Lord is upon me, because he hath anointed me to preach the gospel to the poor; he hath sent me to heal the brokenhearted, to preach deliverance to the captives, and recovering of sight to the blind, to set at liberty them that are bruised. To preach the acceptable year of the Lord. And he closed the book, and he gave it again to the minister, and sat down. And the eyes of all them that were in the synagogue were fastened on him. And he began to say unto them, This day is this scripture fulfilled in your ears." (Luke 4:18-21)*

Jesus always knew what the Father had called Him to do. But He didn't jump the gun. When he spoke the words recorded in Luke chapter 4, he was at least thirty years old. Although He had known His destiny for thirty years, He waited on the Father's timing before he went out to accomplish that destiny.

I knew it was my destiny to reach out to the Jews, but I also knew God had not called me to do that just yet.

I got on the plane in Tel Aviv and prepared for the long, bumpy journey back to New York City.

The flight was no shorter than it had been on my way to Greece, and it was no less bumpy, but somehow, it seemed to pass faster and smoother.

As the plane approached the United States, I could see the skyline of New York City in the distance on the horizon. I had never lived in the city, but right now, no place had ever looked more like home to me.

When the plane touched down, I could hardly wait to get my carry-on bags and deplane. I knew that below was my family, probably awaiting my return just as anxiously as I was.

I peeked out the window and saw Theresa holding little Susan with one hand, and holding onto little David's hand with her other hand as he stood right beside her leg. They hadn't spotted me inside the plane, so they didn't know I was looking at them, but I had never seen a more beautiful sight than my little family standing there waiting for Daddy to get off the plane.

As I got off the plane, the first thing I did was pull the pockets of my pants out, exposing their empty contents. We all cried together.

As I began ministering around the nations of the world, it became something of a joke in our family – when I came home, Theresa would see if my pockets were empty to judge whether I had really stayed and ministered long enough.

All I had was a few coins in my hand.

## My Wife Another Barnabas

"This is it," I said, holding out my hand, with the small change in it. "This is the only thing standing between us and our next meal!"

Theresa smiled at me, her beautiful eyes twinkling with joy. I knew within myself that she didn't care at all about the money situation, she was glad to have me home, but I couldn't see how she could be any more glad to have me than I was to be home with her.

We had lost our house, and because we hadn't come through with the money to buy the house, we had also lost the six-hundred dollar deposit we had paid down on the house.

But at that moment, we didn't care at all. We were together again.

Immediately, I set out once again, traveling and preaching with Theresa and the children accompanying me, going from crusade to crusade, preaching everywhere we were invited.

During that year, God blessed us tremendously – beyond our wildest hopes.

Before my ministry trip to Greece, it had taken us four years to save up enough money for the down payment on that little house. That was four years of clipping coupons, scrimping and saving, doing without the little things (and sometimes the big things).

After four years, we finally had saved up enough for that little down payment that we eventually used to continue the meetings in Greece.

But this time, the financial blessings of God flowed in so strongly that it only took us a year to save the same amount!

I remembered how much Theresa and I had looked forward to moving into that little dream home of ours, so one day, almost out of the blue, I said to her: "Theresa, you know, we should go look in the development where we were going to buy a home."

Theresa had obviously been thinking of something else. She gave me a funny little look that urged me to continue.

"We've got enough to buy or build again," I continued. "Let's go see if there isn't another lot in that area."

Theresa liked the idea.

We got into our car and headed toward the neighborhood we had formerly decided to move into, looking for a new lot or a home for sale.

As we drove into the development, which was located in a beautiful, secluded wooded area, we were surprised as we passed by "our house" (the one we had lost).

As we passed by, we were shocked to see a "For Sale" sign in the front yard of "our house."

It was hard to believe that someone had moved and put the house up for sale after only a year. Today, people seem to move more often, changing houses with nary a second glance, but in those days, many people were born and lived in the same house all their lives. It was fairly unusual for someone to buy a house and move away, in just a year.

We decided that we would visit our friend who was a real estate agent and ask him about the house.

Our friend, Jeff Baron (who everyone called "The Real Estate Baron"), was surprised to see us as we walked into his office. He was the agent who had originally sold the house to us, and he had been sad to see that we couldn't get the house at that time.

"Jeff," I said to him, cutting directly to the point. "I see my old house is for sale. What are they asking for it?"

Jeff chuckled a bit, grinned and looked down at some papers on his desk. Then he looked back at me, still smiling.

"That house is the worst mover we have," he said, still grinning. "I've got houses selling left and right all around it, but that house," he paused, "we can't sell."

I couldn't believe it. If I understood Jeff correctly, they had never sold our dream house – no one had bought it after we had backed out.

I wanted to clarify.

"You mean you've never sold it?" I asked.

"No," he replied. "We've sold every house all around it. The same builder has been building all over that development, and his houses are selling like hotcakes, but no one seems to want your house."

"Jeff," I said, looking him directly in the eye and trying to keep a straight face, "how would you like to get rid of that lemon?"

We talked and negotiated for a few minutes. I didn't want to part with more of the money God had blessed us with than I absolutely had to. Every penny I saved was another penny I could put into the work God had called me to.

After a few minutes, Jeff stopped.

"Look," he said. "I'll tell you what I'll do. If you're interested in buying the house, I'll go back to the owners and see what they will do. The houses in that development have gone up in price an average of $3,000."

I didn't want to pay $3,000 more, but I didn't tell Jeff that. I wanted to wait and see what God would do.

It wasn't too long until Jeff called me, sounding a bit surprised.

"Rev. Cerullo," he said. "I can't believe it, but the developers said if you want that house, they'll sell it to you for the old price you built it for a year ago."

I began rejoicing in my spirit, but Jeff was not done.

"Plus," he said, still sounding like he was having a hard time believing what he was saying, "they will even give you back your $600 deposit you lost last year when you couldn't go through with the deal."

Jeff couldn't believe it, but Theresa and I could. We understood that we serve a miracle-working God. We rejoiced when we found out that we would be able to buy our little dream home despite the fact that we had given the money we had reserved for it into the ministry.

We learned a powerful lesson that day – a lesson that would stick with us for the rest of our lives: When we give to God, He is faithful to give back, and bless us beyond our most fervent imagination and hope. The thing you sacrifice to God, God will give back to you!

# Chapter 5

# SON, BUILD ME AN ARMY

After my first overseas meeting in Greece, it would be four years before I had another chance to go overseas and minister again.

Meanwhile, the ministry continued to expand in the United States.

In each city we visited, we inevitably made friends, sometimes with the host pastor, sometimes with other ministers, and sometimes with people who had been touched through the meetings.

Every week, the mailbox in our new little house seemed to be filled to overflowing with letters from the friends we had made throughout the country.

Some people would send praise reports of miracles that God had done in their lives. Some people would write to let us know just how much the ministry had blessed them. Some people would write to request that we pray for them and that we agree with them for God to meet their specific needs.

I knew that each letter, each communication we received from our friends, was a very personal matter to the people who had written. They had taken great care and time to sit down and compose a letter to send to us.

It was important to me that each person receive a personal reply.

Since my calls to preach were ever-increasing and I was away from home more often than I was there, much of the responsibility of replying to these letters fell upon Theresa, who shouldered the work with great joy.

Many times, Theresa would come running into my study, smiling from ear to ear, waving a letter, shouting, "Morris! You've got to read this letter!"

Many of the letters requested that we send the writer information on how the ministry was doing, information on how the meetings were going, stories of the healings and salvations God was performing through the ministry. Each letter writer felt they were a part of the ministry, as they prayed for God to use me and prayed for God to bring many souls to salvation through my ministry.

I was thankful to have so many people all over the country praying for me and participating in the ministry in such a powerful way. Theresa and I developed quite a correspondence list as we regularly began communicating with those friends, giving regular reports on how the ministry was doing, and telling them of all the wonderful works of God.

As God demonstrated His power through the meetings, the attendance was ever-increasing.

Soon, we were filling up the six-thousand-seat circus tent we had purchased, and not too long after we began filling it, the tent no longer would hold all of the people who were coming to the meetings.

We tried many solutions, including placing chairs outside the tent, but nothing seemed to handle the huge crowds that were coming to the meetings.

It was in Lima, Ohio, in 1957 that God hung a banner over my ministry that firmly established its course, a course that has never left, through the ensuing forty-three years.

I had rented a high school auditorium in Lima to minister there after having received an invitation from a local pastor.

Each night, it seemed the power of God was ministering more strongly, more pervasively than it ever had before, and each night, the Presence of God was more real.

Night after night, person after person was healed of all manner of diseases, from cancer to measles, from common colds to cripples walking for the first time and the blind seeing for the first time. Just when it seemed the power of God couldn't get any stronger – it did.

Night after night, many people answered the call for salvation.

The Presence of God was so thick in that high school auditorium, that every night when I left the meeting to return to my room at the YMCA, God's Presence remained with me – it was all I could do to make it all the way to my room before I fell on my face praising God!

One night, after I had returned to my room and spent an especially worshipful time with God, I climbed into the little twin bed that was in the room, and gradually dozed off to sleep, still recounting the tremendous miracles that God had worked that night in my mind.

I don't recall exactly when I went to sleep, but I know I fell into a very deep and sound sleep.

But that sleep was unexpectedly interrupted by an intense light that filled the room where I was sleeping. The room had been completely dark before I fell asleep, and the contrast between the darkness and the now-brilliant light was very difficult for my eyes to adjust to quickly.

"Surely it's not morning already," I thought to myself. I usually don't sleep very long at night, maybe three to five hours, but I still felt very tired, as if I hadn't even gotten that much sleep. I looked over at the tiny little window in the room and realized that the drapes were closed, and that behind the drapes it appeared to be a lot darker than the light that was in my room.

The room's single bare light bulb hung directly down from the ceiling. I glanced up at the bulb and noticed that it wasn't illuminated.

I knew then that this wasn't any light produced by a natural source.

I immediately lost any residual grogginess I had been experiencing as I got out of bed and fell down, realizing that a supernatural manifestation of God had entered the room and was very near me.

I could feel the incredible nearness of the powerful Holy Ghost as it permeated the room – it was the same feeling of holiness I had felt when I stood in the Presence of God in the vision He had given to me when I was fifteen years old. I could not ignore the fact that I was privileged to again be in the personal Presence of the living God.

I lay prostrate on the floor before God, not knowing why He was here or what He wanted, but knowing that I was in His Presence and that He certainly had a reason for this visitation.

I could hear my heart pounding in my ears…Ka-thud. Ka-thud. I could feel it pounding in my chest. I could even feel my pulse pounding in my wrists as blood coursed through my body, propelled by the accelerated pace of my heart.

As I watched, the walls of this little YMCA room disappeared before my very eyes, and I saw a great horizon toward the edge of my vision.

Above the horizon appeared huge banks of white, billowy clouds, moving in slowly from the peripherals of my vision toward the center of the horizon. The clouds were clearly heavy and ready to drop their cargo at any time.

As the clouds all moved into place, tremendous, large drops began descending downward, but they did not flow like water, they flowed more like oil.

I did not understand what I was looking at. What kind of clouds rained oil, not water? What was God trying to tell me?

"God," I asked. "What does the rain mean?" I truly could not understand the vision I was seeing, and I needed to know what God wanted me to know.

"This rain is the outpouring of My Holy Spirit upon all flesh," God replied to me. "It will be poured out upon all nations of the world."

I began to rejoice in my spirit. I had read the prophecies in the Book of Joel:

> *"And it shall come to pass afterward, that I will pour out my spirit upon all flesh; and your sons and your daughters shall prophesy, your old men shall dream dreams, your young men shall see visions. And also upon the servants and upon the handmaids in those days will I pour out my spirit." (Joel 2:28-29)*

I also remembered the second chapter of Acts, where the Apostle Peter had stood up and proclaimed the fulfillment of that verse, and was instrumental when the Spirit had been poured out on three thousand listeners on the day of Pentecost.

I remembered the stories I had heard of another great outpouring, this one in Los Angeles, California, in 1907, where a group of Christians under the leadership of a pastor named William Seymour had assembled together in a little church on Azusa Street and had prayed until God began pouring out His Spirit again upon them.

Remembering those stories, I began to wonder who God would be using to lead in this next huge outpouring. I began to wonder what great men must be already preparing to lead in the outpouring, how they must be sanctifying themselves even now, preparing for the tremendous and holy work they were about to undertake.

I began to look around in this vision to see the great men that God had called to do this work. But to my astonishment, I saw no one. Everywhere I looked, the scene was the same, clouds on the horizon, raining down huge drops of oil.

"Lord," I asked, confused, "Who will lead this great outpouring?"

I hesitated for a minute and thought about my next question.

"Will I be an instrument that You will use to bring this to pass?"

I wanted to know exactly what it was God was wanting to show me. I didn't know how or what He had planned, but I was ready for whatever He had in store for my life.

"Son," God answered me gently. "You see no man because no man will lead. The work I am about to do will be without human direction. This outpouring will not be the work of a man, but the work of My Holy Spirit."

Immediately I began to understand. As I pondered what God had told me, the vision dissipated, and the walls of the YMCA had reappeared. I don't know how long I had been there in that state, but I know I came away with a clear vision and a clear foundation for the direction my ministry would take for the rest of my life.

This is not the work of a man, but of the Holy Spirit!

With God doing so many tremendous miracles through my ministry, and bringing so many souls to Christ, I knew that my ministry would have to be based upon my relationship with the Holy Spirit and His direction, not upon my personality or the gifts God had given to me.

I remembered the words Jesus had spoken to His disciples: *"And whosoever shall exalt himself shall be abased; and he that shall humble himself shall be exalted."* (Matthew 23:12)

This was God's ministry.

Although He was using a Jewish orphan boy to reach so many souls, it was not this orphan boy's ministry – it was God's ministry. It was not the work of a man, for no matter how hard I worked, I could never replace the action of the Holy Spirit. I could be the hardest worker in the world, but if God did not draw the souls, they would never come to know Christ. I remembered what Jesus had said: *"No man can come to me, except the Father which hath sent me draw him..."* (John 6:44)

From that day forward, I made an extra effort at every opportunity to be sure the people understood Who was to be praised, Who was to receive the glory for His tremendous workings.

I began to repeat what God had taught me every time I got a chance: "This is not the work of a man, but of the Holy Ghost!"

Not only did this revelation give the glory where it properly belonged – with God – but it took the pressure off me. The ministry would rise or fall, not because of my actions, but because of God's actions. He was in charge, He was responsible, He received the glory, and He directed the ministry. It was truly "the work of the Holy Ghost."

That foundation has been the most important plank of this ministry – this ministry that has touched millions of lives all over the world. To this day, many people ask me the secrets to a successful worldwide ministry, but the truth is, there's only one secret. It isn't a ten-step plan, or seven keys to reaching the lost. The truth is, the only way to be an instrument for God is to let God do what He wants, and let Him take the glory for it!

I never forgot that vision, and I was always careful to give God the praise for everything. Every time I stand before the people, every night of my life, as the people clap for me, I am quick to respond the same: "with all my heart, I thank you for your clap offering; I receive it as a token of your care. But I do not receive it for Morris – I receive it for the only One Who is worthy to be praised – yes there is only One worthy to be praised!" Then I ask the people if they can tell me what His Name is, and they all shout "Jesus!"

During the late 1950s, the flow of letters to our little home was increasing exponentially, and our correspondence list grew larger and larger. Even Theresa, who seemed to work all the time, had a hard time keeping up with the correspondence telling our friends how the ministry was doing.

Prayerfully, Theresa and I decided the ministry had to have a home base of operations. It had to be located in an area that was convenient for international flights, and it should be in an area where we could host large groups of people at any time of the year.

We began looking all over the country for a place that might be a good home base for the ministry God had called us to.

When we would begin to find a location that seemed good to us, we would pray, but we never received confirmation from God that we had found the right place.

Finally, toward the end of 1958 and the beginning of 1959, we began praying about a place called San Diego in California.

The warm climate was perfect, and San Diego's location at the southwestern corner of the United States was also perfect for flights to Asia and the South Pacific area that included the Philippines and China.

Theresa and I, after long periods of prayer, decided San Diego was the place to base this growing ministry.

We moved to San Diego, in 1959 and based the ministry there. Our three young children seemed to enjoy the California weather.

We lived in the Stardust Motel in the Mission Valley area of San Diego for six months, before we moved to Cabrillo Palisades, an apartment complex in the Kearny Mesa area.

We still were going out of our way to send out reports on the ministry to all our friends all over the country. Initially, we had a rickety old typewriter, and that's what we would write the letters on. Rarely did a day go by that we didn't spend hours corresponding prayerfully with people who were praying for the ministry.

Even the children got in on the correspondence, sometimes licking stamps, sometimes addressing envelopes.

The children developed games with their part of the ministry, and we had envelope-stuffing contests with the children to see who could stuff the most envelopes in the shortest period of time.

But still, most of the work was done by Theresa, as she worked what seemed to be day and night letting our friends know what we were up to, and what incredible miracles God was working.

I had discovered that having a network of friends all over the nation was a tremendous source of spiritual advice and strength to the ministry. It was as if the web of friends we had made in ministry were serving as a tether line to keep the ministry strong.

Soon after arriving in San Diego, our list of friends had become incredibly large. It became clear that we could no longer write individual reports to each and every person on our list of friends. Even with the entire family helping out, there simply weren't enough hours in the day to write letters to everyone on the list – we would have been doing nothing else, we would have never found the time to minister to the nations of the world, or even at a small meeting at a local church.

It became obvious that we had to find a way to communicate with our friends, but not take up all the time God had called us to use ministering to needy people in crusades and meetings. I still desperately wanted to tell our friends how the ministry was doing, and inform them of God's workings through the world. We could not hire people to write all the letters, either, we knew God had called us to be good stewards of any money we got into our hands and use that money to reach out with the Gospel.

We faced a tremendous dilemma. Some ministries and large corporations had already started a practice of writing one letter, printing that letter on a printing press, and sending it out to multitudes of people.

But I could not bring myself to do something like that. Each of the people on our list of friends had personally invested themselves in prayerful financial support of our ministry; I wanted a way to inform our friends of what was going on in the ministry without sending a letter addressed to "Occupant."

Our dilemma was solved when we discovered a machine called an "autotype." This machine was a huge gadget that would take our letters and type them out, with us addressing each letter to the proper recipient. It operated by sticking a tape, sort of like an audiotape, into a slot on the machine, and the machine would use that tape to determine which letter was printed when. Theresa became quite proficient in using the machines, even learning how to fix them when they broke. In the late 1950s and early 1960s, no one had ever heard of a computer – this machine was cutting-edge technology. It allowed us to still tell each of our friends what God was doing through the ministry in a personalized way, but we wouldn't spend precious ministry time typing hundreds of letters a day by hand.

With the help of that machine, we were able to keep our friends abreast of what was going on so they would know exactly how to pray.

But if we thought that machine would take the work out of the ministry, we had another thing coming. Each letter still had to be folded, placed in an envelope, the envelope still had to be licked, and the stamp still had to be applied. For a little family of five, it was still a tremendous amount of work, a full-time job, especially since it was in our garage!

In 1959, I again received a call to minister overseas, for the first time since my meetings in Greece.

Greece had been a baptism by fire – one emergency after another. It was only through intense fasting and prayer that the meetings even happened. I had been called upon to print handbills and buy advertising, rent the theatre, but I had never really gained a true understanding of the logistics involved in arranging and executing an overseas meeting.

In Greece, I was flying by the seat of my pants, so to speak, reacting to each crisis as it arose, relying on God to move miraculously and still bless the people.

But God had impressed upon me to more diligently prepare for future overseas meetings.

> *"And Paul, as his manner was, went in unto them, and three sabbath days reasoned with them out of the scriptures..." (Acts 17:2)*

Paul had a plan when he went into a city. He didn't just walk in blind and begin winning the lost to Christ; he carried with him a specific plan, and he followed it and reaped great rewards because of his organization.

The troubles in Greece had taught me that I had to inspect what I expected. I had to make sure that what I expected would actually get done. I had to be a good steward not only of the money God had entrusted to me, but the time God had entrusted to me.

So when I received the call to minister in Hong Kong and the Philippine Islands, I knew I had to work diligently to organize the meetings beforehand.

This time, Theresa would be able to go along with me.

As we prepared to leave for Hong Kong, and then the Philippines, we knew there was a mountain of work to do. Two ministers were to accompany us to preach during the daytime services, Gordon Lindsey and Lester Sumrall.

As I began making arrangements, I found out I knew next to nothing about things as simple as getting handbills printed in Hong Kong. The culture there was completely foreign to me.

In Greece, the culture was different from the culture in America, but in Hong Kong, the mentality was even more completely different. Even getting handbills printed and distributed seemed to be an insurmountable task, a task that took literally weeks to get finally rolling.

The logistics of setting up a meeting in Hong Kong were staggering. We had thought of the major things, such as advertising, renting the venue and creating posters – and those things were hard enough.

I knew absolutely nothing about renting a stadium. The stadium we rented in Hong Kong, the South China Football Stadium, was immense, with a capacity for  some forty-thousand or fifty-thouosand people.

We had no idea the sheer amount of money and hard work it took to set up an overseas meeting of any size. Greece had been easy compared to starting a meeting from scratch. While renting the Kentragon Theatre and doing all the advertising had cost only a few thousand dollars in Greece, renting the stadium in Hong Kong would cost quite a bit more.

After we found out how much it would be to rent the stadium and made arrangements in faith to do so, we had to figure out how to build a platform in the stadium.  Every stadium has rules as to what you can and can't do on their turf. Because sports are played in nearly every stadium, you have to be careful not to do damage to their carefully cultivated turf.

We hadn't realized the complexities of even what we considered simple things, like arranging for power to be in the stadium so we could run the sound equipment and the lights. A permit had to be obtained, and we had to deal with power companies to be sure they would be able to get us power when we needed it.

Little details took us completely by surprise: we had to make sure the platform had a pulpit and had chairs. We had to make sure the stadium floor had enough chairs to seat the people who would come. We had to make sure the ministers who would be joining us would have airfare to get to Hong Kong and airfare go get back to the United States. We had to make sure they had hotel reservations. We had to make sure they had transportation from the airport to the hotel, and from the hotel to the stadium. We had to have a place to minister to those who would accept Christ during the meetings. We had to make sure someone would follow up later with the people who would accept Christ. We had to arrange for ushers to help the Nationals who would be attending. There were so many more details than this that it's hard to remember them all forty years later. There were details upon details, and every one had to be arranged by people who had no experience setting up such details. It was a daunting task for young ministers from America to try and accomplish in a nation so completely foreign.

But when we were working out the details, we discovered we hadn't even thought about getting a sound system capable of reaching the entire stadium. A stadium, besides being simply huge, is notoriously hard to set up sound in. Because of the sheer size, if you don't set the sound system up just right, people in the front will hear the message a second or so before people in the back, and when the people in the back are hearing the message, people in the front are hearing echoes of the message in the back.

I was completely naive. I had no idea the kinds of things that had to be done to set up an overseas crusade, and the tremendous logistical details that had to be worked out in advance.

We had to get permits to have an open-air meeting, which I knew next-to-nothing about. Once we got the permits, we were not certain we would be able to keep them. At the whim of just about any official in the bureaucracy of a foreign nation, permits that are granted one day can be repealed the next day – or even sooner – for no reason at all.

Living in the United States, most people have no idea how powerful foreign governments are in the everyday lives of citizens of their countries. The word of government officials is law, and in countries that are grumpy about the Gospel – or even downright hostile – it can be months of work just to get a permit to hold a meeting, and even after all that work, there's no guarantee the permits will be there when you get ready to do the meeting.

These were all details I didn't know when I was preparing to go to Hong Kong and the Philippines to minister.

I had to pick them up in "on-the-job" training. It was an eye-opening experience, and the sheer expense of making all these details come to reality completely floored me. I knew that to operate in a ministry that consistently ministered to foreign nations of the world, I would have to be an extra-careful steward of the funds God entrusted to me. The staggering expense of foreign meetings demanded that every penny be made to count when arranging those meetings, every dollar to stretch like it was five.

To top it off, we didn't know anything about the climate in Hong Kong. We went to minister in that island city in February, the middle of winter, when the temperatures were literally freezing – for open-air meetings.

It was a bit discouraging and intimidating that we had to concentrate on so many little details to make the meetings happen. I was still only a young man ministering for only my second time overseas and really my first time in a truly "foreign" country.

When we arrived in Hong Kong for the meetings, however, we forgot the little details that had dogged us while we were preparing the meetings.

Hong Kong was a fascinating place. The entire country was a little island off the coast of China. Nearly everything on the island centered around the fact that it was surrounded by water. It seemed everything happened by boat.

Hong Kong was a British colony at that time, so some signs were written in both Chinese and English, but many were not. Hong Kong, like Greece, was a study in contrasts. Some people were dressed in traditional Chinese regalia, and others were dressed in Western attire, working in modern-looking buildings and driving modern cars. And everywhere, the influence of Communist China was evident. The Communist party was strong in Hong Kong, and it was not uncommon to see people walking down the street dressed in the unmistakable uniform of the Communist party.

As soon as we arrived in Hong Kong, I immediately felt led of God to pray. No sooner had we checked in to the hotel and gotten into our room than I began to seek God, praying for the souls we would be ministering to, praying that God would work tremendous miracles, but most of all, the miracle of salvation.

If we were to have any effect at all, I knew we couldn't minister without the Presence of God coming into the services.

Unless He came, we could sing the prettiest songs, preach the most theologically correct sermons, and make as much noise as we could, but the people would never be touched. We needed the Presence of God.

Every day, the ministers who had come with me would minister to the multitudes of people. Every night, I was scheduled to preach the services.

Every night, the services were packed with tens of thousands of people. I had never preached to crowds so large.

Theresa had a little Keystone camera that she used to take pictures.

The weather was terribly cold, but once the meetings got going and the power of God began to flow, I no longer noticed the cold, even though I had to preach in an overcoat.

It amazed me, however, that the throngs of people stood outside in that cold, not seeming to mind, for hours on end to receive the Word of God.

Thousands of people gave their lives to Christ, but most amazing were the scores of Communists, who doubtlessly had come to revile the meetings, who came to the altar to give their lives to Christ – which is strictly against the principles of Communism. When the word of the meeting spread, many crossed over the Communist border and sneaked into the meetings.

God was faithful to show up with His healing power – the miracles in Hong Kong were simply incredible, as people with all manner of diseases were healed instantly.

I remember one crippled man who came up for prayer. As I was about to pray for him, God impressed upon me to lay the man's legs on my own and pray. As I did, his legs were instantly healed, and he walked off the platform rejoicing and praising God.

But still, the most tremendous miracles of all were the salvations. Thousands of people answered the call to make Jesus Lord of their lives, and as they did, I couldn't help but weep for the incredible commitment they were making.

Later, we spent a few days ministering to the new converts in a theatre, teaching them the principles of their new life, and the importance of a deep relationship with Jesus.

It was at one of these meetings that we met a precious Chinese lady named Nora Lam. This lady related to us how she had been touched in the meetings, and we quickly became friends with her. So many people had been led to Christ during these meetings, that it became apparent the new converts needed a place to meet for weekly services.

None of the local churches in Hong Kong would have been able to handle such an influx of new believers – it would have simply overwhelmed them.

I didn't know what we could do to help these people to have a house of worship, so I did what I always did when I didn't have an answer to a pressing question.

I went back to my hotel room and fell on my face before God. During that intense time of prayer, God told me that the ministry should obtain a place for this new congregation to worship.

It was a tremendous step of faith. To find a place large enough to accommodate a significant number of Christians and to pay for it in a foreign country having never dealt with real estate in that country was certainly a tremendous proposition.

It would be nothing short of miraculous. But God's will was clear, so we set about to prayerfully find a suitable location for these new believers.

It wasn't easy. Hong Kong is not only a bustling island state, it's also tremendously crowded. Finding real estate is no small task.

After much looking and quite a bit of negotiating, we finally found the fourth floor of a building right on the Hong Kong harbor. The floor's size would be perfect for both a worship center and church offices.

We made arrangements to purchase the floor and turn it into a church – the New Life Temple. Nora Lam, the lady we had met in the believers' meeting, agreed to stay on as our secretary at the church, handling administrative functions and doing the day-to-day work of running a church.

She proved herself a capable and willing secretary, and a tremendous servant of God for the years she stayed with the

New Life Temple. Years later, Nora became world-famous when she wrote her life story of struggle in Communist China in the book, *China Cry*, which also later became a Hollywood movie.

When we closed the meetings in Hong Kong, our next stop was the Philippines, the meetings about which I wrote in Chapter One of this book. Again, the simple logistics of setting up the meeting were tremendously complicated. These two early meetings prepared me for a lifetime of often difficult and always expensive preparations for overseas meetings.

Truly, even through these first two really foreign meetings, I had seen nothing yet.

But if I thought those meetings were battles – through working out the logistics and praying intensely for salvations and miracles – I had no idea what a battle was, yet.

In 1960, I had become acquainted with a ministry called the Full Gospel Businessmen's Fellowship International, a worldwide outreach to men, based in Costa Mesa, California.

The group's founder, Demos Shakarian, had given me a personal invitation to minister in a crusade in the Caribbean island of Haiti.

Haiti is one of the poorest nations in the world. The people there live in unbelievable poverty and in conditions we in America have a hard time even imagining.

But once a year, during a seven-week period, the people of that island gather together in one of the most depraved, wicked displays of human sinfulness that can be imagined anywhere in the world.

The Mardi Gras celebration in Haiti is absolutely vile. It continues seven consecutive Sundays, with people dancing in the streets in drunkenness, and open sexual sin. We even received reports that five thousand girls were raped in one night, and no one did anything to stop it.

# Son, Build Me An Army

And with the revelry of Mardi Gras always came the witchcraft. Most people on the island claim to be Catholic, but the reality couldn't be further from the truth. They may attend Catholic church services, but most don't follow the teachings of that church; after they attend church, they may go straight to the local witch doctor to practice their superstitious religion, voodoo.

At the time, I knew nothing of voodoo. I didn't know of its practices rooted in witchcraft, of its use of religious charms called "fetishes." I had no idea that voodoo priests believed if they burned someone in effigy, or if they stuck pins in a representation of that person that real harm would come to the person the icon represented.

The people fear the voodoo priests, whom they call witch doctors. They fear that the witch doctors might use their magic against the people, so to appease them, the people do pretty much whatever the witch doctors want. I had no idea this kind of fear and superstition gripped the island; I was just a young evangelist. All I knew was I was there to preach the Gospel during a five-day crusade.

In the natural, the timing of our crusade couldn't have come at a worse time. We were scheduled to begin right in the middle of Mardi Gras, the height of voodoo's pagan year. Little did we know that our very presence was stirring up a hornet's nest among the island's witch doctors, who got together and decided to organize against us.

By 1960, we were getting used to the logistics of arranging overseas meetings. Our practice had become to send out posters ahead of time to be posted all over the area of the meetings, advertising the upcoming crusade.

In Haiti, the posters had been put up all over the island. This stirred up the voodoo priests even more.

153

## Son, Build Me An Army

When my airplane touched down in Port-au-Prince, the capital of Haiti, I was immediately met by a string of dignitaries and high-ranking officials in a long motorcade of limousines.

As soon as I stepped off the plane, I knew something was different about Haiti – something was not right. I wanted to hurry to my hotel room and pray, but I didn't want to offend the dignitaries by rushing off, so I agreed to take part in their motorcade, which was to parade through town and in front of the president's house.

As I sat in the back of the limousine with a general and Senator Arthur Bonhomme, the motorcade began its trip through the streets of Haiti.

I began to feel sick. I turned to our crusade soloist and said, "Swen, if you don't mind, please help me. I want to go to my hotel. I don't want to go in this motorcade."

My hosts didn't initially understand, but they obliged, pulling the car out of the motorcade and taking me to my hotel.

The sickness seemed to be permeating my entire body. As soon as I got into my hotel room, for which my hosts had pre-registered me, I fell to the floor as one dead and began praying to God.

"Lord, what is it?" I cried out to God. "What do I feel inside me?"

"Son," God said, "this is not a physical sickness, but a spiritual discernment I have allowed for a reason. I want to talk to you. Tonight there is going to be trouble."

I had seen trouble before, to be sure. Many religious leaders had opposed our meetings, and many times we had extreme difficulty getting everything in order to make the meetings happen, but I sensed that the trouble God was speaking of was different from the troubles I had faced before.

"What is it, Lord?" I asked.

"There are hundreds of witch doctors who are already mad at you," God said. "They are coming to kill you. They have organized to break up the meeting."

The words rang in my head for a bit: "They are coming to kill you." This was the first time that my life had been directly threatened in the course of ministering to the nations of the world. I was a little bit surprised to find out that I could feel no fear within myself. I felt none of the trepidation I would have assumed I would feel. I felt no need to postpone the meetings or cancel them. In fact, I felt a tremendous inner strength and a special apostolic anointing.

"Well, now, Lord," I replied. "I'm glad You told me. If I'm supposed to die, fine. I'll be a martyr for Your sake."

Little did I know this was the first of many times I would have to say this during my life as radicals from countries all over the planet threatened and planned to kill me, and I had to face audiences knowing there was a very real possibility I might be killed.

"If this is what You want," I continued, "it is all right with me. But what should I do?"

I was prepared to die for God's sake, but I wanted to know what He had planned for me to do. If that plan was for me to be martyred, I was fine with that, but if that plan was something else, I needed clarification from Him as to exactly what it was.

God showed me how I was to identify them in the crowd – where they would stand, and then He spoke.

But what God said to me was unexpected, and awe-inspiring in its implications. He had never said anything even remotely close to this to me before, and I have never heard Him say anything like it since:

"Son, the word that you speak will be exactly as if I had spoken it, and that word will come to pass."

Although it took a minute for what God had said to sink in, I knew exactly what He had told me. God was letting me know that this night, I had the power of life and death in my mouth.

What a tremendous and heavy responsibility! I thought of the apostle Peter, who also had apparently been in charge of this kind of responsibility:

> *"Then Peter said unto her, How is it that ye have agreed together to tempt the Spirit of the Lord? behold, the feet of them which have buried thy husband are at the door, and shall carry thee out. Then fell she down straightway at his feet, and yielded up the ghost: and the young men came in, and found her dead, and, carrying her forth, buried her by her husband." (Acts 5:9-10)*

It was not a responsibility to be taken lightly. It was not an authority to be used at the whim of a man, after all, "*...it is not the will of your Father which is in heaven, that one of these little ones should perish...*" (Matthew 18:14).

God's will was not for the people who had planned to kill me to perish. His will was that they "*...may know him, and the power of his resurrection...*" (Philippians 3:10). But God had placed in my hands the tools to ensure that His will was accomplished in the rest of the people at the meetings. If the few were standing in the way of salvation for the many, God had made it clear to me that He would not stand for that kind of disruption.

It wasn't very long until there was a knock on my hotel room door. As I opened the door, I saw many of the local ministers in Port-au-Prince who were hosting the meeting. As I looked on each of their faces, I saw the same thing in all: fear.

I could immediately tell that some of these ministers believed in the power of the witch doctors. They began to tell me what I already had learned by the power of God.

"Brother Cerullo," one of the ministers said. "We don't want to tell you what to do. But we don't think you should have a Sunday night meeting."

The man's face was furrowed with worry, and it was sincere. I could tell he believed every word he was saying, and he was genuinely concerned for my safety.

"A Sunday night meeting will conflict with the Mardi Gras celebration," the minister continued, gesturing with his hands as he spoke. "In Haiti, that is the most important celebration of the year. The witch doctors would not like it if you interrupt that celebration with a Gospel meeting. Already, they have torn down your posters all over Haiti."

He paused and seemed to be pondering within himself whether he should tell me what he had to say next.

"Some of the posters they have burned in effigy," he continued, obviously deciding he should go ahead and tell me everything. "The only posters they have left up are the posters they have poked with their voodoo pins, which they believe will inflict actual harm on you. Already, they are calling their evil spirits down on you to keep you from conducting the meetings."

I could tell from the faces of the other ministers that they agreed with what this sincere man was telling me.

"If you decide to have Sunday meetings, we will come with you," the minister said. "But we don't think you should."

I sat back for a minute and tried to think of just the right words to use to explain to this minister why I would not only hold meetings on Sunday, but why I had to. But just as I was about to speak, C.C. Ford, a friend of mine, and one of the executive directors of the Full Gospel Businessmen, spoke up and answered before I could.

"Let me tell you something about Brother Cerullo," Mr. Ford said gently, in the most reassuring tone I had ever heard him use. "One thing about him you will come to understand is that he is not consecrated unto life."

Mr. Ford let that statement sink in, and I could tell by the puzzled looks on the faces of the ministers that they were in a hurry for him to explain what he meant.

"Brother Cerullo is consecrated unto death. He has no fear of death, nor of your witch doctors."

I couldn't have said it better myself. Mr. Ford had articulated exactly what I wanted to say to these concerned ministers. God had called me to preach the Gospel, and if that included dying in the course of that calling, I was ready to die. Certainly, I didn't want to die if it wasn't in the will of God, but death held no fear for me. I could completely understand what the Apostle Paul was thinking when he said, *"for to me to live is Christ, and to die is gain."* (Philippians 1:21)

Paul had no death wish. He wanted to live in the action of the Gospel. But he also understood that if he was to die, it would be a gain to him as he knew he would wake up in glory, face-to-face with the King of all creation.

I had nothing to lose. If I lived, I would live to Christ. If I died, I would die to Christ – either way, I won.

The ministers who had come to warn me didn't seem too convinced, but they respected our decision to hold the meeting anyway.

I laugh a little bit when I think of what these precious ministers must have thought at that moment – "nice knowing you."

But I had a promise from God…

I knew God intended to bring souls to salvation that night, and He wouldn't let a few measly witch doctors stand in His way.

Haiti's president, Francois Duvalier, had invited the Full Gospel Businessmen and me to come to his country and conduct these meetings.

So when we arrived at the stadium, nearly two hundred dignitaries and high-ranking military officials came and sat on the platform with their wives as the crusade opened.

It looked more like a royal revue than a miracle crusade to look at the bevy of dignitaries who were sitting on the platform. Many of the military men were wearing their full dress uniforms, decked out with gold and medals, ribbons and other symbols of recognition of their valor and skill at military affairs.

That first night, five thousand people were jammed all around the platform, which had been erected in the middle of the stadium. Another ten thousand people were crammed into the stands that surrounded the open area in the center of the stadium.

The crowd was by far the loudest and wildest I had ever faced.

In those days, church crowds were much different from what they are today. No one was moving around during the service. There was a reverent silence during most of the services, and people sat attentively watching everything that went on.

But this service in Port-au-Prince was the exact opposite of the subdued reverence I was accustomed to.

The crowd was in havoc. Many people were laughing and jeering, making faces and intimidating other people in the crowd.

Some were waving their arms around and making strange noises. Others were pointing at the platform and shouting and laughing.

It was a mess.

Milling about through the crowd were three hundred witch doctors. God showed me where each one was. It was as if they completely stood out in the crowd. I could tell every single one. As they made their way around in the crowd, people around them gave them plenty of room. It was clear the people of Haiti weren't interested in incurring the wrath of these voodoo priests.

When I was introduced, the mayhem in the crowd quieted down just a little bit. Many of the people who had been laughing and jeering quit what they were doing just long enough to hear what was said about me.

I approached the microphone and looked out into the crowd. Every eye was upon me.

"I greet you tonight in the Name that is above every name, Jesus Christ, the Son of the living God," I said into the microphone.

It was as if I had fired off a pistol at the start of a track meet.

In the midst of the crowd, in little pockets positioned everywhere, the witch doctors started to chant.

Boom, ba boom, ba boom, ba boom.

Boom, ba boom, ba boom, ba boom.

Boom, ba boom, ba boom, ba boom.

The chant swelled, as the people around the witch doctors began to take up the chant and amplify it by adding their own voices, whether out of compliance or outright fear of crossing the witch doctors.

The witch doctors began to move about the stadium, coming down from the bleachers and heading toward the platform.

Boom, ba boom, ba boom, ba boom.

Boom, ba boom, ba boom, ba boom.

Boom, ba boom, ba boom, ba boom.

I called for quiet.

But the witch doctors and the people who were following them stopped for a moment, then ignored me.

Boom, ba boom, ba boom, ba boom.

Boom, ba boom, ba boom, ba boom.

Boom, ba boom, ba boom, ba boom.

I called for quiet again. I knew what God had called me here to do, and I knew the lengths to which He was willing to go to ensure His message came across, but I hoped it wouldn't come to that.

The witch doctors, stopped again, and then ignored me again.

Boom, ba boom, ba boom, ba boom.

Boom, ba boom, ba boom, ba boom.

Boom, ba boom, ba boom, ba boom.

The chants were increasing in volume. We had set up speakers to amplify my voice to reach the huge crowds in the stadium, but as the chanting built in volume, it was hard for me to hear myself when I called for silence a third time.

Still the witch doctors stopped and resumed their chants, their chants building even more in volume.

Boom, ba boom, ba boom, ba boom.

I tried one last time, and called for quiet.

The chants increased even more.

Boom, ba boom, ba boom, ba boom.

The dignitaries on the platform looked worried. Some were looking around, as if searching for a quick way to exit the platform before the entire place broke out in a riot. There was no escape, however, the platform was built in the middle of a sea of people.

The ministers who were hosting the meeting appeared frightened, and they, too, seemed to be looking for a way out.

Inside me, a righteous indignation rose up like none I had ever experienced. It was as if the Spirit of God completely overwhelmed my being and took over.

My interpreter at this meeting was a Bible school boy named Nelson. I turned to Nelson and sternly pointed my finger at him.

"Son," I shouted to him over the noise of the witch doctors and their cronies. "I want you to interpret exactly what I say – every word! Don't you dare change a single word. Not one syllable!"

Nelson's eyes were wide with fear. "Yes, sir!" he replied. "Yes, sir! Yes, sir!"

I turned to the crowd and began to speak.

"People of Haiti, this is the last time I am going to speak. I have asked for reverence and quiet three times now to be able to give you God's Word. I want you to know that I didn't just decide to come to Haiti. God sent me here. The true and living God sent me to you. He gave me a message of love. He gave me a message of healing for you. He loves you. He wants to save you. He wants to forgive your sins, to bless you and heal you. Now that is the message He sent me here to bring to you. But that God is also a God of judgment."

The crowd's noise quieted a bit, and I could tell they were paying attention to what I was saying. I continued.

"Today, in my room, God showed me that there were hundreds of witch doctors who would be here tonight to destroy this meeting." As I spoke, I pointed to some of the red-shirted witch doctors who were milling about the platform.

"I am going to be here in this city for some time," I continued. "We had better find out tonight – this first night – whether you and your devil have more power than I and my God!"

162

I could tell the Spirit of God had their attention, especially all the witch doctors. But the righteous indignation that had risen up in me wasn't finished. God had a point to make. I turned to look at the dignitaries who were assembled on the platform.

"Now, I serve notice that I take no responsibility for what happens from this point on. The NEXT PERSON IN THIS STADIUM who opens their mouth and says one word to hinder or destroy this meeting, I will take no responsibility before all these dignitaries on the platform when they carry you out of this stadium...DEAD!"

Immediately, the stadium was filled with silence.

No more chanting. No more "boom ba boom."

I didn't even hear crickets chirping. Everyone was so silent, if someone had dropped a hairpin on the ground, I believe everyone could have heard it.

It looked as if some people might not even be breathing.

The witch doctors apparently did not want to find out if God actually would kill them for disrupting this service after they had been warned.

I began to preach a powerful message of salvation under the anointing of God.

For fifteen or twenty minutes, my voice and the voice of my interpreter were the only sounds that could be heard in this massive stadium, the only words that circulated around the fifteen thousand people gathered were words of life flowing directly from the Bible.

After I had been preaching that length of time, a sudden scream from the back of the crowd pierced through the night air like a hot knife cutting through a stick of melting butter.

Many in the crowd turned around to look, as a commotion that began in the back began to work its way through the crowd toward the front.

As I peered over toward where the noise was coming from, I could see many people with their hands over their heads, and they appeared to be passing a little baby over the tops of their heads, one by one, moving the baby toward the platform.

The place was erupting in commotion.

I turned to Nelson and said, "What is going on?"

"Brother Cerullo," he answered, "while you were preaching a child back there who was born blind can now see and is grabbing for his parents' eyes, nose, ears and head. The place is going wild."

They continued to advance the child toward the platform, over the heads of the people, who were passing her forward.

Finally, she reached the platform.

The little girl was gazing in awe at the commotion all around her. She had never seen anything before, and she was amazed at everything.

Her parents were pressing through the huge crowd of people who were assembled around the platform. When they arrived, they began testing her vision, waving their fingers in front of her little eyes. Her eyes followed their fingers everywhere.

A few moments later, a large grin came over the little girl's beautiful little face, as she saw her daddy's nose and began grabbing it. Her father, tears in his eyes, smiled and laughed as his daughter played with his nose.

The little girl's mother was worshiping God, tears pouring from her eyes in what seemed to be torrents.

Behind me, one of the high-ranking Haitian officials stood up and began to shout out some words in his language.

I turned around to my interpreter and asked him what this man, whose uniform was decked with all kinds of gold bars and braids, was saying,

"He's saying, 'My God! That's my neighbors,'" my interpreter said.

God had begun demonstrating His power to this crowd of people, who formerly were so afraid of the witch doctors.

I had issued a challenge earlier, telling the witch doctors that we would find out whether God was more powerful than the devil they served.

In the eyes of the crowd, the question was settled.

Revival began to break out in that crowd of fifteen thousand, as more healings began to take place all over the stadium.

God poured out His Spirit into this group of spiritually starving people.

But God was not done.

If He had simply healed these people and demonstrated to the masses that they had nothing to fear in the witch doctors, it would certainly have been enough to ensure the salvations of many thousands upon thousands of people.

After all, they had tried their worst, and nothing had happened. God, on the other hand, had shown the people that He is alive, and still working in the affairs of mankind.

But I began to remember the Scripture I had thought of in my hotel room, that God didn't want even one person to perish.

As I did, I saw the most amazing thing...

Some of the witch doctors – wearing red shirts – were weeping and crying at the sight of this little girl's healing.

And all over the crowd, from my vantage point on the stage, I saw witch doctors drop to their knees, lift their hands and pray to Jesus to save their souls.

They had for years practiced a religion that promised them power and held them on a pedestal of fear in the eyes of all the people, but this night, they had witnessed the power of a very real God and they realized they had given their lives to the wrong side.

That meeting ended with a tremendous altar call where thousands of people gave their lives to Jesus. The dignitaries behind me could hardly believe their eyes, and many of them also gave their lives to Jesus.

The next night, the stadium was filled to capacity, as word of the witch doctors' defeat spread throughout the island. Thirty-five thousand people crammed themselves into the stadium to receive from God.

The sky was very overcast, with heavy-looking gray clouds looming over the stadium, threatening rain at any minute.

My hosts explained to me that Haitians are very superstitious, and being rained upon was a sign of bad luck. When the dark clouds filled the sky, the crowds at the meeting began to run out of the stadium, not wanting the bad luck of being rained upon.

I grabbed the microphone and shouted into it: "In the Name of Jesus, I command you to stop running and stand still!"

Again, the words just spewed forth from my mouth, under an incredible anointing of God's power and direction.

It was as if I had thrown a gigantic power switch. The people who had been running in superstitious panic suddenly stopped in their tracks, as if a movie playing the scene had stopped dead in the projector.

"In the Name of Jesus, turn around and look at me," I shouted into the microphone. Everyone turned around to see why this preacher was talking to them like this. "You see those dark clouds?" I continued. "Now you are going to know what kind of prophet of God I am. IT WILL NOT RAIN while the service is going on!"

I don't know if the people were just curious to see if what I said was true or not, or if they stayed because they believed what I had said, but the people stayed, and I began preaching, and preached an entire message, about an hour and a half to two hours long.

After I had given the altar call and prayed for salvations and for the sick, the blind saw, the deaf heard and the crippled walked. I spoke into the microphone one last time.

"People of Haiti, the service is over. After I pray, if you don't want to get wet, you should leave quickly, because it's going to rain."

After I had closed the service in prayer, the people began filing out of the stadium quickly. About ten minutes later, the sky opened up and rain began to pour down in the stadium in torrents.

God had once again demonstrated His power to the Haitian people, who so desperately needed the Gospel and the saving knowledge of Jesus Christ!

Indeed, the meetings, which were only supposed to last for five days, ended up lasting for three weeks, during which dozens and dozens of witch doctors gave their lives to Jesus, and thousands of other people also gave their lives to Jesus. As each witch doctor or believer in voodoo gave their lives to Jesus, they would bring their pagan fetishes to the altar and cast them upon the altar as a sign of their new commitment to the living God. By the end of the week, thousands of fetishes had been thrown on the altar by voodoo practitioners who had given their lives to Christ.

One evening, during the middle of the first week, several people connected to the crusade came up to me and wanted to speak to me.

"Brother Cerullo," one of the men said to me. "The leading witch doctor in Port-au-Prince wants to speak to you. This is the witch doctor that holds all the others in fear. He is the one to whom all the others answer."

## Son, Build Me An Army

I wondered what this witch doctor wanted with me. But as C.C. Ford had said the other night, I was not consecrated unto life, I was consecrated unto death. No matter what this man wanted, I knew when he requested to see me that I had to go.

We got into several cars and headed out to the house where the witch doctor lived, in the middle of town. His house had all kinds of voodoo items placed at strategic locations, whether to scare others or work some kind of magic, I never found out, but it was not hard to tell that someone who had believed strongly in voodoo lived in this house.

When we got into the man's house, he told a tremendous story. He and his entire family had been at the meetings we had held during the first week, and they had seen the power of God and had been miraculously converted! As a testimony to his newfound life in Christ, we meticulously went through every room in his house, collecting the relics, fetishes and other charms related to his voodoo practice, and we piled them all up in a giant pile in the middle of the street in front of his house.

As we did, we could see the eyes of curious neighbors peeking through the windows of their homes, some through cracked front doors. Some brave neighbors actually came out and stood in front of their houses to see what was going on at the house of the chief witch doctor in town.

We finally got everything voodoo-related out of the new Christian's house, and made a final pass-through to make sure we hadn't missed anything. When we were sure everything was collected in this huge pile in front of the house, we doused the pile with gasoline, lit it on fire and began to march around the giant fire that sprung up, singing "What can wash away my sins? Nothing but the blood of Jesus!"

The former witch doctor joined in with us, his formerly scowling face that had inspired fear in thousands now cracked wide with a toothy smile as he repeated the words to the old hymn and rejoiced over his new life as the relics of his old life burned in the center of the street.

After the second week of crusades, the usually raucous Mardi Gras no longer had enough people to be significant. Too many people had given their lives to Christ! There were no longer enough people willing to participate in the ungodly displays of Mardi Gras to keep the celebration viable!

The rapes and drunkenness had stopped! The witchcraft and voodoo were no longer readily apparent. God had wrought a mighty change in that tiny island nation.

God had birthed a spiritual revival in that nation that they never would forget, and many souls were won to the Kingdom of God.

From that point forward, the ministry seemed to explode. Everywhere we went, crowds got larger and larger, reaching into the hundreds of thousands.

Everywhere I went, thousands upon thousands of salvations followed. Truly, I was fulfilling the vision God had given me when I was fifteen years old to reach out to the nations of the world, but even though at the age of thirty I had one of the most successful ministries in the world, it didn't feel like that to me.

Every time I saw someone get saved and commit their lives to Jesus, I stood in humble awe of the providence of God. I will never, as long as I live, get over the humbling feeling of knowing that God is doing His most incredible miracle – and He's letting me be a part of it!

Every time someone is born again, I feel almost overwhelmed that God has allowed me to be in the presence of His greatest miracle.

As I began to witness thousands and thousands of salvations in each of the meetings we were holding all over the world, I began to have a concern deep in my spirit, although I couldn't yet articulate it. We were winning thousands of souls to Christ, but what was happening to them afterward?

We did the best we could, giving these precious souls Gospels of John and following up as closely as best we could with literature and all other means, getting names on decision cards so we could keep up with them, but I felt as if there was more we could do.

I began to wonder and pray about how we could more effectively be a help to the tremendous influx of souls that were being won to the kingdom.

I didn't know it, but God was preparing to answer my prayers in a dynamic and life-changing way that would forever provide a guiding framework for my ministry.

In 1962, I had been called to Porto Alegre, Brazil, to preach a crusade in the huge Exposition Grounds.

I was in Porto Alegre for ten days. The newspapers were covering the accounts of the miracles in the meetings on the front pages. People were bringing the sick in from miles around on carts, beds and couches. The streets were lined all day long with those wanting miracles to heal their infirmities. About five days into the meetings, I had been in intense and powerful prayer for God to bring His Presence into the service. After an hour or two, I felt God's Presence and knew He would minister in a special way in the service and bless the people.

As I got into the car to go to the Exposition Grounds, I knew God was about to change lives – but I had no idea how He was about to change mine.

By the time I got to the Exposition Grounds, the music service was already well under way. The music seemed to flow in a rhythm of incredible spiritual synchronicity – everything seemed to fit together like the pieces of a jigsaw. Already, I could see the Presence of God fill the Exposition

Grounds to minister to the fifty thousand people who had crammed themselves onto the field.

The heat was almost overwhelming, like opening an oven in a hot kitchen in the middle of summertime. I hadn't even gotten to the platform to speak yet, but my clothes were already starting to get damp.

By the time the song service was over, a tremendous atmosphere of praise had permeated the entire Exposition Grounds.

My crusade director stepped up to the platform and began to address the people. The congregation listened in reverent silence, and then the crusade director introduced me and called me up to speak at the microphone.

The microphone was placed squarely in front of a small board that had been nailed to the railing of the platform that I was to minister from. That was the only pulpit that was available to me, so I set my Bible on the little board and greeted the crowd in the Name that is above every name, Jesus.

I knew God had already begun to minister to this huge congregation, so I launched right into my message, a message on salvation, healing and miracles. Between phrases, my interpreter would translate my words into Portugese, following each of my gestures with gestures that exactly matched.

I had been preaching for about ten minutes – everything was flowing in an awesome demonstration of God's power.

But suddenly, I was stopped cold in my tracks, as what felt like a hot butcher knife seemed to slice through my chest, directly into my heart.

When my tooth had been chipped as a young boy, I had never felt such pain. When my jaw and cheekbone had been broken by a line-drive softball, I had never felt such pain.

171

This pain was so intense that my very legs wanted to give out from beneath me. It was only sheer willpower that kept me on my feet. For a few seconds, my mind went completely blank. I could think of nothing but the pain – intense, penetrating and devastating pain.

The pain continued to intensify from that point to where it was almost completely unbearable.

I grabbed onto the little board that was serving as a pulpit to keep myself from falling down.

My entire body was now racked with pain. I was completely doubled over, and the pain only seemed to be intensifying.

"Am I having a heart attack?" I thought to myself. I was only thirty years old – far too young in my estimation to be having a heart attack, but I could think of no other explanation.

"Am I going to die?" I thought as the pain increased in intensity. "Is God going to take me home now?"

I had never envisioned myself dying of a heart attack. But if God was going to take me, I was ready, only I didn't want to die on stage in front of fifty thousand people, who needed God's salvation and healing power.

I reached over and grabbed my crusade director by the arm.

Using the very last of my strength, which was being sapped by the debilitating pain, I pulled him to the microphone and whispered to him: "Finish the services. I must go back to my hotel room."

He looked bewildered, but the look in my eyes must have convinced him, because he immediately took over the service. I somehow made it to the back of the stage, where the car I had arrived in was parked, and I literally fell into the back seat.

The driver rushed me back to the hotel room.

When I opened the door and entered my room, I didn't even take time to remove my clothes, which were now completely soaked.

The pain had not subsided at all, in fact, it was still just as sharp and piercing as it had been on the stage.

I fell onto my face in the middle of the hotel room and began to cry out to God.

"Lord," I asked, gasping for breath between words. "Are You going to take me home?"

Sometimes God speaks to me in an audible voice, just as clearly as one person talking to another. Sometimes, He speaks to me through His Word. Sometimes, God gives an inaudible impression in my spirit, which is just as real as His audible voice – because I know Him, I understand that it is His voice.

This day, when I asked God if He was about to take me home, He let me know that this pain was not for the purpose of finally taking me home.

God let me know that He had allowed this pain to happen to me for a special reason, to get my attention in an undivided way.

He said to me: "Son, I have permitted this to happen to you for a purpose."

Personally, I would have preferred another way of getting my attention, but who was I to argue with God? In any case, I noticed that the pain had left my body completely. To this very day, more than thirty-seven years later, I have never had a recurrence of that pain, or anything that even slightly resembles it.

If God had gone to such lengths to get my attention, I knew He must have something very important to tell me; I wanted to give my full concentration to what it was He wanted to say.

"Lord," I said to Him, "please teach me."

God began speaking to me in an audible voice, and He called me by name:

"Morris, what do you want out of this life?"

God had almost always spoken to me in unexpected ways, with unexpected messages, but this was the most peculiar question I had ever been asked by Him. I thought within myself that it was readily clear what I wanted out of this life, with the single-minded dedication I had given to winning souls all over the world at any cost, even facing death to ensure those souls were reached. But obviously God had a reason for asking me this peculiar question, so I asked him:

"God, why would You ask me that? You know the dedication and the consecration I have made to You; why would You ask me what I want out of this life?"

And then I began to think of what it was that I really wanted out of this life. I could have said that my only desire was to reach souls, but I was already doing that, and I knew that there was something more that I needed to be doing.

So many times, I would receive requests from ministers and hosts where I was preaching to "stay, stay and minister the Word of God to us."

Most of the time, I would stay as long as I possibly could. I would take along a certain amount of money, and when that money was gone and I could continue no longer, I would return home to raise money to plan the next meeting I could minister in. But my real desire was to do more than just reach souls.

I blurted out my desire to God from the depths of my innermost being, from the deepest part of my being:

"Lord, there is only one thing that I ask of You in this world – only one thing. God, give me the ability to take what

You have given me, the power and anointing that is upon my ministry...and give me the ability to give that to others."

God had taught me in such a powerful way in Lima, Ohio, that this wasn't the ministry of a man, it was the ministry of the Holy Spirit. It was not Morris Cerullo who was leading so many salvations and healings all over the world, it was the anointing of God that had been imparted into my ministry. It was God Who was causing the success of our rallies, Who was bringing thousands and thousands of souls into the kingdom of heaven.

If I could impart that anointing and power to those I went to reach, they would not need me to stay and minister to them – the same anointing would be on their own lives, and they could more effectively reach their neighbors than I could ever hope to do.

At the time, there was a tremendous movement afoot in many of the foreign countries of the world to reject foreign ministers who came to the countries to hold crusades. Many people resented these foreigners coming in and trying to reach their populations. I understood that an African would be far more effective at reaching Africans in the long term than I could ever hope to be.

I knew that Brazilians would be more effective in the long run reaching out to their own nation than I could ever be holding large national crusades.

Both were needed, but I knew that it would be only through duplicating what God had done in my life that the world could be reached.

I knew that my only hope of impacting the world, my only hope of realizing the vision God had given me when I had looked through His footprints and seen the multitude of souls burning in hell, the only way I could ever make a lasting mark on the world was to train others to reach out as I had and bring the lost to Christ.

## Son, Build Me An Army

It was then, on the floor of a seedy hotel in the middle of downtown Porto Alegré, Brazil, in 1962 that my life and the course of my ministry would forever be changed.

I knew in myself I was standing on the precipice of a fundamental change in the way I was to do ministry. I understood that what was about to transpire would forever modify the way I had grown accustomed to doing things. But I was ready.

God spoke to me in an audible voice the words that would change history:

"Son, Build Me an Army!"

This is a photo of me when I was just a young man in Bible college.

When I met Theresa LePari, I knew she was the woman I'd spend the rest of my life with. This photo was taken in 1951.

I began attending Bible college soon after I met Theresa – and I left married to her.

This is the Daughters of Miriam Jewish Orthodox Orphanage where I spent much of my childhood, and where I received the message that Jeshua (Jesus) is the Messiah.

This crusade in Erie, Pennsylvania, also in 1956, lasted seven weeks, with hundreds of people saved and healed by the power of God.

In 1956, as in this crusade in Pennsylvania, God was already performing many miracles and salvations through my ministry.

Theresa and I pose with Mrs. Ethel Kerr Davis, who obeyed the Lord in the face of all opposition to bring the Gospel to a Jewish orphan boy.

This is an actual photo of one of the crowds in Athens, Greece, in my first overseas evangelistic journey. God moved mightily in Greece, as in New Testament times, saving souls and healing bodies using a Jewish preacher.

This is a photo of Theresa and me, which I sent to Mrs. Kerr shortly before Theresa and I were married in 1951.

This is a photo taken at Christmas in 1956, just a few days before our miracle baby, Mark, was born. From left are Theresa, little David, me and "daddy's girl," Susan.

When I took my first "real" overseas missions journey to Hong Kong and the Philippines, Theresa came along with a Keystone camera as the photographer. This photo of a man from Hong Kong testifying of his healing is one of the many photos Theresa shot in the bitter cold.

In Haiti, after God moved sovereignly through the crowd to silence many murderous witch doctors intent on killing me, many of the witch doctors received Christ as their Lord. Here, surrounded by smoke, one of the chief witch doctors and I burn the implements of his demonic craft after his conversion to the Lord.

By the time I preached in Porto Alegre, Brazil, in 1962, the crowds attending our meetings were reaching immense proportions. It was shortly after this photo was taken that God told me, "Son, Build Me an Army!"

God performed many miracles in Brazil, and in what became a familiar sight, many people who were healed cast off crutches and other items they no longer needed as a testimony to the power of the living God.

In 1966 in Rosario, Argentina, I was arrested for practicing medicine without a license. When I testified before the magistrate, I was cleared of all charges and allowed to go.

An integral part of our ministry has always been to get the word out by any means possible – radio, television, satellite, newspaper advertising and handbills. This handbill is from a crusade I preached in Holland in 1960.

This is a reproduction of a front-page article that ran in the West Indian newspaper in Grenada, giving an account of the tremendous miracles God worked there in 1964 through the ministry.

This flier came from a revival in Chicago in 1959, showing me and my associate ministers, R.F. Bender, Sven Bjork, Lester Sumrall and Gordon Lindsey.

Israel has always been near and dear to my heart. From the time I first met the Messiah, I longed to reach out to my brethren after the flesh, Israel. In 1967, that dream came to pass.

One of the fulfillments of our call to the Jews was when God led us to film *Masada*, a prime-time television special recalling the heroics of a band of Jews who resisted Roman oppression in the desert stronghold of Masada.

When God asked me what I wanted in this life, I answered that I wanted to be able to impart the anointing He had given to me into the lives of others. From that day in 1962 to this, I have always made it a point to impart the anointing in my services.

Hundreds of thousands of people have attended single meetings I have preached overseas, as in this photo from Surabaya. God's power has always been able to change the lives of hundreds of thousands of people at the same time.

This is a photo of our entire family taken before my son Mark passed away. From left are Benjamin, David, Barbara, Becky, Morris, Theresa, Marissa, Susan, Bob, Michael, Dena, Roseanne, Mark, Joseph, Theresa Ann, Grandma LePari, Lucille.

No one was as surprised as I when I discovered the Billion Soul Crusade had been completed years ahead of schedule! It was the faithfulness of my partners that allowed me to accomplish God's mandate so quickly!

When a translator and preacher are in the spirit, it's as if one man is preaching and interpreting. The interpreter follows every action, every mannerism of the preacher, as demonstrated here by Argimero Figueiro, my crusade director for decades.

Part of the plan of building God an army is continuing training through the ministry of *Victory Miracle Living* magazine, which I am passing out to dear Nationals in this photo.

It all began in 1967 when God spoke to Brother Cerullo on an airport bus in South America, *"Son, now is the time to turn your eyes to the Middle East and begin to work for My people, Israel."*

**1968:** First Mass Mailing in Israel to 400,000 Jewish homes

**1968:** Historic First Israel Deeper Life Conference where 150 Jews received Jesus as Messiah

**1970:** 500,000 Jewish homes receive the book *Hear, O Israel*

**1971:** 500,000 Jewish homes receive the *Book of Daniel* in a new Hebrew translation

**1972:** Weekly Radio Broadcasts cover the entire nation of Israel

**1973:** Second Israel Deeper Life Conference

**1974:** Third Israel Deeper Life Conference where more than 100 Jews received Jesus as Messiah

**1975 to 1976:** *Masada* TV Special where more than 200,000 people responded

**1977 to 1980:** Mass distribution of *Two Men From Eden* in five languages worldwide.

**1978:** Correspondence course reaches more than 25,000 Jews throughout Israel

German      Portuguese

ZWEI MÄNNER AUS EDEN      DOIS HOMENS DO PARAISO

LOS DOS HOMBRES DE EDEN      שני אבשים מעדן

French      Hebrew

Spanish

**1981:** *Sound of Trumpets* aired targeting Jews throughout North America

**1982:** *Advent II*, an end-time prophecy film aired throughout North America

**1983 to 1985:** Two major Schools of Ministry conducted in Israel

**1985:** Historic Global Satellite Network was broadcast form Mount Meggido throughout the world

**1987 to 1989:** Launching of Phases I and II, where 150,000 copies of *Two Men From Eden* were distributed in Israel

**1989 to 1990:** *Victory Miracle Living* spiritual warfare training program initiated to thousands of Messianic Jews

**1990:** First Inaugural International SOM in Israel

**1991:** More than 100,000 copies of *Two Men From Eden* translated into Russian distributed to Russian Jews

**1992:** More than 100,000 Jews reached through the European Super Channel

**1994:** *Victory* Television launched in Israel with Arab subtitles

**1995:** Israel Leadership Training Meetings train 1,400 key Israeli leaders

**1996:** One million copies of the book, *The Messiah* (titled *The Peace* in Hebrew) is mailed to one million Jewish homes in Israel!

**1997-1998:** Participated in major national ad campaign to defeat a proposed law to prohibit distribution of Messianic literature in Israel. This bill was defeated in 1998!

ДВА ЧЕЛОВЕКА из ЭДЕМА

Моррис Серулло

VICTORY MIRACLE LIBRARY
Morris Cerullo

השלום

**1999: THE GRAND UNVEILING OF THE TOP SECRET ISRAEL PROJECT...THE RABBI**

Thousands of Nationals received training to reach their nations for Christ at the El Cortez School of Ministry. Those SOM graduates are still doing the work of the Gospel in the nations of the world to this day. Many have gone on to build the greatest, largest churches in the world.

God had engendered such a deep love for the Nationals all around the world in my heart that I think about them and pray for them constantly.

One of the most integral parts of a School of Ministry is anointing the Nationals to carry out the ministry themselves. Here I am laying hands on a National as he ministers under the power of the Holy Spirit.

# Chapter 6

# HOW THE VISION CAME TO PASS

Suddenly, I had a new plan, a new way of looking at ministry. God had commissioned an army – not a group of converts, but an army, trained to march forward and decimate the ranks of the enemy; but instead of taking prisoners of war, this army would be trained to free the prisoners of the enemy – a new breed of God's people.

I had heard the cries of the world for help.

Every day, those cries echoed in my spirit. I remembered the anguished cries of the millions of souls I had seen in hell, and I knew this new way of ministry would help me reach many more to prevent them from ending up there.

I knew I could not preach enough in my entire life to reach as many souls as I needed to reach. I could preach morning, noon and night, every day, seven days a week, until I was one-hundred years old, and I still would not make a significant enough impact on the world. There were more people being born every hour. Those were people who eventually would need to be reached. I knew that even combining the efforts of all the world's major evangelists – Billy Graham, Oral Roberts, A.A. Allen, T.L. Osborne, myself, and others – we would never be able to reach the world as thoroughly as it needed to be reached.

Each man could draw crowds in the tens or even hundreds of thousands, but this earth is crowded with six BILLION people! To put that number in perspective, the entire nation of the United States has only about two-hundred and seventy million people. That means there are twenty-two people in the rest of world for every one person in the United States.

On that floor in Porto Alegre, Brazil, in my pool of sweat, I had seen the key to a closing world – how we literally could reach the world.

Think of every person you can think of in the United States...your mother, your father, your children, your spouse, your cousins, your friends, your neighbors, your co-workers, the people you see on television, the people you read about in the newspapers...

Add all those people up, and for each one of those people – for every person you can think of – there are twenty other people in the world – and that number is increasing every day.

That means that reaching that gigantic number of people is impossible for just one man, or even a crowd of well-known men who can draw hundreds of thousands of people at the same time – it just isn't possible.

I remembered back to the vision God had given me in Lima, Ohio, when I had looked all over for a man to lead the outpouring that God had shown me was going to come.

Though I had looked all over, I could see no man – God was saying that the major evangelists, though they were needed, would never be able to reach the world, would never be able to touch all the souls who so desperately needed touching.

But on the floor in that hotel room in 1962, I began to see how I could be instrumental in reaching the billions of souls on this earth, how I could truly fulfill the vision that God had given me.

I knew that a National could reach out to his home country and be more effective than I could ever hope to.

A National could get to areas of his country I might never see. He could reach people who would never come to see an American evangelist.

God showed me that to reach the world, I would have to raise up an army of spiritual warriors, people who were not just trained preachers, but lay people...doctors, lawyers, ditch diggers, plumbers, farmers, ranchers, carpenters, housewives, sailors, factory workers, household servants – everyone was a potential minister! These people could be anointed and trained to go to their own villages, their own cities, their own countries and saturate them with the Word of God, winning thousands and thousands to Christ.

A famous advertising slogan at one time was "How do you cook an elephant?" The answer, of course, was "One piece at a time."

That became the crux of the vision – that each National could take one piece of the huge whole and, piece by piece, we could do what otherwise would be impossible – reach the world.

To accomplish this incredible task, we would transfer the anointing to the Nationals we ministered to, and we would train them in evangelism with a period of intensive training aimed at preparing them for the task they faced.

God had taught me another fundamental truth in Porto Alegre – all truth is parallel. For every natural truth we can mention, there is a spiritual truth to match it. For every spiritual truth we can mention, there is a natural truth that matches it.

I began to think of God's command to build Him an army.

What I had been doing through the first years of my ministry was recruiting soldiers into that army – an army I hadn't even yet known existed. I had been looking for a way to do more, and God had shown me the way.

No army recruits soldiers and sends them out into battle without training.

First, the army sends its soldiers to some kind of basic training, where the new recruits learn everything from scratch.

Young people who have done things a certain way all their lives have to re-learn everything.

They eat what the army decides they'll eat, and they eat it when the army decides they'll eat it.

These new recruits may come into the recruiting depot with any manner of different haircuts, some with long hair down to their shoulders, some with hair parted on the side, some with hair parted in the middle. Some people even come in with wacky haircuts spiked up a few feet off the tops of their heads.

But once these recruits get into basic training, no matter what kind of hair they came in with, they all walk out of the barber shop looking the same – heads all-but shaved. They don't have a choice to say, "just a little off the sides, please."

The new recruits must even re-learn how to dress.

When they were at home with their parents, they usually were allowed to wear pretty much whatever they wanted, whenever they wanted.

But when the recruits come to basic training, they learn quickly that the army has a way of dressing for every occasion. When inspection comes, they'd better have their shirts pressed just so, their belt buckles polished and shiny, their shoes so clean and buffed that the sergeant can see his face when he looks down at their feet.

When it comes to bed time, the soldiers can't wear pajamas with little pictures of Superman on them – they have to wear what the army gives them, and they have to wear it how the army tells them to wear it.

Each soldier is taught exactly how to make his bed, how to make the corners look just right, how to fold down the blanket and the sheets, how to place the pillow, and they have only a certain amount of time to get it done.

Each soldier, no matter how proficient with the weapons of war he may be when he comes to basic training, must re-learn everything, using the army's way. He is taught how to properly hold a rifle, how to aim it, how to squeeze the trigger, and how to disassemble his rifle and clean it to ensure it's always in top condition. He's taught that he must also disassemble, clean and reassemble the rifle in an allotted amount of time. He is taught the difference between a rifle and a sidearm. He must be proficient in the usage of both – for different kinds of combat.

He must learn to depend on his teammates, those who are in his platoon, to help him in every aspect of military life. The loner can no longer run off by himself and expect to accomplish anything. He must now depend upon his fellow soldiers to provide a support structure for everything he does.

Each soldier, no matter how good his physical conditioning is when he comes into the army, must learn how to keep himself ready for battle. Each soldier must do pushups when the sergeant says, must do pull ups, must run an allotted distance in an allotted amount of time. Each soldier must complete obstacle courses designed to replicate the conditions of battle.

In effect, the army takes a young recruit and completely changes his lifestyle, retraining him so that he might do things the army's way when he goes into battle.

They thoroughly train a young recruit to face the battles that certainly lie ahead and to face those battles in a time-proven method.

As God had shown me, all truth is parallel. This natural metaphor had a spiritual companion that was no different.

When a new believer is won from the world into the Kingdom of God, he must re-learn how to live so that he may conduct himself accordingly when he goes into battle.

He must learn how to eat: where he formerly filled his mind and spirit with the things of the world, from television to worldly publications and chatter, he must re-learn to feed his spirit with the things of God.

The new Christian must learn to depend upon his fellow Christians to provide a support infrastructure of fellowship and glorifying God.

Where the new Christian may have been accustomed to waging war against his enemies with his fists or weapons, he must re-learn to do battle in the spirit world, with the weapons of Christian warfare, not against flesh and blood, but against spirits.

He must learn to dress himself in spiritual armor.

Everything in the new Christian's life must be re-learned, and that process is very difficult without the help of a mature Christian who has learned at the feet of God the proper way to conduct life as a new Christian.

If a Christian does not re-align his entire life after the way God intends, he will have a very difficult time being effective for God. When the battle comes, he will be unprepared, and will have to feel his way along by trial and error, and he greatly increases his chances of failure.

This army, unlike any earthly army, would transcend nationalities and ethnic groups. It would be an army without borders, a force the like of which mankind had never seen. Truly, the army would be as Jesus said: *"That which is born of the flesh is flesh; and that which is born of the Spirit is spirit...The wind bloweth where it listeth, and thou hearest the sound thereof, but canst not tell whence it cometh, and whither it goeth: so is every one that is born of the Spirit"* (John 3:6,8).

This army's conquests would not be kingdoms or nations of this world, its goal would not be to overthrow despots and dictators or to bring natural revolution against the governments of this world – this army would conquer the devil's workings in the lives of men, it would overthrow the dictator of men's souls!

I began to think about the need to train ministers to bring the Gospel to their own nations, their own cities, their own neighborhoods.

In the natural world, I saw a cry rising up from the nations:

Africans for Africa!

Asians for Asia!

Indians for India!

South Americans for South America!

## How the Vision Came to Pass

The entire third world had been ruled by first-world countries for centuries, but centuries of imperialism were slowly being rejected by country after country as they declared independence. Their cries began to ring out:

"Yankee, go home!"

"British, go home!"

"French, Belgian, Dutch, go home! We don't want you to rule our countries any more!"

But now, with National ministers training their own people, those cries would no longer ring out – the Nationals would be welcomed in their own countries – they were the sons and daughters of local people; fluent in the local language and the local traditions.

Our single-minded focus had suddenly become clear: To build God an army of trained, motivated soldiers to win the world for Jesus Christ.

Ideas began racing through my head at lightning pace. This army would literally change the face of ministry all over the world – and I was humbled and awed that God had allowed me to be a part of it.

Immediately, we began to change the focus of our meetings. To be sure, we would still hold crusades; after all, how can you build an army if you don't recruit?

But we began to hold National Training Institutes in 1963, immediately after God had given me the mandate to build an army.

At these meetings, we began to focus on raising up ministers, teaching them the basics of holding crusades like the ones we held, and at the end of our training sessions, we would call the Nationals up to the platform to be anointed with oil – a point of contact by which I could give to the Nationals what God had given me: the anointing to reach multitudes of souls.

Toward the end of our intensive Institutes, I would step back and a National would come to the platform to preach the message, using the lessons he had learned through the transference of God's anointing.

Another National would give the altar call, inviting those in the congregation to come forward and receive what God had for them.

Another National would pray for the sick, the lost and those who had other needs.

This on-the-job training prepared the Nationals to go and do the exact same thing in their own villages and cities, to not be afraid to operate in the anointing of God and the power of His might!

Immediately, the new focus of the ministry on raising up an army of trained, dedicated Nationals began paying off. New ministers were inspired to begin ministering the Gospel to their families, their neighbors, their villages, their cities and their entire nations.

Many of the Nationals who attended our initial National Training Institutes went on to pastor and build from zero churches to thousands and thousands of members, imparting into those members the same ministry truth that God had imparted to them through God's servant.

At the same time the ministry was exploding with the expansion that came with the National Training Institutes, the list of friends that Theresa and I were mailing to became larger and larger.

More and more people wanted to know what the ministry was doing from day to day, and we had begun forming partnerships with many of our friends, who faithfully supported the ministry in prayer and finances.

In 1964, Theresa and I prayerfully decided to form a new magazine to explain to the people what we were doing. *Deeper Life* was born.

# How the Vision Came to Pass

*Deeper Life* contained reports from the mission fields of the world as we ministered to ever-growing crowds all over the nations. Our new staff photographer, George Ekeroth, began to accompany us everywhere so we could report and show our partners and friends exactly how God was moving through our crusades and National Training Institutes all over the world.

Many Nationals wrote to testify of the tremendous works God had done through their ministries after they had attended the intensive training of the National Training Institutes.

In keeping with the tremendous amount of work Theresa had always taken upon herself, she became the editor-in-chief of this new magazine, and under her guidance, it became a world-class glossy publication with photos on every page showing the tremendous works of God.

Almost immediately, thousands of people all over began to send testimonies to *Deeper Life* describing how God had used the ministry to touch their lives – they wanted the whole world to know what a powerful God we serve.

The ministry had long since outgrown our little garage. I had initially built a wall in our garage, one half was used to store the children's bicycles and other items you would expect to find in any family's garage, and the other half contained the implements of running an ever-expanding ministry, with tables to fold letters and stuff envelopes, and the huge autotype machines on which Theresa became so proficient.

Finally, when the ministry clearly had become too large to house in the garage, we moved the ministry into its first building, on Lamont Street in San Diego, where Theresa had found a suitable building.

It was from Lamont Street that *Deeper Life* was originally published. It didn't seem possible that such a tremendous, high-quality magazine could be published from such a relatively small office, but Theresa put her heart and soul into it and made *Deeper Life* successful and inspiring through her hard work and prayerful dedication.

Because we had to conserve every penny to make the most efficient use of the money over which God had placed us as stewards – we wanted to save every little bit we could to use in ministering to the nations of the world. We hired one of our first employees, a man named Lowell Warner, who ran a little print shop in the Lamont Street office. David, who by this time was getting older, even worked as an apprentice to Lowell, learning all the ins and outs of shooting negatives, making printing plates, operating the press and cleaning up afterward. (These days, David, who remains great friends with Lowell, jokes that he got to do all the jobs Lowell didn't want to do, like cleaning out the press's ink wells.)

As an interesting sidebar, that experience would come in handy later for David in the 1980s, as we were holding a School of Ministry (which you'll learn about later in this chapter) in Brazil. At the last minute, we discovered that we didn't have any diplomas for the graduates, so David, every bit as industrious as his mother, took an old diploma we happened to have with us and searched all day until he found a print shop. It was a weekend, and everything in the city was closed. But David convinced the owners to open the shop and let him run the press. Using that old diploma, David shot a new negative, made plates and printed up enough diplomas for all the students at the School of Ministry.

As our group of friends and partners around the world continued to grow, it didn't seem possible, but we also began to fill up the Lamont Street office. Desks, tables, printing equipment, letters, fliers and files were everywhere.

As unbelievable as it was, it soon became clear to us that even the Lamont Street office was no longer big enough to house our ministry, which was ever being expanded by the providence of God.

## How the Vision Came to Pass

For the first time, the ministry was in a position to actually buy a building to do the work of the ministry – a tremendous boon, because in the long run, buying a building is almost always less expensive than renting one of similar size.

As Theresa and I prayerfully looked all over the San Diego area for a suitable building that we could obtain for a reasonable price, we finally settled on building what, at the time, seemed to us to be a huge building on Mercury Street. The building was around ten thousand square feet, and it seemed to us that we would never be able to fill that much space – it seemed downright palatial.

In November of 1969, we moved our offices to Mercury Street, into the new building that seemed like a huge office complex to us.

But because of the tremendous growth of the ministry and the ever-expanding ministries of the Nationals who had learned through the National Training Institutes, the impossible happened; the Mercury Street building soon became too small to house our extremely busy ministry, and we had to erect another building onto the back of the existing building. Even though we soon began to outgrow even the new building that we had added on, but we would not move from the Mercury Street location for another ten years.

In 1962, I had begun immediately acting on God's mandate to build an army. For a few years, my initial concentration was on bringing Nationals through a spiritual boot camp, training them how to defeat the devil in prayer and how to bring the Gospel to their nations. But soon, I began to realize that spiritual boot camp was not enough.

The National Training Institutes were working very well, and they were very successful, but I began feeling an unction in my spirit to do more – to invest even more of what God had invested into me to the Nationals in whatever way I could.

## SON, BUILD ME AN ARMY

God deals with different people in different ways. To some people, like some of the old testament prophets, he gives specific, step-by-step, one step at a time directions, "do this. Now do this, next do this."

But to other people, such as the Apostle Paul, God gave simple plans; He gave a directive – preach the Gospel to the Gentiles – and many of the details were left up to Paul from that point. God gave Paul a goal, and Paul was responsible for getting to that goal by the strength and anointing of God.

I find that more often than not, God directs me as He directed Paul. He gives a goal, a directive, and it is up to me to use the wisdom and anointing He has given me to get to that goal.

God had given me a directive: Son, build Me an Army.

From that point forward, relying on prayerful strength from God, it was my job to do whatever it took to make that goal become a reality, by the anointing God had placed on my life.

After we had started the National Training Institutes, I realized that we had not yet completed the vision that God had given me.

I began thinking again of the parallel truth of a natural army. A natural army, once it has trained its soldiers in basic training, does not just send them out into a field of battle with no weapons, no armor, no air support and tell them, "OK, go fight a battle – and we expect you to win!"

No, the army that behaved that way would quickly find it was doomed to failure as its ill-equipped soldiers faced opponents who were better equipped and supported by firepower from the air and land.

The army that wanted to be successful would equip its soldiers, giving them the most accurate rifles, the healthiest rations, the most efficient battle plan and support from other branches of the military.

## How the Vision Came to Pass

All truth is parallel. Through this analogy, God showed me that we had to do more than just train the Nationals to reach their nations.

Many of these Nationals lived in some of the poorest nations of the world. Most of these nations are so poor that even upper-class people do not have running water. Their excuses for streets are little more than dirt roads with gigantic mud holes every ten or fifteen feet.

To get electricity for some meetings, we had to set up generators of our own, because no place close had electricity.

It is not uncommon to find people whose only home is one they've made out of mud and grass.

For millions of people around the world, bathing is a luxury reserved for only the rich. Meat simply is not eaten – it's too expensive for the average person.

So to train these soldiers and then turn them loose with only a directive to "win the battle" and reach their nations was not as effective as we desired. We wanted National ministers who could reach people we could not reach, but we didn't want to send them out into the spiritual battle unequipped.

We formulated a plan, that, once we had thought of it, seemed so simple. To ensure that the Nationals we trained would be optimally effective, we would sponsor National Evangelistic Crusades. There the Nationals who had been trained and anointed at our National Training Institutes could use the training they had received to minister to their own nations in crusades that followed the pattern of our own crusades.

World Evangelism would provide financial assistance to the Nationals, who then would use the money to print handbills and posters, build a platform and rent sound equipment to conduct their own crusades. In addition, we would print and give the ministers "how to" manuals that laid out the fundamental teachings God had inspired us to impart to these precious Nationals.

Our partners and friends all over the world rushed in to support these tremendous National Evangelistic Crusades. At our seminars and Deeper Life meetings, our partners and friends would swarm to a large scholarship board we had set up with photographs of the ministers we wanted to sponsor. Our partners would choose a minister to sponsor, and they would donate whatever they could so that National ministers could lead crusades to their own people after they had been trained and anointed.

The response and results were beyond our wildest dreams.

In just ONE YEAR alone, World Evangelism partners sponsored 4,098 National Evangelistic Crusades. In addition, they established 3,060 churches or evangelistic stations overseas.

But the most astounding number, a number that was staggering to think about, was the number of recorded decisions for Christ that came as a result of just one year of this incredible ministry outreach: 1,692,356!

More than one-and-a-half MILLION people gave their lives to Christ as a result of just one year of National Evangelistic Crusades sponsored by our friends and partners' generosity!

Those numbers were only the decisions for Christ that were recorded! Who knows how many more went unreported!

At last, the vision of reaching the world through building God an army was producing results on a massive scale!

Those National Evangelistic Crusades continue to this day, although they are no longer called National Evangelistic Crusades.

In the 1970s, I again began to feel a rumbling in my spirit that we could do more – we could equip ministers for lifelong service in God's Victorious Army that God had called me to build.

Again, I began to think of the natural parallel to the spiritual truth we were living through the National Evangelistic Crusades.

We were recruiting soldiers in this great army through the crusades we conducted nearly everywhere we went, with attendance ranging upwards into the hundreds of thousands, and decisions for Christ sometimes numbering in the tens of thousands a night, by the grace of God.

We were taking the new soldiers through spiritual boot camp in the National Training Institutes that we were conducting to impart the anointing and train the Nationals.

We were sending the Nationals out into battle with the National Evangelistic Crusades as we provided the weaponry for them to succeed.

But I believed something was still missing.

In a natural army, after a soldier completes boot camp, he is not yet ready to go out to the battlefield. Almost any army in the world has a second training camp, a second level of instruction called advanced training.

It is at this second level of training that the raw soldier hones his newfound life of military service into a razor-sharp, well-oiled battle machine.

It is at advanced training that the raw soldier becomes a tank driver, or an aircraft mechanic, or an anti-tank gunner or a pilot, flying multi-million-dollar aircraft with the capability to destroy entire cities. It is at advanced training that the raw, faceless soldier learns a specialty, whether that be cooking for infantry or sitting up in trees with a sniper rifle or communicating in coded messages to the top command.

Advanced training is necessary for modern warfare.

Without advanced training, armies would be forced to fight as they had in the Middle Ages – groups of men armed with swords and clubs who would rush at each other, hacking and chopping away until one army had more men standing than the other. It was a brutal way to wage war, and inefficient in both manpower and equipment, not to mention the hideous mess that had to be cleaned up afterward by someone.

Advanced training changed that mob of brutes into a team that worked together as intricately as the inner workings of the most expensive grandfather clock, each cog, wheel, gear and spring working together to produce a perfectly running machine.

I knew the spiritual parallel to advanced training well:

> *"For the body is not one member, but many. If the foot shall say, Because I am not the hand, I am not of the body; is it therefore not of the body. And if the ear shall say, because I am not the eye, I am not of the body; is it therefore not of the body. If the whole body were an eye, where were the hearing? If the whole were hearing, where were the smelling? But now hath God set the members every one of them in the body, as it hath pleased him. And if they were all one member, where were the body? But now are they many members, yet but one body. And the eye cannot say unto the hand, I have no need of thee: nor again the head to the feet, I have no need of you. Nay, much more those members of the body, which seem to be more feeble, are necessary. And those members of the body, which we think to be less honourable, upon these we bestow more abundant honour; and our uncomely parts have more abundant comeliness. For our comely parts have no need: but God hath tempered the body together, having given more abundant honour to that part which lacked." (I Corinthians 12:14-24)*

Each part of the machine – the Body of Christ – had its part, and all parts were necessary to fulfill the goal of ministry: to win souls to the Lord. One person could not do the job of another, each person was selected and set apart to fulfill the specific role God had determined for them since before the foundation of the world.

I knew that God had separated these body parts – these soldiers who would go into advanced training – into five main divisions:

> *"And he gave some, apostles; and some, prophets; and some, evangelists; and some, pastors and teachers. For the perfecting of the saints, for the work of the ministry, for the edifying of the body of Christ." (Ephesians 4:11-12)*

My job was to equip and perfect this fivefold ministry, this five-fronted attack force, with the tools and training they needed to effectively operate as a finely tuned army, destroying the works of the enemy, each person fully trained to implement the role God had intended them to fill.

I knew that to accomplish this monumental task, we needed a more intensive and exhaustive training than the National Training Institutes, with their limited time schedule, could accomplish.

Advanced training required a more intensive, more expanded and more individualized training plan. Those who had been turned into soldiers would now have to be turned into well-tuned ministry juggernauts who would be members of the special forces in God's army.

The School of Ministry was born.

But we needed a place to house the students who would be training at this new School of Ministry. In addition, the offices on Mercury Street were bulging at the seams. The ministry had continued to grow and expand exponentially, and we were running out of room. Both the School of Ministry and World Evangelism needed a new home.

The El Cortez Hotel had been a historic San Diego landmark for years. In 1979, we were able to purchase the hotel to bring in Nationals from all over the world for intensive training at the complex.

But first, the hotel needed major renovations.

The El Cortez was really a five-block complex in downtown San Diego, including several small motels and a convention center. But the centerpiece was the historic and majestic hotel, which overlooked the beautiful city of San Diego like a sentry standing guard over a sleeping palace.

This building, which was designed to serve as a five-star hotel for the hoards of people and for kings and presidents who flooded to San Diego each year to vacation in one of the world's most beautiful and temperate cities, had to be completely renovated and redesigned to fit the purpose for which we intended it; to house Nationals in dormitory rooms.

Each step of the way, we had to completely re-do something. By the time we were finished, we had nearly completely gutted the entire building and re-built it from scratch.

We got rid of anything the hotel had that we couldn't use. In fact, one humorous story came from the renovations.

My son David had just finished college at Oral Roberts University in Tulsa, and was in charge of the El Cortez renovations. He developed a plan for renovating the front of the building and decided to have an auction to dispose of some of the hotel's equipment that was no longer needed, and to raise some money for renovations in the meantime through the sale of the items.

Over the years, many people had taken their honeymoon or a memorable vacation at the El Cortez, and those people were extremely interested in obtaining memorabilia from the hotel.

194

# How the Vision Came to Pass

The auction was very successful, and David was able to finance many of his smaller renovation projects with the proceeds from the sale. One of the things David sold, however was the set of doors on the front of the hotel.

But renovations at the top floor of the hotel, which was to become a 24-hour-a-day prayer center, took longer than expected, so David never got around to the renovations at the front of the hotel he had been planning when he sold the front doors.

At that time, a woman named Pat Hulsey had become my administrative assistant, and when she got into the office vacated by her predecessor, she found a stack of letters that needed to be read and dealt with. One of the letters, she was shocked to find out, was from someone who claimed to own the doors to the El Cortez, and in no uncertain terms, he explained that he wanted to come get his doors as soon as possible.

Not too long afterward, I was overseas conducting a crusade, and Pat got a call from security at the El Cortez:

"Pat, come quick," the security man said. "Someone's here taking our doors!"

Pat rushed downstairs to the front of the building and witnessed a scene she described as straight out of the Indianapolis 500, as a crew of men had jumped out of the bed of a truck and feverishly begun dismantling the El Cortez's ornate front doors as quickly as a pit crew would change the tires on a race car.

Pat, not sure what was going on, had called our lawyer and the police, and they had all shown up at the front of the building. The police determined that the man had the paperwork that said he indeed owned the doors, so there was nothing they could do to stop him from taking the doors. Pat and the security man stood by helplessly as the man took the doors he had bought and put them in his truck.

To make matters worse, a local television crew had been filming the whole fiasco from across the street, and broadcast it on the evening news.

The doors had been oversized, and the hotel crew found out it would take two weeks to get new doors made that would fit the hole the man had left in the front of the building, so for two weeks, the front was boarded up with a tiny door built in until the new doors arrived.

But the setbacks – humorous as they were – were small and infrequent. The El Cortez was renovated to become a state-of-the-art learning center where Nationals could receive intensive training for a six-month or three-month session, and then take that knowledge back to their own nations and replicate themselves there, building up God's Army throughout the nations of the world, one on one, even quicker than we had imagined.

Each National attended the School of Ministry on full scholarship provided by our partners. Room and board were provided, as well as meals, which were served in the completely renovated cafeteria, which was designed to serve one thousand students in less than thirty minutes.

Through the generosity of our partners, thousands of National ministers received in-depth ministerial training to go and reach their own nations for Christ – and the fruits were incredible.

To this very day, many of the graduates of the El Cortez School of Ministry are on the frontlines of doing the work of the Gospel all over the world. Many times, when I travel to the nations of the world, I find that graduates of the School of Ministry are hard at work, tirelessly canvassing their entire countries with an unending zeal for the Gospel, winning souls everywhere they set foot, just as God told Abraham, *"...Every place whereon the soles of your feet shall tread shall be yours..."* (Deuteronomy 11:24), these Nationals were making inroads into countries that had never been reached before, and everywhere they went, they were winning that area to the Kingdom of God.

As with overseas crusades, the logistics of running a School of Ministry were nearly overwhelming. Students were chosen from a group of National Training Institute graduates – those who had been demonstrating the teaching in their own ministries. Then arrangements had to be made to bring the students to the United States for six or three months – no small feat, many times. Many countries have very strict laws regarding travel overseas, and most countries have a currency limit, meaning the students in the School of Ministry couldn't bring very much money; they were almost completely dependent on the partners of World Evangelism to provide for their every need.

After the students arrived in the United States, they had to be fed and housed – no small task for a school with more than a thousand students. Many of the students who came from seventy countries had never been to the United States, and even being in a room with a radiator was a completely new experience to them. Some students even hung their clothes to dry on the radiators in the El Cortez's rooms – and had to be taught why that was not a good idea by the School's staff.

The upstairs area at the El Cortez had previously been a bar where people went to imbibe alcohol and carouse in drunkenness.

But we renovated the upstairs into a 24-hour-a-day prayer center, complete with phone banks, called the I Care Prayer Center. Part of the training of the School of Ministry was to teach the students how to counsel and pray for people who needed those things, so each student served some time in the prayer center ministering to the needs of the thousands of people who called with prayer requests.

Students attended classes every day, all day, and then on Monday and Tuesday nights, special generals of the Gospel such as Kenneth Copeland, Dr. Fredrick K.C. Price, Pat Robertson and Dr. Walter Martin would come and address the students.

During the day sessions, School of Ministry staff, including Pastors Dr. Charles Blair, Alex Ness, Paul Trulin and Ed Cole would teach the students the advanced spiritual principles they needed to become generals in God's Army.

In classes, the students had a state-of-the-art student response system built into the armrests of their chairs. Whoever was lecturing had a console in front of them that showed them who was in attendance, and if the teacher had asked a question, he could immediately see which students had answered which answer. This allowed the teachers to tailor their instruction to the specific needs of the students who were present at any given time. Projection screens were built with the capability to project lesson points even in direct sunlight.

The cost to run this incredible, ground-breaking school was immense, costing well over $500,000 a month for the day-to-day expenses of housing and feeding students and teachers and providing them with the advanced spiritual training we knew they needed to be lifelong, effective ministers in their own nations.

In fact, it was such a massive operation, that a good friend of mine, Rex Humbard, came to visit us in San Diego one year. As he was touring the facility, he continued to remark to my son David, "Praise God, bless God" and other such remarks.

Finally, David could contain his curiosity no longer and asked Rex what he was praising God for.

"I'm praising God that this is yours and not mine," Rex said.

But the effort paid off in the fruit. Those key leaders who were trained at the El Cortez School of Ministry are still to this day producing fruit in the nations of the world.

The school was indeed producing tremendous results, and God began to show me that we needed to take the limits off the School of Ministry.

We were having a tremendous impact within the four walls of the School of Ministry at the El Cortez center in San Diego – training many for lifelong service.

But up to this point, if someone wanted to attend the School of Ministry to receive this tremendous advanced training, they had to come to America, stay for three or six months, and then go back to their countries. Not everyone could make arrangements to attend the school, for various reasons, not the least of which was getting international visas.

God began to reveal to me a way we could consolidate the teachings of the School of Ministry and take it in a new brevity to the nations of the world, using existing facilities in those nations to host this advanced training. Truly, it would become a school with no walls, giving intensive training to the key leaders all over the world who would then impart that training to their own nations. The training would last for extended periods of time in these new Schools of Ministry without walls; sometimes for a week, sometimes for two or three weeks of focused, concentrated training they would be able to get nowhere else.

That way, people in every corner of the world could receive the training of the School of Ministry without having to come to America to receive it.

Besides its obvious advantage of training on the move, this mobile School of Ministry opened doors to this ministry that have never been opened to anyone else. Indeed, because the nature of the School of Ministry was to equip Nationals to reap results in their own nations, not to bring in foreign missionaries and evangelists to do the work, presidents and prime ministers of nations were inviting me to come and train their people how to be effective ministers.

While I was teaching a Ministers' Institute in Nairobi, Kenya, the president of Ghana sent an invitation to me saying, "I want Rev. Cerullo to come and train our National ministers to lead our nation in righteousness."

The Schools of Ministry quickly became more urgent for the ministry than the crusades; for in a mass crusade, I could preach the Gospel to hundreds of thousands of people, of which tens of thousands might give their lives to Christ in any given night.

But a powerful ARMY of dedicated, trained and anointed National ministers who had been trained in a School of Ministry in their own nation could effectively reach MILLIONS of souls in a small amount of time!

From the Schools of Ministry, I began to concentrate on how I could reach even more people with the intensive training of the School of Ministry to increase the penetration this Army we were building would achieve.

This focus and intensification led to one of the largest one-night outreaches in the history of mankind, the Million Soul Crusade.

When I had seen the vision God had given me of footprints, the time was before man-made satellites were even invented. Little could I have known that later a technology would be developed that not only would allow one person standing in one place on the earth to be seen simultaneously all over the globe, but that the area into which that signal would be broadcast would be called a FOOTPRINT.

When a signal goes up into a satellite, it travels through a piece of technology called an uplink. It then is received by the satellite and is bounced off, both to other satellites and down to the earth in patterns called footprints.

People on the earth who have the right equipment can interpret that satellite broadcast using their television sets. All of this happens in a split second – while the speaker is still forming his words, television sets all over the globe are seeing the minister speak the words and hearing his voice come through their television's speaker.

In 1984, in the midst of a time of intense prayer, God revealed to me that by broadcasting via satellite, I could send a School of Ministry to nine cities at the same time, and I could broadcast a huge international Day of Miracles to millions of people live via satellite all around the world.

When I received this revelation, I began to get excited. We would, for the first time in history, hold the largest spiritual meeting that had ever been imagined.

Like all things associated with bringing the Gospel to a lost and dying world, however, the conceptualizing was much easier than the actual implementation.

The logistics of a simultaneous linkup of satellite technology all over the world is daunting enough, but add to that the special needs of a School of Ministry and crusade service, and the logistics boggle the mind.

We had to have a team in each city, both in Brazil, where the broadcast originated, and throughout North and South America, where the crusade would be broadcast.

There were more than sixty cities in the U.S. alone, and a dozen in Canada.

In each city, at each site, we had to have technicians to run the equipment that would receive the satellite signal. We had to have an usher chairman, prayer counselors, testimony workers and announcers, who would speak before the satellite broadcast began.

Each city had to have a bank account set up to hold the finances for making the meeting happen – every little aspect of a crusade meeting takes money. In addition, each city had to have decision cards and Gospels of John.

To top it all off, we had to have a huge phone bank in Brazil to receive calls from each of the more-than a hundred sites at the beginning of the broadcast. Each site had to confirm to us that they had sound, they had video, and if they didn't, we had to have qualified technicians on hand to help the site work out the problems – all these calls and troubleshooting technical discussions had to take place in a matter of minutes, all at the same time.

Many people, who think of something like a satellite broadcast, never think of the tiny details that must be in place to make that broadcast happen, but we had to deal with each of those details, and we had to be prepared for any contingency.

As always, our partners in the ministry were faithful to God's call on their lives to reach out to souls and build Him an army – they faithfully supported the Million Soul Crusade vision and it was due to their support that the vision actually became a reality.

For an entire week, in which thirty thousand people took the School of Ministry, we broadcast the School of Ministry from São Paulo, Brazil, to eight cities all over Brazil. The signal was beamed by state-of-the-art satellite technology across the dense rain forests of the Amazonian jungle to Rio de Janeiro, Belo Horizonte, Belem and five other cities throughout the huge nation of Brazil – an entire week of intensive, directed, anointed teaching directly from the Spirit of God to a gathered congregation of Brazilian Nationals hungry to be used of God to reach their own people.

But this historic satellite School of Ministry was only the beginning of that miraculous week God led us to minister.

At the end of the School of Ministry, on June 23, 1984, hundreds of thousands of men, women and children gathered into churches, auditoriums and civic centers all over Brazil and North America, during our crusade, called the Day of Miracles. Our Gospel-carrying signal did not just float into North and South America, however. The same signal that preached the life-changing Gospel of Jesus Christ to the Americas also sent the signal to Hong Kong, and most miraculously, into the depths of Red China – our signal literally blanketed that closed country with the Gospel of Jesus Christ!

As live miracles were coursing through the arena in Sao Paulo, the anointing virtue of God was at work throughout the entire world as people were being healed and saved all across Brazil, the North American continent, China and Hong Kong – all at the same time!

That night, I had no way of knowing it, as I prayed for salvations throughout the audience, but more than one-hundred and twenty-five thousand people in Brazil alone answered the call for salvation and gave their lives to Jesus...all at the same time! God performed His greatest miracle – salvation – one-hundred and twenty-five thousand times in an instant in the most awesome display of His power I have ever personally witnessed.

Even before I began to pray for physical healings, miracles began to break out all over the arena in Sao Paulo, where we were hosting the hub crusade. Immediately, I recognized what was happening. God had personally stepped in and taken over the meeting. I no longer had any control whatsoever of what was happening in that arena that night. All I could do was stand and praise God as His Spirit ministered in such a powerful way and healed hundreds and hundreds of people. There no longer was any need for me to minister; God Himself had taken over completely.

When I was finally able to begin leading prayer again, the huge platform we had built in the arena was literally filled with people who had been touched in the precious, awesome move of God that night.

God had made a tremendous point to me that night. The power of satellite technology gave wings to the ministry He had entrusted me with, and allowed me to reach far more people than I in my wildest dreams had ever imagined I would be able to reach.

Through this new tool, I would even be able to reach into closed countries, with the life-changing Gospel...and there was nothing the despotic rulers of closed countries could do to stop the signal!

Over the years, I had been tremendously blessed and given favor by God to reach into many countries that were closed, but there were still some countries that did not welcome anyone preaching the Gospel. But through satellite technology, I could reach into those countries by the power of God and make inroads that were completely impossible before satellites.

The incredible harvest of souls we had been privileged to see saved in the Million Soul Crusade supercharged and energized our ministry. We began an intensified campaign to bring the School of Ministry to even more Nationals and to bring in even more souls through crusades throughout the world.

God had shown me that this new satellite technology was one key to accomplishing my final training dream for the Army He had called me to build.

I knew that the only way to maintain an effective and battle-ready force was through ongoing training.

A natural army doesn't just send its soldiers to boot camp and to advanced training, although both are necessary. If the army keeps its soldiers very long (and we intended to keep ours for their entire lives), it doesn't just let them sit around on bases, watching television and eating C-rations. No, the army invests in ongoing training, turning privates into corporals, corporals into sergeants, sergeants into lieutenants, lieutenants into captains, captains into majors, majors into colonels and colonels into generals.

Each soldier has a program of ongoing training to make even the best soldier better.

God showed me that I could institute a plan of ongoing training to God's Army's soldiers all over the world utilizing the same technology that had made the Million Soul Crusade successful, and by implementing a policy that each month, we would infuse our School of Ministry graduates with more advanced training to equip them to become better soldiers all the time.

This new plan came to be known as the Global Satellite Network, with as many as three-hundred sites in strategic locations all over the world – hubs for ministry activity and learning – that would receive training materials on a routine basis, via, videotape, audiotape and printed media.

Each month, I would send teaching materials to these locations of teachings that God had laid on my heart to share with these Nationals who were on the front lines of world evangelism.

Each month, video and audio teachings containing anointed messages to encourage, build up and train these soldiers, the Nationals would also receive another important tool, the *Victory Miracle Library* (later *Victory Miracle Living* magazine), packed with teaching materials – marching orders, if you will – that infused the Nationals with the manna of God's direction for the army we were building. Just as natural armies communicate with their soldiers via many forms of communication to let them know what's going on, we would send our communiqués out to God's Army to communicate God's directions for the army on a month-to-month basis.

With the addition of the Global Satellite Network, the infrastructure of building God's Army was complete:

* Crusades would win souls and recruit soldiers.
* Intensive Schools of Ministry would take the soldiers through basic and advanced training.
* Ongoing communiqués via the Global Satellite Network would continually train the soldiers to become ever more effective in reaching the world, one nation at a time.

But if I thought the Million Soul Crusade and the Global Satellite Network were the best this vision would get, I was completely surprised in late 1988 when God again spoke to me, this time giving me a goal I would never have dreamed of in my entire lifetime, a goal that seemed so large it was almost beyond comprehension.

As the School of Ministry and Global Satellite Network strategies were achieving unbelievable success, I realized in 1988 that by the grace and providence of God, we had been able to train and equip more than four-hundred and ninety thousand Nationals to reach their nations for Christ! From the early days of the National Training Institutes and the El Cortez School of Ministry, I would never have imagined such a tremendous impact. If someone had asked me in 1962 if I could possibly train almost five-hundred thousand ministers by 1988, I would have told them I didn't think such a thing was possible. But God never calls if He doesn't also equip, and by His power, that's exactly what He had enabled us to accomplish!

God spoke to me very clearly and said, "Son, you must take the strategy I have given you to build Me an army and use this strategy to fulfill this new mandate: REACH ONE BILLION SOULS BY THE YEAR 2000!"

One billion souls.

Even the thought nearly knocked the breath out of me.

## How the Vision Came to Pass

I had never even considered such a tremendous challenge. One billion souls. To say the number, our minds often don't even conceive of the immensity of such a task. Most normal people can't even visualize the number one billion in their heads. Most people, if given a billion dollars, couldn't even spend that much, much less count it.

One billion people is one-sixth the population of the entire planet. That means that for every six people on the planet, God had commanded me to reach one through the strategy of Schools of Ministry...ONE out of EVERY SIX people on the entire planet.

Not only had He told me to reach this gigantic number of people, but He had given me a deadline: the year 2000.

For days, I was staggered by the immensity of the task that God had set before me. I knew that God wouldn't have called me to do the task if He wasn't prepared to equip me to accomplish what He had called me to do, but I still could barely conceive of the sheer unimaginable immensity of the task of reaching one-sixth of the population of the planet.

It would clearly be the most challenging thing I had ever set out to do.

Each time we held a crusade, the costs could run into the hundreds of thousands of dollars by the time the crusade actually happened. Each School of Ministry's cost was even higher, and the cost of conducting the ongoing Global Satellite Network was so high I dare not even mention it.

That, coupled with the sheer logistical details of each phase of the army-building operation, from the smallest School of Ministry with a few hundred students to the largest crusade with hundreds of thousands of members to coordinating dozens of Global Satellite Network sites each month, made the task of intensifying that to reach a billion souls seem even more difficult.

But I sat down and began working on numbers to see exactly what would be needed to reach one billion souls. I knew that I could not afford to overestimate in my calculations – I would have to use the most conservative figures I could; I would rather reach too many people than not enough.

I calculated that each National – conservatively speaking – would reach an average of 1,200 souls after they had been trained by the School of Ministry. Some Nationals would reach many more than twelve-hundred, and some would reach many fewer, but the low-estimate average from reports we had received through the years was that on average the School of Ministry graduates reached twelve-hundred souls apiece.

That meant that if I was to fulfill the goal God had given me, I would have to train 850,000 Nationals before the year 2000!

Considering the fact that in the twenty-six years from 1962 to 1988, I had only trained 490,000 Nationals, a twelve-year window to reach 850,000 was a daunting task, indeed.

But I knew that with God's help it could be done, and so immediately, I began working feverishly, stepping up the pace of ministry to a new high, completely intent on reaching one billion souls before the year 2000. The Billion Soul Crusade was born.

The entire World Evangelism team stepped into high gear, working nearly around the clock to arrange crusades overseas, arrange Schools of Ministry all over the globe, and recruit more members into God's Victorious Army.

Throughout this fast-paced acceleration of the plan God had given me, our partners also stepped up their support, their prayers and their intercession on behalf of World Evangelism and the Nationals who were in the streets and alleys overseas preaching the Gospel.

## How the Vision Came to Pass

We worked almost non-stop, using every precious minute to forge ahead into uncharted territory. No one had ever even attempted to reach so many souls, but God had not called us to be attentive of precedents – through the strength of the foundation of the partners God had called to this ministry, the Billion Soul Crusade quickly became the rallying cry for hundreds of thousands of Christians all over the world whose desire, like mine, was to be part of this tremendous army God was building all over the world.

In 1995, God began speaking to me a new, even more ambitious direction for the ministry. One day, when I was deep in prayer, I heard the voice of God as clearly as I had ever heard it: "Son, reach the entire world before the end of the year 2000!"

But I couldn't understand exactly when God wanted me to start this new focus He had given me. The year was 1995, still four years before the deadline of the Billion Soul Crusade.

I didn't understand at the time what exactly God was trying to tell me.

But I found out a few months later.

Late in 1996, Lynn Hodge, who at that time was the executive vice president of the ministry, came into my office looking flabbergasted.

Lynn handed me a spreadsheet document with a string of numbers on it, wanting me to double-check his figures.

As I looked at the spreadsheet, I understood what had Lynn worked up so. According to the numbers on Lynn's spreadsheet, by the middle of 1996, we had already reached our goal of one billion souls – three years before our deadline!

That announcement caught my attention.

Lynn and I began to meticulously go over all his calculations, one number at a time, checking corroboration and details. Each time we checked, we came up with the same number.

To double-check, we sent the spreadsheet to several other vice presidents and directors in the ministry to see if they came up with the same number.

The verdict came back the same: Somehow, by the grace of God, we had fulfilled God's mandate to reach one billion souls – three years before our deadline!

My heart was deeply touched by the faithfulness our dear partners had shown to enable us to minister so effectively all over the world. The expenses of the Billion Soul Crusade were simply staggering when taken in perspective, and our partners had faithfully met every expense, every need had been met.

As I write this book more than three years later, I still cannot help but wonder how many crowns await our partners who gave and sacrificed so much to reach out to one billion souls all over the world.

> *"He that receiveth a prophet in the name of a prophet shall receive a prophet's reward; and he that receiveth a righteous man in the name of a righteous man shall receive a righteous man's reward. And whosoever shall give to drink unto one of these little ones a cup of cold water only in the name of a disciple, verily I say unto you, he shall in no wise lose his reward." (Matthew 10:41-42)*

Our partners had truly earned a prophet's reward. Though they had not been able to go overseas themselves to reach out face-to-face, they had been there through their giving and their prayerful support – nothing that had been done could ever have been done without them. It was truly a miracle of God, and when the story is finally told at the end of time, I'm convinced many will be shocked when they learn of the sacrifices made by so many people during the course of the Billion Soul Crusade!

But I didn't have very much time to reflect or to savor the satisfaction of having completed such a tremendous God-given goal.

God, Who had known in 1995 when He began speaking to me to reach the world that the Billion Soul Crusade would soon be completed, had given me a new goal, and a new deadline: the end of the year 2000.

The goal was even more immense than the Billion Soul Crusade. This time, God wanted me to reach the ENTIRE WORLD before the end of the year 2000.

As I began to fast and pray together with the staff at World Evangelism, God began to give me a clear vision of how to accomplish this Mission To All The World...

It all came back to that old advertising slogan: "How do you cook an elephant? One piece at a time."

To cook this gigantic elephant, the entire world, we would break it up into smaller pieces and cook them one at a time, metaphorically speaking.

The world would be divided into ten major regions, with smaller sub-regions inside those regions.

Each region would be targeted with a massive effort to both preach the Gospel, through crusades and satellite television broadcasts, and to train an unprecedentedly large number of National ministers through intensified Schools of Ministry in each of the regions and sub-regions.

In addition, God showed me that to reach the world, we would literally need to blanket the entire planet in prayer by raising up a Global Prayer Strike Force of committed families who would turn their houses into Prayer Command Centers, where they and their friends and neighbors could meet to pray for Mission To All The World...and something that God had never directed me to tell my partners to do before: to pray for the soon return of Jesus.

The last recorded prayer in the Bible was only six words long: *"Amen. Even so, come, Lord Jesus."* (Revelation 22:20)

But that prayer is one of the most powerful in the Bible. It declares that the person praying it is completely consecrated, separated and awaiting the Lord's return. God told me to stress everywhere that His will was that His army begin praying for Jesus to return to the earth to meet with us in the air.

I began to see a prophetic picture develop. Jesus had clearly said that He wouldn't return until the world had been reached: *"And this gospel of the kingdom shall be preached in all the world for a witness unto all nations; and then shall the end come..."* (Matthew 24:14)

I knew that although no man knows the date Jesus returns, we know He won't return until the Gospel is preached to the ends of the earth. After that day, Jesus can return at any time. It may be days, it may be years, but the way for His eventual return will be cleared.

With this Mission To All The World, we would actually be partaking and participating in end-time prophecy; we would be part of the prophetic machine God was using to fulfill the words that Jesus had spoken nearly 2,000 years earlier to a group of society's outcasts in the hillsides of Israel.

Immediately, I began gathering ministers and team members to go forth and set up the immense infrastructure we would need to fulfill this latest, most incredible goal God had given us. We would have to work diligently and quickly; we only had four years to accomplish the most difficult goal we had ever aspired to reach.

Other ministers joined forces with me as well, completely putting their own lives on hold to participate in this, God's end-time plan and His directive to us.

It had come such a long way since the early days of the ministry when I was preaching to groups of ten or twenty people in a small church in New Hampshire. It had even come such a long way since 1962, when God had come to me as I lay in a sweaty pile on the floor of a hotel room in Porto Alegre, Brazil.

God had taken this ministry through a series of steps that had positioned it to be in the privileged position of participating in the fulfilling of prophecy that had been spoken from the lips of our Lord Himself when He was in His physical ministry on the earth.

To this day, I am humbled and awe-stricken that God has allowed me to be a part of such a momentous end-times ministry. I never would have believed or imagined that I would be in such close proximity with so many wonderful moves of God in my lifetime. But truly, God uses the weak things of this world to confound the strong.

But the building of God's Army has not been the only outreach God has involved this ministry in.

Ever since I was a lost, little boy in a Jewish orphanage crying, "It's real and you can't take it away from me," I have had a heart for my physical brethren, the Jews.

As I stood on Israeli soil for the first time in 1955 after my first overseas crusade in Athens, Greece, I knew that God would call me one day to reach out to my brethren after the flesh. As you turn the page, I'll tell you the story of how God made that come to pass.

# Chapter 7

# ISRAEL – LAND OF MY PEOPLE

Ever since I received the Messiah as a little boy in the Daughters of Miriam Orphanage, I hungered to reach out to my brethren, the Jews.

Even as the rabbi was trying to convince me to renounce this new Gospel I had received, believed and held near to my heart, I was aching to make him understand that Jesus was the Messiah who had been prophesied throughout the Old Testament, the hope of Israel .

From that day forward, I harbored a deep spiritual desire to bring Jews to Christ throughout the world. After all, He had come to the Jews first, and offered the Gospel to them first. Only when the Jews had rejected Him and His message did Jesus command that the Gospel be preached to the Gentiles.

Through the centuries, many Christian leaders believed and taught that the Jews had missed their chance, that Israel was hopelessly lost and could not be redeemed. That kind of preaching led to all kinds of anti-Semitism and killing.

The misinterpretation and hatred reached a boiling point in the early centuries after Jesus' passion with "Saint" John Chrysostom, who said "It is incumbent upon all Christians to hate the Jews."

The crusades of the Middle Ages were not so much a quest to seize the Holy Land as it was a crusade against Jews everywhere. But by far, the most virulent anti-Semite before Adolph Hitler was Martin Luther, the founder of the Protestant reformation.

Luther wrote a tract called "On the Jews and their Lies," in which he spewed forth the most vile filth against God's chosen people that had been committed to paper nearly in all of history.

In this vile tract, Luther demanded that the Jews' synagogues be burned, their books destroyed, their homes wiped out, their money confiscated, their tongues be cut from their throats and that "young and strong Jews and Jewesses be given the flail, the ax, the hoe, the spade, the distaff and spindle and let them earn their bread by the sweat of their noses as is enjoined upon Adam's children..."

Luther also concluded in his tract, "Know this, Christian, you have no greater enemy than the Jew."

This, from the founder of the Protestant Reformation!

No wonder Jews resisted listening to ministers who tried to preach the Gospel to them! No wonder an enmity had built up between those who were heirs to Abraham's covenant and those who had been adopted in through the covenant of Jesus Christ!

I could quote many more anti-Semitic "Christian" sources, but the above makes my point: to reach the Jews, I knew I would have to overcome the tremendous wall that had been built between Jews and Christians for more than a thousand years.

I knew this wall was a tremendous shame; Christianity had been very Jewish in the beginning. Christianity had been designed by the Father as the culmination of the Jewish covenant, as the fulfillment of His initial promise to Abraham thousands of years before in the dusty sands of a region that would come to be known as Canaan.

> *"And said, By myself have I sworn, saith the Lord, for because thou hast done this thing, and hast not withheld thy son, thine only son, that in blessing I will bless thee, and in multiplying I will multiply thy seed as the stars of the heaven, and as the sand which is upon the sea shore; and thy seed shall possess the gate of his enemies. And in thy seed shall all the nations of the earth be blessed; because thou hast obeyed my voice." (Genesis 22:16-18)*

216

Jesus had been the ultimate fulfillment of this promise, and though some early Jews had rejected this blessing, others like Peter, John, Paul and the other New Testament apostles had received it with great joy.

As I reflected on the difficulties that were inherent in reaching out to my natural brethren, I began to understand how the Apostle Paul felt when he penned these words:

*"I say the truth in Christ, I lie not, my conscience also bearing me witness in the Holy Ghost, That I have great heaviness and continual sorrow in my heart. For I could wish that myself were accursed from Christ for my brethren, my kinsmen according to the flesh, Who are Israelites; to whom pertaineth the adoption, and the glory, and the covenants, and the giving of the law, and the service of God, and the promises. Whose are the fathers, and of whom as concerning the flesh Christ came, who is over all, God blessed for ever. Amen"* (Romans 9:1-5)

My heart, as Paul's, was heavy with the difficulty of reaching my brethren with the Gospel. It seemed that no one really had much success reaching the Jews with the Gospel of Jesus Christ. So mighty had the walls between Jews and Christians been built through years of anti-Semitism.

Even Muslims, who many perceive as the Jews' most bitter enemy, had treated Jews in Israel, during the time they ruled the land, much better than Christians had treated the Jews. Why would any Jew respond at all to a Christian?

I knew that if I was to reach the Jews, I would have to rely solely upon God and His mercy and grace; only a supernaturally conceived plan implemented exactly as God commanded could ever hope to break down this tremendous wall.

When I visited Israel on my first overseas missions trip in 1955, I knew that I would one day be back to preach the Gospel and win Jews to Christ through the power of God.

In 1959, God had led me to print a brief testimony of my life; how I had been converted to Christianity in an Orthodox Jewish orphanage. That testimony had been printed in Hebrew and distributed to one-hundred thousand people in Israel. But even though I wanted to follow up that mailing with more ministry, God would not give me a release to do so. Instead, He had stressed to me that my ministry at that time was to the Gentiles.

I obeyed God and continued ministering to the Gentile nations of the world, but day after day, I would pray, "God, is now the time for Israel?"

But as I prayed, I would never hear God give me the OK to go ahead and begin ministering to my brethren after the flesh.

In February of 1967, I was in Florianopolis, Brazil, preaching a crusade. Thousands of people had answered God's call for salvation and had given their lives to Jesus. I had completed the ministry there and was en route to Buenos Aires, Argentina.

Argentina is very close to the equator, where seasons of the year are somewhat different from the Northern Hemisphere, where I live. In February, much of the United States and Europe are blanketed in snow, and people venture outside the comfort of their heated homes and cars only if they are sufficiently bundled up in a parka, a scarf and mittens.

But in Argentina in February, it was summertime – hot and sticky.

I was traveling on what seemed to me to be an ancient bus. As I bumped along the ride, I couldn't help but be amazed by the bus I was riding in. I became convinced that inside the bus was at least 20 degrees hotter than outside, even though the windows were all open, allowing outside air and lots of dust to billow into the bus with every bump. The bus either did not have shock absorbers, or the ones it had were at least as old as the bus itself. Each bump was like an earthquake, and on some of the "bumps," I actually came out of my seat as the bus left the ground for a few split seconds.

The ride was to be very long and arduous, so despite the flies that occasionally decided to swarm around the sweaty passengers on this uncomfortable bus ride, I felt compelled by God to make my way to the back of the bus to pray.

So I made my way to the back seat and stretched out to pray.

Quietly, so that I didn't draw any unnecessary attention, I began to pray to my Father, to thank Him for the miraculous wonders He had just done, and to give Him the glory for the incredible ministry He was doing every day. As I prayed and glorified Him, I began quickly to forget about the barbaric ride I was enduring. I forgot about the dust that I inhaled with every breath. I forgot about the blistering heat that had soaked my shirt and my socks.

I found myself lost in the glory of God, and there's never been any place I'd rather be, no matter where I am physically. I was completely focused on God and on His incredible Presence. Suddenly, God spoke something to me I would never have expected to hear from Him on a dusty, crowded, steaming hot bus in the middle of Argentina.

"Son," God said to me gently. "turn your eyes to the Middle East, for now is the time to work for My people, Israel."

Immediately my mind snapped to attention and intense scrutiny on what God was telling me. God had often spoken to me things I had not expected, but this case was completely different. My heart had ached for Israel for so long, and I had never heard anything from God regarding ministering to Israel, but here I was in Argentina and God had given me the directive to minister to Israel – I was in rapt attention.

219

"The time is now…go to Israel!"

Israel hadn't been in my plans for this ministry trip. I had scheduled other stops, but not Israel. I knew that in my long-term plans, I would minister in Israel, but this was unexpected.

"Son," He continued. "Do not be afraid. Go; I will open a door for you in Israel unlike I have ever opened."

God had answered my question before I ever asked it: "How will I reach the Jews, Lord?"

He knew the desire of my heart, and He had alleviated my fears before I could even mention them. God had assured me that, just as He had told me before, this is not the work of a man, but of the Holy Spirit. His Spirit would be in charge of ministering to the Jews, and He would draw them to Himself.

> *I immediately began to think of the scripture in the book of Psalms: "Thou shalt arise, and have mercy upon Zion: for the time to favour her, yea, the set time, is come." (Psalms 102:13)*

God began, like lightning, to reveal His plan for reaching the Jews…His plan to "have mercy upon Zion."

Because the Jewish religion is based upon the law handed down by God to Moses, the Jews are very literate people – some of the most literate people on the entire planet. To follow the law, one must read it, and to read the law, one must be able to understand and implement what one reads…therefore, one must be literate.

Many Christians had tried through the years to reach out to Jews by standing on a corner or outside a synagogue to hand the congregation a tract or to preach a sermon to them as they entered or left. But I knew that wouldn't reach into the heart of a Jew and open it for Christ.

As God revealed the plan for the Jewish World Outreach, I reached inside my baggage, grabbed a pen and a piece of paper, and began writing down God's plan to reach the Jews.

Part of the plan was so simple I was surprised I had not thought of it before. The original plan of building God an army was more necessary with Jews than it was in almost any other country! No Jew wants a Gentile preaching to them. God showed me that I would need to raise up Jews to reach the Jews, just as I trained Argentinians to reach Argentina and Africans to reach Africa. God made it clear to me that I was to make plans to hold a Deeper Life Conference in Israel (Deeper Life Conferences were the predecessor to the modern-day Schools of Ministry) to train Israelis to reach their own nation for Christ.

The second part of the plan God gave me to reach the Jews in Israel involved a concerted, sustained effort to minister through literature to these most literate of people to the truth about Jesus, not the lies they may have heard over a lifetime of propaganda.

As soon as I had finished my scheduled crusade in Kumasi, Ghana, I made arrangements to fly immediately to Israel and begin implementing the plan God had given me.

The climate in Israel was not geared to be receptive to the Gospel message. Even though the Israeli constitution granted religious freedom, most Jews interpreted that to mean that Jews could worship as Jews, Muslims could worship as Muslims and Christians could worship as Christians.

It was very direly frowned upon for one religion to try to convert members of another – especially for Christians to try to convert Jews.

In addition, the prevailing thought in Israel at the time was that it was impossible to separate a Jew from his religion, Judaism (even though we had no intentions of doing so, the Jewish perception was that to become a Christian meant no longer being a Jew).

But a few Jews were experiencing a stirring in their spirits that told them there was something more…

One rabbi had even stated so in the *Jerusalem Post*: "We know that something is taking place right now in the stream of our religion," he wrote, "but we are frustrated because we do not know what it is."

Months before the June 1967 Six-Day War in which Israel liberated Jerusalem from Jordan, I was in Israel publishing my first Messianic booklet, entitled *Besorat Shalom*, which means the Gospel (or good news) of Peace.

I mailed this first booklet to twelve thousand Jewish homes in Israel, and the response was tremendous. From that first mailing, more than two thousand Jews responded – a phenomenal response rate of 16 percent!

But God was not done with the Gospel of Peace.

Someone gave me the name of a mailing house in Tel Aviv where I could mail my booklet to even more homes, so I visited the owner of the mailing house.

When I arrived, I placed *Besorat Shalom* on the man's counter in the front of his business and, point blank, I said, "Sir, I would like to mail this literature to whatever names you might be able to rent me."

The man looked at me with a strange look on his face, as if no one had ever asked a question quite the same way. He looked down at my booklet, and then back up at me.

"Who are you," he asked me, matter-of-factly.

"I'm a Spirit-filled Jew," I replied to him. I figured a point-blank question deserved a straightforward answer.

His look grew even more puzzled as he seemed to be pondering what I had just told him. I'm certain it wasn't every day this man met someone who called themselves a Spirit-filled Jew.

"What is a Spirit-filled Jew?" the man finally asked, looking a bit amused by this time. His body language had relaxed a bit, too. He appeared to be intrigued by both the title of my booklet and by the straightforward answers with which I was handling his questions.

I began to slowly explain to him that I had been orphaned and raised in a Jewish Orthodox orphanage, and that I had, after much study and many questions, come to understand that Yeshua (Jesus) was the Messiah that had been prophesied throughout the Torah and the Prophets, and that I had become a believer in Jesus Christ as my Lord.

The man looked at me again, and then back down at my booklet. Once again, he looked at me, as if sizing me up to see if I was pulling his leg. It was obvious by his hesitation that this man didn't deal with Christian Jews very often, if at all, and he was mentally chewing on all I had just told him.

Finally, he sighed and looked at me again.

"Look," he said, "I'm a businessman. I don't believe religion should be governed by the state or anything else. If you want to mail this literature out, I will mail it for you."

I was elated. Finally, I had found a way to reach a significant number of Jews through literature that explained exactly Who Jesus was.

The man and I began to talk about how many names we would be able to mail the booklet to, and how much it would cost. The man explained to me that he only had one list to rent out to me, a list of thirty thousand Jewish professional people.

Thirty-thousand seemed to me like a good place to start, but I knew it was only the tip of the iceberg. I knew that God had called me to reach every single Jew, and I knew that eventually I would be given the opportunity.

I decided that thirty thousand was a foot in the door toward my eventual goal of reaching every Jew, so the man worked up a contract to distribute *Besorat Shalom* to the thirty-thousand professionals.

I thanked the man and said good-bye, preparing to leave and make arrangements to have thirty thousand copies of the booklet printed and delivered to the man for distribution.

But as I was about to leave his business, the man stopped me.

"Mr. Cerullo," he said, with a puzzled look on his face. "Don't ask me why, but I have the strangest feeling that I am supposed to do something else for you."

My ears immediately perked up.

"How would you like to send your literature to every single registered voter's home in Israel?" the man asked.

If it was physically possible, my jaw would have hit the ground right there in that man's shop. I was flabbergasted. EVERY VOTER'S HOME in Israel? It was beyond my wildest expectations. I wanted to make sure I had heard him correctly.

"I beg your pardon," I said to him, I'm sure the look on my face was comical with surprise.

"I have only one list for rent," the man continued. "And that's the list you rented. But I also manage and control the list of voter registration for every Jew in the entire nation of Israel."

Numbers began to fly through my head. A minute ago, we had been talking about thirty-thousand names, which was staggering enough – more than enough to populate a small town. But now this man was talking about mailing my booklet to every single voting Jew living in Israel.

"There are more than four-hundred thousand names on the list, representing every registered voter's household in Israel," the man continued. "Are you interested?"

Interested? I was ecstatic. I could hardly believe my ears. I had been prepared to leave with my foot in the door, but it appeared that God was ripping the door completely off its hinges right before my very eyes.

"How do I get permission to use this list?" I asked, Surely there would be months and months of red tape and paperwork. I knew from my years of dealing with foreign governments that nearly any bureaucrat along the lines of any situation had the power to stop a deal dead in its tracks, simply upon a whim.

This deal sounded almost too good to be true. Certainly there would be a complicated process to go through and many bureaucratic hurdles to be cleared. I thought that even though this man's offer was generous, I would have to go higher to get permission from someone to use this massive list.

"I can give you permission to use the list," the man surprised me by saying. Again, I could hardly believe my ears. The miracle God was working was beyond my comprehension to grasp. Not only would I be able to mail *Besorat Shalom* to thirty-thousand professional Jews, but if what this man was saying was true, I would be able to mail to four-hundred thousand Jews all over Israel, and all I needed was this man's permission! It was one of the most incredible breakthroughs I had ever seen in such a short time.

But it's a good thing I don't faint easily, because my surprise was about to become shock. The man continued speaking:

"In fact," he said. "I will let you use the list for free."

Have you ever been in the middle of an important situation and just felt like jumping up and down and shouting "Praise the Lord!"? If you have, you know how I felt at that moment. No sooner had the man offered to let me mail the *Besorat Shalom* booklet to every house in Israel – without a charge for the use of the mailing list, than God's words came back to me clearly from the dusty bus in Argentina: "Do not be afraid. Go; I will open a door for you in Israel unlike I have ever opened..."

Instantly, I knew that my meeting with this man who owned the mailing house was a fulfillment of this promise God had given me in Argentina.

I remembered what God had shown me on my first visit to Israel twelve years earlier – that everything should be done in the timing of God. Now that God's timing had come, the pieces of the puzzle began falling into place almost effortlessly.

After I thanked the man and began arranging details, I immediately set about making arrangements to print and deliver four-hundred thousand copies of *Besorat Shalom*.

The timing couldn't have been more perfect.

In the time it took to get four-hundred thousand copies printed and arrangements made to deliver them to the mailing house in Tel Aviv, the nation of Israel had been attacked from all sides by armies of its neighbors, but in six days in June of 1967, the Israeli armed forces had defeated all their foes, who had them greatly outnumbered.

Even though this victory was tremendous and miraculous, a foreboding quickly settled in throughout the land of Israel, as the people realized that they still weren't at peace with their neighbors, and the threat of all-out war loomed never more than a few bullets away.

When a booklet titled *The Good News of Peace* began to arrive in their homes in September and October of 1968, Jews all over Israel immediately read it all the way through to see what this booklet had to say about the peace they felt was so elusive after their quick and decisive war.

But if I was surprised at the miracle God had worked in allowing us to mail the booklet to so many homes, I was completely overwhelmed when the responses began pouring in by the thousands. Thousands of Jews all over Israel were writing to me to tell me that they had received Jesus as their Messiah after reading *Besorat Shalom*.

But I didn't have any time to rest in the awesome miracles God had performed in our first mass mailing to Israel. Part of the plan God had given me on that bus in Argentina was to hold a Deeper Life Conference in Israel to both strengthen the Christian walk of Jews who had received the Messiah, and to reach out to those who had not received Him yet.

Again, however, I knew we would need a direct miracle from God for a Deeper Life Conference to even get off the ground. After all, even though I was a Jew, most Israelis never saw past the "Christian" label, and it would seem very unlikely that any Israeli would rent a place large enough to me to hold a conference of any size.

When I was in a hotel in Jerusalem, I saw a man I thought I recognized from twelve years earlier, during my first trip to Israel. If I was correct, the man had been a desk clerk at the same hotel all those years ago. I was surprised he was still working at the hotel.

I approached the man, and as I neared him, it became clear to me that he was indeed the same man I had met and befriended in 1955.

"You used to be the desk clerk here," I said to the man as he looked up at me, recognition spreading over his face. "What are you doing now?"

The man smiled and looked at me.

"I'm not the desk clerk any more," he said, the smile still beaming on his face. "My brother and I own the hotel."

Again, I could feel God's providence intervening to open doors in Israel. First, I had found favor by the grace of God from the man at the mailing house, and now I had miraculously found a man I had befriended twelve years earlier who now owned a hotel that would be perfect for hosting a Deeper Life Crusade.

"I want to rent your hotel," I told him. "I want to rent the kitchen, the dining room, every room – the whole hotel."

The smile disappeared from the man's face as he leaned forward a bit, as if to see if I was kidding. It was probably quite unusual that someone would request to rent the whole hotel. I didn't know it at the time, but that hotel in the heart of Jerusalem was considered one of the most staunch Orthodox Jewish hotels in all of Israel, because of its proximity to Hechal Shlomo, the seat of the chief rabbi of the state of Israel.

"You must be crazy," he said to me. "What do you want my hotel for?"

"I want to have a religious conference," I replied. I knew the next statement would catch him by surprise, but I had to continue and be as forthcoming as I could so that everything was on the table. "You know I'm an evangelist, and I preach and pray for the sick and miracles take place. I want to have a meeting like that in this hotel."

The man laughed out loud. But as he looked at me, he could see I wasn't joking, so a more serious look came over his face.

"I've never heard anything so ridiculous in my entire life," he said. But then he got a puzzled look on his face as he continued. "But I will talk to my brother and see what he says about it."

I knew right then that God was preparing to give favor again to our meetings.

He had called me to hold a Deeper Life Conference in Israel, and He was about to make it happen before my very eyes.

I began praising God silently for the victory that I was sure would come at any time after the man had a chance to consult with his brother.

I went on about my business and went to bed that night, both praying for the outcome I desired and praising God for the miracles I was sure He was performing on behalf of the Jewish souls we were destined to reach.

The next day, when I saw the man in the hotel lobby, he came over to me and pulled me aside.

"I don't understand it," he said. "I talked to my brother about your idea, but he didn't think it was crazy at all. We talked about it, and decided to rent the hotel to you."

I was no longer surprised at all, because God had worked so miraculously in securing the list of every Jewish registered voter's home in Israel. This miracle fell into place in just the same way. Clearly, God was at work, and He had a plan for the Deeper Life Conference.

The day I signed the contract to rent the hotel was just six weeks before the Six-Day War – who could have known at the time the prophetic significance of the time we were living in, and the time in which God had moved me to begin ministering to the people of Israel?

When I left Israel, I flew immediately to a crusade in Orebro, Sweden. When I left that tremendous crusade, I flew immediately to Michigan, where I was scheduled to host two eight-day Deeper Life Crusades during May.

The schedule of a Deeper Life Crusade was packed full, with hardly any time for things such as a prophetic sermon, but in Michigan, God began to urge me to deliver a prophetic sermon.

"God is about to return the old city of Jerusalem to the Jews," I told the congregation that was gathered. "His prophetic time is NOW!"

At the time, no one expected Jordan to enter into the conflict that was building in the Middle East. Egypt and Syria were expected to attack Israel, but it was Jordan that controlled Jerusalem, and Jordan was living in relative peace with Israel.

June 5, 1967, only a few short days after I preached that sermon in Michigan, Israeli Premier Levi Eshcol sent a communication to King Hussein of Jordan, assuring the king that if Jordan did not enter the war that was brewing, Israel would not attack Jordan.

But when King Hussein received the communication from Premier Eshcol, his warplanes were already in the air, and he had no way to call them back.

Six days later, Israel had recaptured the old city of Jerusalem – a city that had not even been expected to be a part of the war between Egypt, Syria and Israel.

When the smoke cleared in September of 1967, I began to busily prepare for the Deeper Life Conference. I knew it would be no walk in the park. We had to convince believing Jews to risk ridicule or even more serious consequences to attend a meeting with an American evangelist, and we had to believe God to bring in nonbelieving Jews whose hearts would be ripe to receive the Gospel of Jesus Christ.

Because we would be training prospective ministers, we wanted to be sure we invited everyone who should come.

But as preparations proceeded, many began to ask the same question: "Do you think anyone will come?" After all, it was Israel, and even those who desired to come might be afraid of their peers.

When the day of the meeting came, Orthodox Jews assembled outside the building to protest the Christian meeting that was scheduled to go on inside, but their protests did not stop a sizable crowd  from assembling and packing the hotel to enter into a Deeper Life – it was standing-room only.

I took my message that night from Isaiah 53: *"Who hath believed our report? and to whom is the arm of the LORD revealed? For he shall grow up before him as a tender plant, and as a root out of a dry ground: he hath no form nor comeliness; and when we shall see him, there is no beauty that we should desire him. He is despised and rejected of men; a man of sorrows, and acquainted with grief: and we hid as it were our faces from him; he was despised, and we esteemed him not. Surely he hath borne our grief's, and carried our sorrows: yet we did esteem him stricken, smitten of God, and afflicted. But he was wounded for our transgressions, he was bruised for our iniquities: the chastisement of our peace was upon him; and with his stripes we are healed. All we like sheep have gone astray; we have turned every one to his own way; and the LORD hath laid on him the iniquity of us all. He was oppressed, and he was afflicted, yet he opened not his mouth: he is brought as a lamb to the slaughter, and as a sheep before her shearers is dumb, so he openeth not his mouth He was taken from prison and from judgment: and who shall declare his generation? for he was cut off out of the land of the living: for the transgression of my people was he stricken. And he made his grave with the wicked, and with the rich in his death; because he had done no violence, neither was any deceit in his mouth. Yet it pleased the LORD to bruise him; he hath put him to grief: when thou shalt make his soul an offering for sin, he shall see his seed, he shall prolong his days, and the pleasure of the LORD shall prosper in his hand. He shall see of the travail of his soul, and shall be satisfied: by his knowledge shall my righteous servant justify many; for he shall bear their iniquities. Therefore will I divide him a portion with the great, and he shall divide the spoil with the strong; because he hath poured out his soul unto death: and he was numbered with the transgressors; and he bare the sin of many, and made intercession for the transgressors."*

Everyone before the meeting had seemed to have questions. Would Israelis who actually did come to the conference respond to the message? Was the veil lifted? Was it really God's time to move upon Israel to minister to the hearts of Jews? Even as I had left my hotel room that night on my way to the service, someone had spoken to me and said, "Brother Cerullo, no one ever gives altar calls in Israel, because these people will not go forward to altars in response..."

But as more than 150 previously nonbelieving Jews risked everything, including possibly their lives, and gave their hearts to Jesus, accepting Him as their Messiah during the altar call, those questions were answered!

They risked castigation of their friends, hostile crowds who had gathered outside the conference, possible loss of their jobs and maybe even being disowned by their families! They were willing to sacrifice all to come to a deeper knowledge of the Messiah, who had sacrificed Himself for them!

Perhaps the biggest breakthrough besides the salvations that happened was the fact that, just months after the Six-Day War, where Jews and Arabs had viciously fought each other, in the Deeper Life Conference, Jews and Arabs worshiped God together, in peace and harmony!

Truly, as God had promised, he had thrown open the doors of ministry in Israel to World Evangelism...but these tremendous breakthroughs were only the beginning.

In 1969, I led a tour group of World Evangelism partners through Israel, to see the Garden Tomb, the Upper Room and many other sites in the land where the Bible had been written.

One Saturday night, I was in my room preparing for the message I was to deliver that night to the tour group during a communion service at the Garden Tomb, where we would remember the blood Jesus shed for us and the flesh that was torn for us.

I began earnestly praying to the Lord for our infant ministry in Israel. He had shown us great success and incredible breakthroughs, but what did He want us to do next? The seed of ministry had been sown in Israel, but I was sure that wasn't all He wanted me to do.

For three hours, I sought the Lord like that in prayer.

Finally, He answered:

"Son, prepare a special Bible correspondence course and send it to all those who are interested in knowing more of God and His Son, Jesus Christ!"

It was a tremendous revelation – an overwhelming sense of "Of course!" Sometimes when God speaks to us, we later find it hard to believe that God had to point out what He had said to us – the idea was so simple.

Many years before, in the early years of my ministry, with my heart yearning to reach out to my physical brethren, I had spent days and days preparing an exhaustive study outline on Christ as revealed in the Old Testament Scriptures.

It was this outline that became the basis for the Bible Correspondence Course, which was sent to 2,000 Jews in Israel, who signed up to receive it.

Each issue dealt with salvation and the new walk in Christ from a Jewish perspective, building a strong foundation for the messages in the Old Testament and then showing how those messages were carried through in the New Testament. As the correspondence course continued, more and more Jews signed up to receive the teachings, which were designed to both lead the unbelieving Jew to Jesus and to build a solid foundation for the Jew who had already accepted Jesus.

In 1970, we embarked on our second mass mailing to Israel, this time with my book, *Hear O Israel*, which taught, that Jesus was the same God who was in the Old Testament; that Jesus was indeed the Messiah that God had promised to send to redeem Israel and to be King in David's seat. The book did not reveal the voice of a 20th Century preacher from New Jersey, but the timeless witness of Isaiah, Jeremiah, Ezekiel and Daniel, who all testified of the coming Messiah!

After I had sent out the first mailing to four-hundred thousand homes of *Besorat Shalom*, I assumed that tension in Israel would close that door to me forever, but when we prepared to mail out *Hear O Israel*, we were shocked to learn that the same mailing house owner offered to make his list available to us again, but this time, the list contained five-hundred thousand names! This mailing was sent out to one-hundred thousand more homes than our initial mass mailing of four-hundred thousand.

The size of *Hear O Israel* was double the size of *Besorat Shalom*, meaning the cost of typesetting it, translating it, printing it, binding it, and mailing it would also be doubled.

But those logistical details did not stop the most expansive outreach that had ever been attempted in the history of Israel.

It was a tremendous breakthrough at a time when a book that sold five-thousand copies in Israel was considered a best-seller. But no sooner had the book hit the mailboxes of a half a million homes in Israel than letters began to pour in to our office in Jerusalem responding to *Hear O Israel*. The list of people receiving the Bible Correspondence Course expanded from its original two-thousand to more than fifteen-thousand, and then twenty-two-thousand Jews, receiving teaching about Jesus the Messiah!

One important aspect of *Hear O Israel* went barely noticed by us when it initially was printed and distributed. Every one of the Old Testament prophets we quoted were required reading for every Jew in Israel when they went through the school system – except for one prophet, Daniel.

The lady who translated our book into Hebrew was a born-again Jew who also was a Hebrew teacher in Israel.

As she was painstakingly translating the book from the English in which I had written it into the Hebrew that would reach into half a million homes, she noticed a problem. The translator did not have a copy of the Book of Daniel written in Hebrew – without which she could not guarantee an accurate, word-for-word rendering of the Scriptures for the Hebrew edition of *Hear O Israel*.

This precious lady spent many weeks searching, scouring old libraries and resale shops until she finally was able – at great effort – to obtain a Hebrew translation of Daniel, and at last *Hear O Israel* was finished and mailed.

A few months later, the man who was my project manager for Operation Israel, George Ekeroth, was visiting with some Jewish friends in Jerusalem late one evening. The friends all gathered together in a discussion of the prophets, and the Jews displayed a stunning knowledge of all the Old Testament prophets – after all, they had learned about the prophets all their lives. But when the conversation turned to Daniel, George's Jewish friends looked puzzled.

They were not familiar with Daniel's prophecies, and asked George what was so significant about Daniel. As I had written in *Hear O Israel*, the Book of Daniel was one of the most important prophetic books, because it pinpointed the exact time of the arrival and death of the Messiah!

When George shared that revelation with his Jewish friends, they were shocked.

When George shared that story with me, it confirmed what God had been speaking into my spirit. Though they are some of the most educated and literate people in the world, most Jews had never read the prophetic chapters of Daniel, because those chapters had never before been translated into Hebrew and distributed in Israel!

Daniel had been written in Aramaic, the language of the captivity in Babylon, not in Hebrew, so most Hebrew scholars had never read these most important prophecies from one of Israel's most powerful prophets!

The only existing translations of Daniel into Hebrew were extremely rare, and the average Jew did not have access to them. One of the most stringent import laws for Bibles in Israel was that the passages of Daniel that were written in captivity be kept in the language of the captivity – Aramaic. Most Jews could not read Aramaic, though, so they were left out of some of the most powerful passages in the Bible.

God confirmed to my heart that I needed to provide a new translation of this powerful prophetic book into Hebrew and distribute it to Israel – for the first time in history! Literally for the first time ever, Jews in Israel could now read the Book of Daniel in its entirety and understand how Daniel had prophesied the coming Messiah! It was a breakthrough of tremendous significance! Half a million Jewish homes, for the first time in history, had a copy of the Book of Daniel in Hebrew, eight and a half by eleven inches for display of great art with charts and commentaries for easy understanding!

As we intensified our efforts to reach the Jews through literature, I knew that we had only just begun.

Only when a point is demonstrated using the Scriptures will a practicing Jew give it any credence. It must be biblically sound, or the entire publication will be ripped to shreds as intelligent Jews point out flaws and unsupported statements.

So with each publication we sent to Israel, the entire ministry team spent hours in prayer, in study and in checking facts and statements over and over again, going over the publications with a fine-toothed comb so that we were sure everything we said was air-tight.

We didn't want our human flaws to come in the way of our goal, bringing Jews to Christ through the publications with which we were flooding the Holy Land.

But our outreach did not end there, and it did not end with publications. God had called me in Argentina to begin an all-out campaign to reach every Jew on the face of the planet, and I knew that to accomplish this goal, I could not rest for a minute, I could not slack off or relent in any way. I had to keep up the intensity of the effort, for it was persistence alone that would produce results in a culture so predisposed to reject Christianity.

In 1972, I began a weekly radio broadcast to Israel on a signal that covered the entire country, saturating it with the saving knowledge of Jesus Christ to a nation that so desperately needed Him.

Initially, the broadcast originated in Jordan, but we quickly found out that the signal did not transmit as clearly as we desired, and it was not as reliable as we desired, so after much prayer and negotiations with the authorities, we moved the broadcast to a medium-wave radio station on the island of Cyprus, which is in the middle of the Mediterranean Sea. What this new location meant was that practically anyone with a tiny transistor radio would be able to receive our transmissions that testified of the Messiah of Israel.

In 1973, I was able to hold my second meeting in Israel at the Baptist campgrounds, where hundreds of Jews came to hear the preacher who was raising all the ruckus through his mailings and radio programs.

As I ministered under the anointing of the Holy Spirit, the effects on the audience were tremendous; many Jews were touched by the Word of God, and they received a powerful witness of the resurrection of Jesus Christ – one they could not deny.

In 1974, I again was afforded an opportunity to conduct a meeting in Israel, at which more than one-hundred Jews bravely stood to accept Jesus as their Messiah, despite the fact that they knew they would face almost certain persecution from their friends and possibly even their families for the decision they had just made.

Such public displays of receiving the Messiah were very dangerous, especially given the fact that leading rabbis in Israel had begun to denounce Christian ministries and begun to angrily demand that Jews ignore any Christian missionary materials. This was in response to reports that more and more Jews were making decisions for Christ and becoming believers in Jesus as their Messiah. But that persecution did not stop the effectiveness of the ministry God had called me to.

God had promised in 1967 on the back of that bus in Argentina that He would open a door like none had been opened before, and the Jewish ministry was a testimony that He indeed kept His word!

God was blessing and prospering our Jewish World Outreach beyond our wildest dreams. Not only had we been granted unprecedented access, the stories were pouring in of Jews who had received Jesus as a direct result of our persistence, but we had not even really gotten going yet – God had more direct and powerful plans for us to reach His chosen people.

In 1975, God began dealing with me to produce a television special targeted at a Jewish audience that would tell the story of one of the Jews' greatest military defeats and moral victories that became a rallying cry for an entire nation of people that such a massacre would never happen again. That special dealt with the story of the Roman razing of Jerusalem and one dedicated band of Jews who holed up in the desert fortress of Masada, holding off the vaunted Roman empire for months.

Many Jews who are now living in Israel saw *Masada* when they were still living in America, and it was broadcast on prime-time television all over the nation. Responses to the powerfully anointed *Masada* special poured in like nothing we had ever done before in the history of the ministry. Literally two-hundred thousand responses came to our offices in San Diego of people who had either given their lives to Jesus or wanted more information.

In 1977, God dealt with me that it again was time to send a mass mailing to the Jews – not only in Israel, but those in America, too. Even to this day, the largest concentration of Jews anywhere in the world besides Israel is in the United States of America.

God led me to write one of the most powerful witnessing tools to Jewish people in the history of the Christian Church. In this anointed book, God led me to compare the lives of two men who, although they lived four-thousand years apart, led very similar lives, except for the fact that one had become a total failure and the other had become a total success.

The book, *Two Men From Eden*, compared the lives of the first and second Adam – Adam, the first man created, and Jesus, the man who redeemed all mankind.

*Two Men From Eden* demonstrated how Adam was created in the image of God and how Jesus was the image and likeness of God, how Adam was created to be God's companion and Jesus had always been the Father's companion, how Adam was formed of the earth and Christ was of Heaven, not earth. The book showed how Adam received his life from God, and how Jesus Himself was that life.

*Two Men From Eden* was our most ambitious mailing project to date. We sent this powerful prophetic ministry tool to three million, two hundred Jewish homes in North America.

Even today, I am staggered by the immensity of mailing such a book out to so many people. Many best-sellers in the publishing world would be ecstatic if they sold and distributed a million copies, but we sent three and a half times that out at no cost to the recipients!

More than ten-thousand Jews responded to that initial mailing of *Two Men From Eden*, testifying that they had received Jesus as their Messiah as the result of reading the book.

When I wrote *Two Men From Eden*, I knew that it was to be a ministry to the world, not just to North America or Israel. So, in 1979, at the leading of the Holy Spirit, we had *Two Men From Eden* translated into five languages: Spanish, French, German, Portuguese and Hebrew, so that people who read only those languages could receive this powerful and timely message in their own language and receive Jesus as the Messiah. The book ended with a powerful call to make a decision for any Jew reading the book – now that they were fully informed as to the biblical truth that Jesus of Nazareth was indeed the Messiah Who had been promised, they had to make a decision – would they serve Him or not...

And thousands upon thousands did indeed make that decision and turned their lives over to Jesus Christ as their Messiah.

But as we prepared to mail *Two Men From Eden* into Israel, new laws were passed forbidding mass mailings to Israelis. It appeared that the doors were closed.

But God had a plan and we stepped out on faith in 1980 and began mailing twenty-five thousand copies of *Two Men From Eden* to strategic homes throughout Israel in a test to see if we could pull off the new strategy God had laid in our hearts.

We found that we could mail the book in increments of twenty-five thousand throughout Israel, and in 1980, we did just that. The response was astounding as scores of testimonies flowed into our offices of lives that had been changed by the Second Man from Eden!

In 1981, the ministry that had been flowing to Israel from the United States became a two-way street, as I traveled to Israel to film *The Sound of Trumpets*, a television series filmed on location at the actual historical and archaeological sites in Israel, recounting the ministry of Jesus and the tremendous miracles and prophetic fulfillments that followed His life on earth.

In *The Sound of Trumpets*, we imported musicians and we also had musicians directly from Israel, who sang powerful songs of praise to God. We filmed from Cana, where the water was transformed into wine and Jesus transformed an ordinary wedding into His first Bible miracle. We filmed from Gethsemane, the garden where Jesus went through the agony of the price He paid for our souls. We filmed from Chorazin and from the Pool of Siloam, where Jesus healed the blind man.

On the video, we interviewed former Israeli Prime Minister Yitzhak Rabin and other dignitaries. The response from the forty television segments of *Sound of Trumpets* was incredible, as Jews from all over North America who had been intrigued by the chance to see the Holy Land also saw the Messiah.

## Israel – Land of My People

In 1983, God led me to hold the very first School of Ministry in Israel, with a time of reverent prayer in the Garden Tomb where Jesus had been laid after His death, and from which He arose three days later. During that tremendous School of Ministry, hundreds of Christians were trained to minister salvation to Jews and Gentiles alike. In 1985, we again held a School of Ministry in Israel, again with tremendous results as many believers received their marching orders to reach the Jew and the Arab with the Gospel of Jesus Christ.

From 1987 to 1989, using the incremental approach God had shown us in 1980, we were able to distribute more than one-hundred and fifty thousand copies of *Two Men From Eden* LEGALLY in Israel, despite the laws that had been passed against mass mailing, because of a loophole in the law that allowed our incremental approach to work. Though these mailings were slower than our initial mailings to Israel in the 1960s and 70s, God's timing was perfect, as testimonies came in a constant stream of people whose lives had been changed as a result of reading *Two Men From Eden*.

But even though our outreach to Israeli Jews had surpassed our wildest imagination, God still was not done reaching out to Jews elsewhere. He had given me a goal of ministering the Gospel of Jesus Christ to every Jew on the planet at least one time before Jesus returns – though I couldn't possibly accomplish such a lofty goal face-to-face with every Jew, through the twin attack plan of literature and face-to-face training of soldiers in His army, I knew that the goal of reaching every Jew was possible.

But one obstacle had always seemed a bit too high to jump. I knew that God wouldn't call me to reach every Jew if He wasn't prepared to provide a way, but I couldn't understand how God possibly expected me to reach behind the Iron Curtain of the then-Soviet Union to reach out to the hoards of Jews who lived under Communist domination.

But in 1991, God miraculously provided a way, as more than one-hundred thousand copies of *Two Men From Eden* were translated into Russian and distributed to Russian Jews in Moscow and Jerusalem by the power of God.

Since 1972, we had been ministering to Israel through radio, with a few interruptions caused by political unrest, but in 1992, God provided us with an open door to reach into more than one-hundred thousand Jewish homes in Israel through a powerful television station called the European Superstation. Through this tremendous open door, God allowed us to minister the Gospel to even more Jews in Israel by daily television.

But by far, the biggest outreach and breakthrough in Israel ministry came in 1996, as God opened the doors wider than we had ever imagined possible.

God had long been dealing with my heart to take *Two Men From Eden* to the next level and write a sequel, a book that would take all the Scriptures of the Old Testament referring to the coming Messiah and then show their fulfillments in the life of Jesus Christ – a daunting task, to be sure, but one that I knew would touch the hearts of countless Jews.

The prospect of mailing books en masse to Israeli homes was still very difficult, and a new anti-proselytizing fervor was brewing in Israel, but I knew I could not ignore God's command, so immediately, I began working on the new book, which I initially titled simply *The Messiah*.

As I completed the initial draft of the book, I ran it by many of my Messianic Jewish friends, including several leaders in Israel, all of whom I asked to read it carefully and look for human flaws that may have crept into the manuscript. After the final manuscript was prepared, I sent the book to a faithful Jewish believer, who translated the book into Hebrew for distribution to three-hundred thousand Jewish homes. Even this three-hundred thousand would be difficult, but I believed God had opened the door wide enough that we could accomplish that goal.

At the time, the Palestinian Liberation Organization and Hamas were again busily bombing Israelis and threatening to break out in war almost daily as Syrians were lofting rockets down on Israeli cities periodically. At the time, peace was the furthest thing from anyone's mind in Israel, but in the midst of this mayhem, God spoke to me very directly to re-name the book from *The Messiah* to *The Peace*.

Immediately, I saw the brilliance in God's plan.

The reality of religious life in Israel was that many wary Jews would see the word *Messiah* on the front of a book, realize that it was a piece of missionary material, and throw it away without reading it. My goal was to break past that initial barrier and at least get the recipients to read the book, and God's plan struck me as perfect – no Jew in Israel would not want to read a book about peace.

As we were arranging to have the book printed and mailed, another miracle came and surprised us even further. Miraculously, we had been offered access to a list of ONE MILLION Jewish homes in Israel – literally EVERY Jewish home in the entire country!

We had never had such an opportunity – never been given such unprecedented access!

Immediately, we changed all our plans. Although printing, binding and distributing a million books would be three times more expensive than three-hundred thousand, I knew better than to ignore the miracles of God when they happened.

We found a printing house in the ex-Soviet Union that once had been used to print Communist propaganda materials to indoctrinate the minds of the populace that had been enslaved by the red beast. But God used this once-nefarious press to print a book about peace, and after a few troubles, we were able to get the books into the mailing house and distributed throughout Israel.

Although we immediately began to hear stories from those who had given their lives to the Messiah as a result of *The Peace*, one thing we hadn't expected was the furor *The Peace* caused in Israel.

Television shows and newspaper advertisements denounced the mailing of the books, and people even held huge bonfires where they piled the books up and burned them in the streets, motivated by the fanatical orthodox forces.

Even more ominous, however, was the fact that the Israeli legislative body, the Knesset, began to consider a law banning all missionary activity from Israel, which could possibly have meant big trouble for the struggling Messianic Jewish congregations in Israel, and any future efforts to evangelize the Jews.

In the midst of the trouble, many people approached the ministry to ask why we had mailed the books to Israel, but I knew God had a plan. Even when things look their worst, even when everyone around can't seem to understand what God is doing, God always has a plan, and He would never do anything to hinder the preaching of the Gospel. Persecution expands the Gospel. Since I had only followed the directive of God in distributing the million books to Israeli homes, I knew God had something He wanted to do in Israel through this uproar.

In a miraculous breakthrough, Nissim Zvilli, member of the Knesset, and the author of the anti-missionary bill, withdrew support for his own bill.

But the anti-missionary fervor was not done in Israel. No sooner had Zvilli's bill been killed than a more restrictive bill was proposed, which would jail those who witnessed for

Christ for a period of three years and make them pay a fine equivalent to thirteen-thousand dollars.

Initially, Prime Minister Benjamin Netanyahu had said he opposed this more restrictive bill, but he shocked many when he voted for the bill himself.

But what the devil intended for evil, God had planned to use for good. In the midst of the fervor that was racking Israel, we teamed together with Messianic churches to sponsor an advertising campaign in Israeli newspapers that not only opposed the anti-missionary bill, but also preached the Gospel of Jesus Christ to EVERY SINGLE SUBSCRIBER to the newspapers in Israel!

It was a tremendous breakthrough for Israel. Once hopelessly divided, the threat of persecution, jail and imprisonment brought the Messianic community together for the first time!

One of the advertisements titled *Who is the Messiah?* said "Rabbi Yochanan said; The Messiah – what is his name?...And our Rabbis said, the pale one...is his name, as it is written 'Surely he took up our infirmities and carried our sorrows – yet we considered him stricken by God, smitten by him and afflicted.' (Sanhedrin 98, page 2) If our Jewish tradition attributes Isaiah chapter 53 to the Messiah – why should we claim otherwise? Yeshua is Israel's Messiah!"

The Messianic Action Committee in Israel was able to run that advertisement in many Israeli newspapers – an advertisement that preached the exact same sermon I had preached in Israel thirty years before! Now they did it openly and without fear!

The anti-missionary law was defeated in the Knesset, and, as of this writing, a newfound freedom for ministering in Israel has been opened – and God only has greater things in store for the Israel outreach!

## Chapter 8

# DIVINE REVELATIONS

Over the course of my ministry, many people have asked me the same question: How does God speak to you?

That's quite a personal question.

It's like the Bible says, *"And he said, Go forth, and stand upon the mount before the LORD And, behold, the LORD passed by, and a great and strong wind rent the mountains, and brake in pieces the rocks before the LORD; but the LORD was not in the wind: and after the wind an earthquake; but the LORD was not in the earthquake: And after the earthquake a fire; but the LORD was not in the fire: and after the fire a still small voice"* (I Kings 19:11-12).

Most times God speaks to me in a still, small voice, deep inside my spirit. Deep calls unto deep. That voice speaks, and because I know Him, I recognize His voice, and I listen.

Other times, as I open up His Word, God speaks to me through a revelation of Him; no matter how many times I read His Word, every time I read it, God reveals something new that I hadn't considered before. His Word is truly alive, and it's one of the most overlooked modes of communication with God in the Church today.

Starting from my experience on the street corner after I left the orphanage, God began dealing with me in a very personal, supernatural way. God will never use anyone without first giving them an experience.

During important times of decisions in my life, such as the experience in Lima, Ohio, when God showed me that the ministry was not the work of a man but of the Holy Spirit, or when He took me into heaven to reveal His ministry for me, He has spoken to me in literal experiences – not intuition, not in my mind, but actual experiences just as God came to our forefathers, Moses and Abraham. That's why there is such a dramatic anointing of God's Presence on my life.

247

Many times, God reveals His will to me through the reading of the Word – Christians can NEVER spend enough time reading God's Word!

Most times, God lets me see something before it happens, like the way God showed me long before it happened that Israel would recapture Jerusalem.

And more often than not, God speaks to me while I'm in prayer to Him. We live in a microwave society, where people want to stick a raw roast in the microwave and pull it out five minutes later to enjoy their meal, but God does not operate on our time schedule – the only way we're going to hear His voice directing us and leading us is by spending time with Him, and lots of it. God taught me that power does not travel in words, but in relationship.

A weak and spiritually debased Church has de-emphasized the closet of prayer and a good, old carpet imprint on the forehead from hours spent on our faces before God. But you will not hear from God if you don't spend time with Him.

God has called me to be a prophetic watchman, to give early information to His Church so that they may prepare for the things to come.

God does not give prophecy to scare people. He gives prophecy to PREPARE people for what is coming.

> *"Son of man, I have made thee a watchman unto the house of Israel: therefore hear the word at my mouth, and give them warning from me."*
> *(Ezekiel 3:17)*

The true test of a prophet is that what he says comes to pass.

> *"When a prophet speaketh in the name of the Lord, if the thing follow not, nor come to pass, that is the thing which the Lord hath not spoken, but the*

*prophet hath spoken it presumptuously: thou shalt not
be afraid of him." (Deuteronomy 18:22)*

In 1955, I was in prayer and Bible study with God, and
God spoke to me and said, "Son, write down what I am
about to tell you."

Right then, I went to my rickety old typewriter and began
taking notes as God revealed what was going to happen:

1. The greatest economical shakeup and transitional
period the country had ever known would be coming. (This
prophecy was fulfilled in the 1970s and early 1980s with
gigantic inflation and huge unemployment and financial
dearth throughout the nation.)

2. Immorality, vice, corruption will not decrease, but will
increase until the age of Noah represents itself. (This
prophecy has been ever-increasingly fulfilled since the mid to
late 1960s, and it builds nearly every day, with every kind of
immorality and base behavior being accepted as the norm.)

3. The Church of Jesus Christ will go through the greatest
sifting process it has ever felt to bring forth all true believers.
(This began to be accomplished with the tremendous trials
through which many famous ministries were dragged,
testing the faith of the people who had put their faith in
ministers instead of God.)

4. Pentecostal people will be clearly noted from all other
people in the world: 1. Those who want the move of God and 2.
So-called sideline compromisers. (This has been fulfilled time and
time again, from the time of the Charismatic renewal that started
just a few months after I wrote this prophecy down to the modern-
day revivals in places like Pensacola, Florida, where Pentecostal
people are standing – sometimes seemingly alone – for the truth
of the Bible and the righteousness of God.)

5. Israel's armies shall march against Old Jerusalem and
recapture it, after hundreds of years of captivity. (This
prophecy was fulfilled in 1967 during the six-day war.)

These tremendous prophecies were revealed to me in 1955, before any of them could reasonably have been expected to come to pass.

In the late 1960s, I was in the West Indies, and I had a tremendous experience with God. I was on an island called Grenada, where more than thirty -thousand people had gathered night after night to come to the meetings. Almost the entire island's population was coming out to our meetings.

In the midst of this incredible outpouring, I began to agonize in prayer in my hotel room. As I was praying, lying on the floor, holding a Bible, I began to cry out to God, "I don't understand why You use me. I am nothing."

The Spirit of God came into the room and God began to gently talk to me.

"Morris," He asked, "why are you so discouraged?"

"I don't know," I said. "Look at the men You dealt with in the Bible. I don't have what they had. If I could only just be like them."

God said to me: "Who do you want to be like?"

"Well, look at Moses, I replied. "He was so meek and humble. I'm not very meek and humble. Why couldn't I be like Moses?" Have you ever said this to God: "God, I'm not humble enough?"

God answered with a question: "Have you ever disobeyed me? Have you ever done something opposite of the way I told you do to it?"

"No," I answered.

"Moses did," God replied. "I couldn't let Moses go into the Promised Land, because he did do something opposite of the way I told him to do it."

He paused and then said, "Next."

Then I said, "OK, let's put Moses aside – I don't want to take anything away from Moses; he was indeed God's called, chosen servant. Let me be like Abraham," I said. "He's called the father of faith. I don't have enough faith. Look at me. My faith isn't strong enough." Have you ever said to God, "I just don't have enough faith?"

God said to me: "Son, do you love your wife?"

"My wife?" I asked, "What does she have to do with faith in God? Of course I love her, God."

God said: "Son, what would you do if in the middle of the night three strong men knocked on your door, told you they understood your wife was beautiful, and wanted to come into your house and sleep with her?"

I thought about it for a second. I knew that I could only answer God with the absolute truth: "God, you know everything. You know what I would do. I'd pick up the nearest chair – I would kill them. Christian or no Christian, they would not get my wife unless it was over my dead body."

God said, "Morris, I know you would. But not Abraham. Twice he took his wife and pawned her off as his sister, and I had to come and intervene, or I would have had to destroy their entire nations. Next – now who would you like to be like?"

I thought for a moment, and then I said: "God, be patient with me. Just one more, Lord. Please be patient. Let me be like David. "

God said: "David? Why do you want to be like David?"

"Look at the Psalms," I said. "Look how David longed for You as the hart panteth after the water brook, so David longed for You. I don't long after You enough." Have you ever said to God, "I don't long after You enough?"

God said: "Did you ever murder anyone? Did you ever take another man's wife?"

"No, never!" I replied immediately.

God said: "David did."

Then, on that floor, I broke down, wept and sobbed as if my heart would break.

"God, I understand what You're trying to tell me. It's not who these men were or what they possessed, it's what You could make of them."

God said: "Son, get ready, I'm going to send a new anointing, and it's going to flow through you upon the world."

At the time, the entire world, especially America, was in an uproar, embroiled in the most embarrassing war we had ever fought, in the tiny country of Vietnam, students were literally tearing our institutions of higher learning apart, riots, racial tension and fighting were racking the nation.

America appeared to be anything but receptive to an outpouring of God's Spirit. Still, God had never steered me wrong, so I began looking for this outpouring for several years.

I began to wonder what this new anointing would be.

I had been to India, but I did not want to go back. Every story I heard about meetings in India ended up the same – the ministers were fortunate if they escaped with their lives. I saw oppression and resistance in India as I had never seen anywhere before. I even told God, "Don't ever send me to India, Lord!"

Nevertheless, God called me in the early 1970s to go to India and hold a crusade. I was not too keen on going, but I have never shied away from a directive God has given me.

I was very apprehensive, and I knew it would be the spiritual fight of my life to go to India. I had fought a tremendous spiritual battle in Haiti, but it was nothing like the battle that waited in this country of three-hundred and thirty million false gods and hundreds of millions of people who were so lost that they would starve to death in the most ghastly of conditions as perfectly edible cows grazed all around them.

I was cognizant of the fact that I could very well lose my life in India, but that was not what made me apprehensive. I knew a tremendous battle awaited – a battle for the souls of many lost and dying people.

My son, David, had just graduated high school, and he had been to several overseas crusades with me so he accompanied Lowell Warner, our technician, to India to set up the crusade before I went.

When I arrived in India, David met me in the airport, and I will never forget the look I saw on his face. He was white as a sheet. He looked more like a ghost than the robust, six-foot boy who had accompanied Lowell to India.

When I got off the plane, I immediately asked him, "David, what's wrong?"

David looked at me as solemnly as he could, and I knew he had been working very hard to get the crusade set up correctly.

"Dad, I don't know what's wrong," David said to me. "There's something in the air, something in the atmosphere of this nation...there's something here that makes me sick. I don't understand it."

I knew what David was feeling. The spiritual oppression was so thick, you could almost feel it in the air all around you. It was as if the devil was so entrenched, so in power, that he was standing, thumbing his nose at God and saying, "Preacher, go home, you have no power here."

I instructed the driver to take me immediately to my hotel room.

As we traveled through the streets on the way to the hotel, I couldn't help but be struck by the awful conditions people in this country had to face. People were filthy, sitting on the streets, missing body parts, begging for change. Some people were too far gone to even look up, but they still had the instinct to hold out their hand for a handout.

Rats were everywhere – rats as big as some dogs in America. The streets were old and worn, with huge potholes everywhere – and drivers swerving to avoid them.

If traffic laws existed, I certainly wasn't aware of them. It appeared that the rule of the road was that the biggest car won – and you had to hope you were in the biggest car.

Fumes were everywhere...fumes from diesel engines, fumes from gasoline engines...

Everywhere, people had the same, faraway look in their eyes. Everyone looked oppressed and without hope.

As I got to my hotel room, I began immediately praying, I didn't even have time to unpack. I began to pray earnestly in the Spirit.

Now, it is my custom to pray for several hours before any meeting in which I am scheduled to preach, but this prayer was different. I began to travail and call out certain things by name. I began to go beyond the actions, and to the root causes.

Where formerly I would pray that God would stop disruptions in the meetings, I now was praying about the spiritual root of the disruptions, that God would silence the evil spirits who were prone to causing disruptions.

Where I once had prayed for diseases and bondages to be healed and loosed, I now began to go beyond the diseases and bondages to their root causes and began to do battle in prayer against their root causes.

I began in the Name of Jesus to bind those powers of the enemy – the spirits of sin, sickness, false religion, false cults, idol worship and false prophets. I found myself binding the power of Satan that was operating in the religious leaders who were working and using their influence to stop the meetings from happening and were trying to destroy the crusade.

As I was praying intensely like this, God spoke to me and said, "Son, the sooner you realize that you have to go beyond the surface and to the root causes, the sooner you're going to have the victory, and the sooner you're going to understand what My new anointing is."

I understood then what God was trying to say to me.

The uprisings in America, the losing war in Vietnam, the tremendous political battles we were going through, were not the problem, they were an effect of the cause of the problem.

God told me that, in America I would have to go to the root causes of those problems to see any results.

The American Church for years had been fighting a defensive battle, just as the American military had been fighting a defensive battle in Vietnam, not going after the enemy, but just trying to keep the enemy from coming into South Vietnam.

All truth is parallel. Just as the physical warriors were prevented from what would have given them victory – pursuing the enemy into their own territory until victory was assured – the Church also was losing the battle because they had not taken the battle beyond the church walls. The Church would sit in its protective barriers each Sunday and pray that the devil would stay outside. They would feel relief that at least within the stained-glass protection of their sanctuaries, they were safe from the devil's evil influence that seemed to be so dominating the world.

But I now knew that if we were going to have any success in raising up disciples in America, we would have to go after the devil into his own territory and defeat him until he kept retreating to the ends of the earth.

That crusade in India turned out to be the most effective crusade by a foreign minister that had ever been held in India up to that point. We had a venue as large as three football fields, and people were packed into it, with more healings than I could count, and more salvations than I would have believed possible before we went to India.

The fourth day of the crusade, God spoke to me and said, "Son, can you see it? Can you see that as soon as you begin to use the same keys to victory in North America that you are using here, the sooner you will see the same anointing in North America?"

That was when I realized that for the first time, I was seeing the side of the devil I wanted to see – the backside of the devil, which is the part we see when he's running away from us. It was time to turn our war against the devil on the offensive and attack him until he couldn't run fast enough to get away from us!

One October morning in 1975, I was in my kitchen in San Diego, praying over some of the hundreds of prayer requests we got every week from partners of the ministry.

Theresa and I had just enjoyed breakfast and she had gone to the sofa to sit, but when I looked over my shoulder, I did not see her head over the top of the sofa,so I went over to see if she was there, and Theresa had laid down and was in a deep sleep.

As I was praying over the needs in my briefcase, I began to enter into a deep, intense period of intercession and travail for these needs, and I began to sense the Presence of God surrounding me and His anointing all around. Suddenly I felt a hand on my shoulder, and I turned and looked around. The manifestation of the anointing of the Presence of God was all over, but no one else was there.

As I mentioned earlier in this chapter, sometimes God speaks to me through His Word, by the revelations He shows me there. Sometimes God speaks to me in the still, small voice in my innermost being. Sometimes God speaks to me by allowing me to see things that will come to pass. And sometimes God speaks to me in an audible voice. This October morning, God spoke to me in an audible voice, just as real as if Theresa had awakened and begun speaking to me:

"Son, tell My people that very soon everything that can be shaken will be shaken. Tell them to fix their faith on two things: 1) That which is infallible, and 2) that which is impregnable."

I took out a long, yellow legal pad and began writing down what God was telling me.

God showed me that ministers would begin to fall, that every ministry that had spiritual problems would be shaken.

From that point forward, people on my staff would bring me newspapers with big, bold headlines, telling the woes of a world headed toward the edge of oblivion, but never once was I surprised by what I read. God had not given me a vague feeling of "things will get worse," but a SPECIFIC prophecy, regarding specific events that would take place. It was as if I could read tomorrow's headlines today, as God was showing me what was to happen.

I immediately began to share this revelation and visit of God with the people in my crusades and seminars and in my ministry publications. I began to teach people of the urgency of the hour, and how we must have a fixed point in our faith, the impregnable and infallible.

Not very much later, the shaking God revealed to me began to happen all over the world and throughout the Church at large.

One by one, each specific prophecy came to pass; ministers were defrocked, ministries fell, but the prophecy was not just about the Church: the American economic system went through one of its toughest periods ever. Earthquakes increased exponentially all over the world. New, more powerful weather patterns changed life for untold millions of people.

Entire governments (such as the U.S.S.R.) collapsed. Entire nations went bankrupt.

Wars began to proliferate in countries like Afghanistan, Nicaragua, Iran and Iraq, and all over the globe.

But God did not just reveal to me gloom and doom.

In 1989, Theresa and I flew into Perth, Australia, on my very first trip to minister to the Australian people. We had finished the meetings in Perth and went on to Sydney, where we were staying overnight, waiting to catch the next plane, to return to the United States.

We were very tired, so we went to bed. I hadn't been in bed very long, though, before God spoke to me, "Morris, get up!"

God said, "Go to the little table in the room, take out the pen – I am going to speak to you."

I took out a pen and began writing what God revealed to me, step by step, line by line. God revealed to me five major crises that were coming in the 1990s, a decade that was still five months away at that time.

That revelation became my book, *5 Major Crises and 5 Major Waves of the Holy Spirit Coming in the 1990s."*

The first of the crises God revealed to me was a coming crisis of change; change in the world's economy, change in the traditional structure of the Church, increased hatred by the world toward Christianity and Christians, intense persecution of the true Church of Jesus Christ, and a change in weather patterns, causing disruptions and natural disasters around the world. These prophecies were all fulfilled. Worldwide economic changes came about in many different ways, and many different times, but one of the largest fulfillment's was the implementation of the euro, the single currency of a unified Europe. The currency got off to a rocky start, but it represented one of the most fundamental changes in world economic practice in the history of all mankind.

The second sub-prophecy on changes was that major changes in the structure of the Church would come about. Specifically, God showed me that denominational barriers and walls would no longer be able to keep Christianity divided, that the move of the Holy Spirit would transcend all denominational, man-made restrictions.

In the 1990s, we witnessed the largest merging of Christians in history since the Protestant Reformation.

258

Though some Christians may attend a Baptist church, others an Episcopalian, others a Pentecostal, the ministry of the Holy Ghost has permeated all Church groups, regardless of the name on the building, and many, many denominational pastors have begun teaching this unity in the Spirit of God.

The third sub-prophecy of change was an increased and intensified hatred toward Christianity. This prophecy was fulfilled through increased media persecution, and by nearly daily assaults on the basic foundations of Christianity by infidels all over the world. Almost daily, television programs portrayed Christians as hateful, arrogant and twisted, sometimes even mentally deranged; and through saturation broadcasts of these perceptions, those portrayals began to be impregnated into the collective consciousness of the world. This perception was intensified by several news exposés of major ministries, sometimes telling lies, other times telling the truth.

The fourth sub-prophecy of change was an end-time persecution of the true Church. This prophecy is fulfilled daily, almost hourly, in the nations of the world, where zealous anti-Christians kill, rape and beat Christians. In Egypt, Coptic Christians are forced to watch as their children are raped. Families are divided and beaten. In Indonesia, rioters literally killed any Christian they could get their hands on, smiling and laughing the whole time.

The fifth sub-prophecy of change God revealed to me was an increase of destruction from natural disasters. Since that time, devastating earthquakes have become commonplace, most recently in Turkey where tens of thousands of people were killed. In addition, weather patterns went completely wacky, with El Niño catching the blame for some and La Niña catching blame for others; increased hurricanes of extreme force, massive tornadoes hitting and wreaking havoc in downtown areas of major cities like Miami, Oklahoma City and Salt Lake City.

The second major crisis God revealed to me in 1989 was a major crisis of the family. God showed me ten sub-prophecies of this crisis of family.

The first was a growing spiritual division between unsaved family members and saved family members. In the 1990s, an unprecedented number of divorces rocked the Church, many of those based upon divisions between Christians and non Christians.

The second sub-prophecy of the family crisis was that moral standards would break down with not only acceptance, but a promotion of promiscuity. Even in the face of AIDS, the most devastating sexually transmitted disease in history, promiscuity increased exponentially in the 1990s; with ever-increasing promotion through media propaganda and a complete loss of morals, from the highest levels of government on down. Teen pregnancies skyrocketed, and surveys showed high percentages of teenagers who were regularly having sexual intercourse while they were still in high school.

Closely related to the second, the third sub-prophecy God showed me was that AIDS and other sexually transmitted diseases would increase tremendously. Some nations are completely riddled with the disease, and some figures estimate that large percentages of single adults in America are either infected with the disease or soon will be. Despite repeated warnings and education campaigns, the disease continues to spread at epidemic proportions.

The fourth sub-prophecy of family crisis was that domestic and child abuse would grow worse. In the decade of the 90s, more child abuse was reported than in any other decade in history. Case workers were overloaded with work, and children were routinely removed from their parents' care to be placed in foster homes. A huge number of spousal abuse cases were reported, with many ending up in murders, either of the abuser or the abused.

The fifth sub-prophecy was that rebellion would increase in the teenagers and young people. Teenagers became completely unmanageable in the 1990s, some even killing their parents or going on shooting rampages at their schools, such as the rampage in Littleton, Colorado, where thirteen ended up dead because of two rebellious teenagers who wanted to go out in a blaze of "glory."

The sixth sub-prophecy was that teenage suicides would increase. Following the high-profile suicides of rock stars Kurt Cobain of Nirvana and Michael Hutchence of INXS, thousands of kids attempted copycat suicides and many succeeded.

The seventh sub-prophecy was that families would find it harder to provide the basic necessities of life for their children and families. Poverty levels in America reached new highs in the 1990s, with more families depending on government assistance of some sort than ever before. Economic woes hit foreign families even harder, with many children dying from malnutrition and disease based upon economic inability to pay for the basic necessities.

The eighth sub-prophecy was that the family would continue to be under assault by the enemy, dissolving more marriages than ever before. Sexual sins hit a new height in the 1990s, with the advent of the Internet and telephone sex lines, many husbands found themselves drawn into an ever more powerful cycle of pornography and unfaithfulness that eventually led to the dissolution of their marriages.

The ninth sub-prophecy was that the foundation of the family would continue to dissolve through New Age philosophies and the teaching of humanism in schools. With the advent of the community philosophy of raising children, parents suddenly found themselves in legal jeopardy for disciplining their children.

261

The tenth sub-prophecy was that the moral values of families would be torn apart through saturation of the devil's evil devices. This prophecy is fulfilled every day, and by just turning on a television set, it is possible to see the complete moral destruction of the values that once ruled American families.

The third major crisis God revealed to me that would come in the 1990s was the shaking of the Church.

God revealed to me five sub-prophecies of how the Church would be shaken. The first sub-prophecy was that intense persecution would begin on a worldwide scale, starting in America. In the 1990s, children were allowed to practice any religion at school except for Christianity. Christians were systematically derided and persecuted in America for their beliefs, and liberal humanists portrayed Christians as twisted, deranged wackos in every avenue they could possibly find.

The second sub-prophecy was that the true Body of Christ would be separated from the uncommitted nominal Christians. In the past decade, nominal Christians were separated as wave after wave of revival encouraged the true Church to come closer to God and to walk the narrow path of righteousness, and the lines of demarcation between committed Christians and the uncommitted became crystal clear.

The third sub-prophecy was that the traditional structure of the Church would be shaken, with the Body raising up ministers from all aspects of life. Many churches moved away from the traditional pastor-dominated structure to one of lay ministers taking care of portions of the congregation's needs, with more and more people becoming ministers to each other, and witnessing to their friends and co-workers.

The fourth sub-prophecy was that new leadership within the fivefold ministry would emerge under the divine leadership of Jesus Christ. In the 1990s, many evangelists, prophets, apostles, pastors and teachers were raised up by God to begin fulfilling the spiritual needs of the Church that was growing beyond the denominational barriers of man-made religion.

The fifth sub-prophecy was that traditions and man-made doctrines would be broken. In the decade of the 90s, many traditional churches broke out of their traditional modes of worship and service, as they embraced the freedom of worship in the Spirit of the living God.

The fourth major crisis God revealed to me in 1989 was a coming worldwide financial crisis that would bring upheaval around the world.

This prophecy began to be fulfilled in the late 1990s when the world's financial markets, starting in Asia, were rocked by Asian economies faltering, starting in Indonesia and spreading throughout Asia, then to Europe, South America and North America. Many people lost their homes, their jobs and their life savings as the world's economic troubles translated into real disasters for them. There is much more to come on this.

The fifth major crisis God led me to prophesy was a coming satanic confrontation of gigantic proportions, with an increase of lying signs and wonders, and many going astray after the lies of the devil.

The 1990s saw the biggest increase in occult activity in history, with even mainstream and everyday people depending on psychic call-in lines for their daily direction, and horoscopes and New Age philosophical books becoming the bywords for an entire generation.

But God did not just tell me to prophesy five coming crises, He led me to tell the Church of five waves of the Holy Spirit coming in the 1990s. Those prophecies also were fulfilled.

The first major wave was a new wave of holiness coming on the Church. The late 1980s found the Church in the aftermath of highly publicized scandals from major preachers who were not living in holiness and not following the principles they taught. This worldliness seemed to pervade the Church, but God showed me a wave of holiness was coming. That wave of holiness began almost immediately in the early 1990s, and has only grown stronger through the decade, culminating in tremendous revivals in places like Argentina and Pensacola, Florida. God's holiness has become the rallying cry of an entire multitude of Christians who are no longer willing to settle for nominal Christianity, but instead want the deeper things of God.

The second wave God told me was coming was a wave of great signs, miracles and wonders. This wave of miracles has resulted in more documented healings, salvations and deliverances than at any time in the history of the Church, with God's power being poured out as never before.

The third wave God led me to prophesy was coming in the 1990s was a wave of true unity through a new covenant relationship. Many Christians of all denominational and ecclesiastical backgrounds came together as never before in a new unity of the Spirit, worshiping God in Spirit and in truth. This unity has resulted in the creation of a more powerful Body of Christ that is stronger than it has ever been in history, and is only getting stronger.

The fourth wave of the Spirit God led me to prophesy was a wave of divine wisdom and discernment in the Body of Christ to deal with the crises that were coming in the decade of the 90s. This wave of discernment and wisdom has been fulfilled in a tremendous way, with many new leaders coming to the forefront in the dearth of leadership that the shaking of the Church has left, many leaders who are filled

264

with biblical wisdom and spiritual discernment to lead the Church into new frontiers of the Spirit.

The fifth wave of the Spirit God led me to prophesy was that restitution and restoration would come on the Church. My files of testimonies are packed with stories of Christians who have received back every penny the devil has stolen from them, and even more, as God takes them beyond the point of blessing into a new realm of pouring out His blessings that they can't even contain. Headings have increased exponentially, and deliverances have increased. God has moved in the most tremendous ways possible, and it's only beginning!

# Chapter 9

# COUNTING THE COST

Preaching the Gospel of Jesus Christ in the nations of the world is at once both overwhelmingly fulfilling and extremely unpopular.

Through my more-than fifty years of ministry, I have had the privilege of preaching the Gospel, face-to-face, to as many people as any man in history. Every day, I stand in awe of the tremendous grace God has shown on my life. I would be overwhelmed by His providence if I had only been allowed to stand by as someone else was preaching to all those people – Just to witness the power of God in such a real way day after day, night after night, is more momentous than any other experience I could imagine anyone having in their entire lifetime.

Many times, as I read the newspaper, I am reminded of the lives of the rich and famous, and obviously envious newspaper reporters and television talking heads gushing over the lifestyles of the people who have been made famous by a world starving for entertainment to block out the nagging in their souls from not having a relationship with the living Christ.

I can take the example of Bill Gates, CEO of Microsoft Corporation, who at this writing is the wealthiest man in the world. At one point in 1999, Gates' wealth was estimated at more than 100 BILLION dollars. That means Bill Gates could give fifteen dollars to every man, woman and child alive on the face of the planet and still have more money left over than most people will earn in a lifetime.

But I would not take the wealth of Bill Gates in exchange for the tremendous triumphs God has allowed me to witness through the years: the salvations, the healings, the deliverances...the army of more than one million Nationals raised up around the world.

Through all the challenges and tragedies I've faced in my life, I have never failed to see God change that challenge or tragedy into a testimony of His ever-gentle power and grace in operation in the lives of men. God's hand is always at work, and though tragedies occur, He is ever standing ready to change those tragedies into both learning experiences and triumphs in the spirit.

I am brought to mind of the words penned by another Jew who lived almost two-thousand years before me. This Jew was beaten, stoned, dragged, spit upon, jailed, derided, lied about and mocked, but instead of lashing out at the people who were persecuting him, this Jew exhibited the character the Lord had so carefully instilled in him when he wrote these words:

> *"Of the Jews five times received I forty stripes save one. Thrice was I beaten with rods, once was I stoned, thrice I suffered shipwreck, a night and a day I have been in the deep; In journeyings often, in perils of waters, in perils of robbers, in perils by mine own countrymen, in perils by the heathen, in perils in the city, in perils in the wilderness, in perils in the sea, in perils among false brethren; In weariness and painfulness, in watchings often, in hunger and thirst, in fastings often, in cold and nakedness. Beside those things that are without, that which cometh upon me daily, the care of all the churches. Who is weak, and I am not weak? who is offended, and I burn not? If I must needs glory, I will glory of the things which concern mine infirmities." (II Corinthians 11:24-30)*

Through more difficult circumstances than we can imagine, Paul forever glorified God in his infirmities and trials.

Peter and John also exemplified the attitude God desires to engender in us when they were beaten for preaching the Gospel:

> *"And they departed from the presence of the council, rejoicing that they were counted worthy to suffer shame for his name. And daily in the temple, and in every house, they ceased not to teach and preach Jesus Christ." (Acts 5:41, 42)*

Throughout the decades of my ministry, countless people have asked me over and over again a very similar question: "Why does God allow bad things to happen to good people?"

After so many years in the ministry, I only have one answer to that question: The things that seem to be the bad situations we endure through the grace of God work tremendous maturing in us, and allow us to witness firsthand the miraculous delivering power of the living God.

From the time of my very first overseas crusade in Athens, Greece, I found out what it was to face opposition to the preaching of the Gospel of Jesus Christ. When I arrived in that country, the people who were there were dejected, resigned to the fact that the government was a higher power that they simply could not move at all.

But in my young life filled with the deliverances and miracles of God, I had learned one lesson if nothing else: What seems to be the immovable object is always proven to be moveable when it meets the truly irresistible force, the hand of the living God.

In the natural, the first reaction of many people to a situation like we faced in Greece is to immediately go through the proper channels, barking your way up the tree of bureaucracy until you finally find someone who will listen and then continue barking until you find someone who can change things. But God has never operated that way, and though I was just a young man, I knew that about God; I knew that He had His own way of solving problems.

> *"For we wrestle not against flesh and blood, but against principalities, against powers, against the rulers of the darkness of this world, against spiritual wickedness in high places..."* *(Ephesians 6:12).*

Though I did not fully understand the concept of spiritual warfare at that time, I understood that I served a God who could change things, a God who was able to break down any door and open any heart.

So while the natural inclination was to seek the remedies of this world, God led me to hole myself up in the little hotel room I rented and pour my heart out to Him day and night until He moved.

> *"And shall not God avenge his own elect, which cry day and night unto him, though he bear long with them? I tell you that he will avenge them speedily..."* *(Luke 18:7-8)*

The battle was won, not in the courtrooms of Greek judges who would interpret arcane laws and render whatever judgments they desired, but in the court of the supreme Judge, who answered the cries of His servant.

It was a lesson that would stick with me for the rest of my life. When our natural inclination is to rely upon the men and women we believe can help us, God's admonition to us is to rely upon Him:

> *"Thus saith the Lord; Cursed be the man that trusteth in man, and maketh flesh his arm, and whose heart departeth from the Lord...Blessed is the man that trusteth in the Lord, and whose hope the Lord is"* *(Jeremiah 17:5, 7)*

When the Lord is our hope, no man, no army, no government, no natural law, no natural wisdom can defeat us – we are His army fighting a battle He has called us to...we WILL prevail!

Though Greece was a challenge and certainly a hurdle, I wouldn't find out what a real run-in with the forces of man's armies could be, until my crusades in Brazil and Argentina in 1966.

I was in a crusade in Fort Aleza, Brazil, pouring out everything in my body into the crusade for ten days. In those days the meetings would go long and we would have day meetings and night meetings and afternoon meetings. Our custom was to go from one meeting to the next to the next until we ran out of money, and then we would come home.

We were scheduled to minister in Mar Del Plata, Argentina – my first meetings in Argentina – after the meetings in Fortaleza, but after ten days of meetings in Fortaleza, I was completely exhausted, so I prayed to God and said, "Lord, I've got two or three days before the Mar Del Plata meeting – I really need some place to rest."

A strange thing happened while I was praying. The Lord showed me a vision of a hotel near the water (Mar Del Plata is on the sea). This hotel had a balcony and a room off the balcony, so I called my Crusade Director Clair Hutchins and sent him to Mar Del Plata, and told him of the place the Lord was preparing for me to rest for two days, and told Clair I would join him after he got to Mar Del Plata.

Clair went to Mar Del Plata and found the very picturesque little French hotel on the side of a hill and asked if they had the room I had described, and the people at the hotel said they did.

The room was just as I described in the vision. Clair booked the room, and as soon as I was done in Fortaleza, the

Lord gave me two beautiful days of sitting on that balcony, praying, communing and writing.

The first night of the meeting in Mar Del Plata, the police had been notified to close the meeting down. We were on an open field. The man they sent to arrest me was standing on the grounds. The meeting had been going on two or three days, with incredible intensity building throughout the city. Many of the strong religious people in the city were persecuting the meetings because the vast majority of their people were coming to the services.

About the third night, the meetings were really going strong. A policeman had brought his blind daughter, who he had standing by his side. Suddenly, the little girl looked up at her father and said, "Daddy, I can see."

The policeman broke into tears when he saw the incredible miracle God had wrought in his little daughter.

At the same time, all sorts of miracles were going throughout the meeting, with canes and crutches flying as people who no longer needed them discarded them.

The policeman, who had been sent to arrest me, was afraid to touch me because of the miraculous power God had demonstrated through the healing of his daughter.

The next day, a police wagon drove up to the hotel and policemen got out and came up and asked for me, so I came down from the room and the policemen looked at me sorrowfully.

"We're sorry," one of the policemen said. "We don't want to do this, but we're under orders, we have to arrest you."

They took me to the station, and I was there all day from the early morning at least ten hours being interrogated by the chief of police. Finally, the policeman whose daughter was healed testified, and the police chief said, "We're going to let you go, there's no reason to arrest you – none of the charges against you can be upheld, you are only speaking God's Word."

So about 7 p.m., they let me go, and I went right to the meeting – we never missed a meeting – and God moved mightily. The blind saw, the deaf heard, the crippled walked and thousands were brought to Christ.

That was the beginning of all the troubles we faced in Argentina. The next place we went was Rosario, Argentina, where a good friend of a friend of mine, Nels Kastberg, was laboring in the Gospel as a missionary for the Assemblies of God of Sweden.

My dear friend, who was the leading Assemblies of God missionary in Porto Alegre, Brazil, had told Nels, "Please, please invite Morris Cerullo to your city – God's power will break your city wide open."

As we prepared for the salvation, miracle, healing crusade in Rosario, we could tell the going would not be easy in Rosario, which at the time had only thirty-five or so Pentecostal believers in a city of more than two million people. We had no workers, ushers or counselors.

My associate minister, Argemiro Figuiro, had gone ahead of me to prepare the crusade, to rent the football stadium, which would hold eighty-thousand people, to place the advertising in local newspapers and to set up all the hundreds of details that had to be arranged for my overseas crusades.

When Argemiro went about to place the advertisements in the newspapers, radio and television, he began to encounter strong resistance. Everywhere Argemiro went, the story was the same: "No, we will not run that ad for you."

Rosario, like much of South America, was predominantly Roman Catholic, and these media outlets had never published any Protestant literature, and they weren't about to start with this minister from America.

Argemiro and I discussed the matter at great length and we prayed earnestly about the situation when we had a breakthrough revelation – we believed God was telling us that Argemiro should go to the Catholic bishop of Rosario.

Argemiro approached the Catholic bishop with our problem, believing that God would provide the breakthrough we needed. After long hours of talking and much negotiation, the bishop agreed to help us with our problem and sent his personal secretary with Argemiro to the media outlets to recommend that they accept our paid advertising.

Those advertisements would turn out to be part of the initial victory of the Rosario adventure...they testified that God's servant would be coming to Rosario to teach that Jesus Christ is alive – that He is the same yesterday, today and forever.

These advertisements may not seem like much in our day and age of ever-more shocking television and print ads, but in November of 1966, ads that promised to show that Christ was alive were very provocative, and they piqued the interest of hundreds of thousands of people in Rosario.

Everything seemed to go smoothly until I arrived in Rosario. The police had been very cooperative, but that Saturday, Rev. Kastberg received a notice that the meeting we were planning on holding in the football stadium had been banned and was not to be conducted under any circumstances.

In the notice, the police stated that they would not be able to contain such a huge crowd as was certain to assemble for the meeting, therefore they could not allow it to proceed.

At this point, I didn't know of the troubles. My ministry team, which included Argemiro, The Rev. Alex Ness and Clair Hutchins, snapped into action and went to the local authorities to discuss why our crusade permit had been invalidated.

But the negotiations were to no avail. The chief of police had gone into seclusion for the weekend and could not be reached. He had left strict directions that no circumstances would be acceptable for changing his orders that the meeting be stopped.

My ministry team, Alex Ness and Clair Hutchins, were already gone, preparing the meeting. When they arrived at the stadium, there were tens of thousands of people waiting for the stadium doors to open three hours ahead of the meeting.

The entire place was blockaded with sawhorses and guarded with machine guns, halftracks with mounted machine guns on their jeeps – stationed all around the stadium. You couldn't get within three or four blocks of the stadium.

Alex went to the stadium's front doors and found padlocks on them. The chief of police and his guard were at the stadium gates.

In my hotel room, I was in prayer and I heard a knock on the door. When I opened the door, my overseas Crusade Director, Clair Hutchins was standing outside my hotel room. He described for me the mayhem that was happening at the football stadium.

"Brother Cerullo," Clair said to me, "we've tried everything, and there's no way they're going to let us hold this meeting."

I looked at Clair and said, "follow me."

Clair never said a word, he simply fell in behind me.

We went to the barricade and walked right through them. At the barracades, a guard looked at us forebodingly and raised his gun and pointed it at us, spoke to the us.

"You cannot go any further," he said in Spanish, I found out later.

"I don't understand Spanish; I only speak English," I said as I continued to pass through the barricade.

As I continued to walk forward, it was like the Pied Piper. People all over the crowd recognized me and began calling out my name, and one by one at first, they began to follow me over the barracide, then more, and finally, it was a sea of thousands of people passing over the barricades.

All around me, people with tremendous needs were gathered together. They had been drawn by advertisements that promised, "The blind will see, the deaf will hear, the lame will walk."

And everywhere I looked all around me, I could see throngs of people who were depending upon those promises being true. On the left was a man with crutches, his leg gnarled and withered, his eyes big with expectation of something supernatural. On the right, a woman was holding the arm of a relative, her eyes whited out by blindness that had certainly afflicted her for a very long time. In front of me, men were communicating with each other using only their hands, signifying to me that they were deaf or mute or both.

My heart began to be moved with compassion for the crowds. So many needs were represented. So many faces filled with sorrow, pain and hunger for knowledge of God. So many lost souls were gathered at the gates of a football stadium, expecting a minister from America to show them that Jesus Christ was still alive.

As I and the massive crowd behind me arrived at the front of the stadium's gates, the police formed a human chain to keep us back. The police were now looking directly into the faces of the people who had gathered. They saw the needs, the desire and the expectation in the eyes of the people, and many of the police began to weep openly. I also was moved to tears by the tremendous expectancy of the people and the sheer mass of needs that were represented in this throng of ten-thousand people who had gathered around me.

## Counting the Cost

Many of the police murmured to each other of their dissatisfaction with the fact that they had to keep these people from being ministered to.

Some high-ranking officers of the police force were nearby and they were sympathetic to our cause, but their hands were tied; they could not reverse the orders of the chief of police. I was forbidden to speak at all.

Rev. Ness made his way through the crowd, and I asked him what the verdict was in the negotiations about letting us hold the meeting.

Rev. Ness just shook his head and let me know that the situation had not changed.

I got up on top of a Jeep and, using a megaphone, I announced that I would move the meeting.

We had put up a huge tent seating two-thousand people, which was to be our daytime convert class. The tent was on our grounds, and the police couldn't do anything about us holding a meeting there.

I told the people that the meeting would move to the tent.

By the time the meeting in the tent started, you couldn't get within half a block of the place, it was so jammed with people singing and rejoicing. We had a powerful service that night, with incredible healings and salvations.

Right after that, the police stopped me and told me I couldn't preach any more, placing me under house arrest and forbidding me to preach, but that tent became the rallying place. Morning, afternoon and night, for more than a year, you couldn't get anywhere near that tent for the crush of people who came there to be ministered to. That tent became a soul-saving healing station. People were getting saved and healed every day by the hundreds – all through the local National ministers.

Afterward, Rev. Kastberg had to buy a theatre that could hold two-thousand people; and from nothing, in one year, he was pastoring a church of more than twenty-five hundred people.

From there, they started dozens of churches all over Rosario.

The next year, I came back to Rosario to hold another crusade. (But I first had to go to trial over the first arrest.)

I went into court and faced all my adversaries – most of whom were doctors – who were there, accusing me of practicing medicine without a license because of all the great healings God had wrought.

The magistrate asked me if I had an attorney present, and I answered that I did. The magistrate then asked where my attorney was.

"Right here," I said.

Of course, the man looked at me as if I had lost my marbles.

But he decided to have the trial anyway, and the trial began, with my accusers laying out the charges against me.

When time came for me to make a defense, the judge said to me, "Do you or your attorney have anything to say?"

"Yes, we do, your honor," I replied.

I started from the Book of Genesis and told him how God created man and how man fell and how sin, sickness and death came into the world as a result of man's disobedience.

I then told him how God did not leave man under the curse, but how He made a plan for man to be redeemed and how Christ paid the price for sin, sickness and death and now we have eternal life through Him.

The judge paused, slammed the gavel down and spoke:

"This man is not practicing medicine without a license," the judge said, looking sternly at my accusers. "This man is a minister of the Gospel. Go preach."

We went right from there and started our second crusade in the same stadium. We were there for five days; the place was packed with forty-to-fifty-thousand people every night.

There were incredible salvations and awesome healings, with the blind seeing and the deaf hearing and the lame walking.

I had never felt such expectancy from a group of people, such a receptiveness. Thousands and thousands of people crammed the stadium, and thousands upon thousands answered the call for salvation.

Argentina was not the only country that offered hurdles for me to overcome and turn into chapters of the book of Acts through the power of the Holy Spirit of God.

In 1981, God had called us to go on a Central American Journey of Love, visiting every country in Central America, South America, Bogota, Peru, Bolivia, Chile, Uruguay, Argentina – holding mass crusades every night. In the daytime, we held training services for believers.

As we came into Nicaragua, when we landed, our plane wa surrounded with Jeeps and machine guns in the hands of Nicaraguan police, who took us off the plane and into a waiting area. My ministry team stayed outside as the police took me into an office where they started to interrogate me for hours, barraging me with question after question.

In the room, they questioned me over and over again, with the same type of questions: "How long have you worked for the CIA? Why are you here to spy? Why did your government send you here? What's your opinion of the revolution? What's your opinion of General Ortega? (Gen. Ortega then was the president of Nicaragua)."

For three hours, they barraged me with question after question. Everyone in the room besides me seemed to be chain-smoking cigarettes, blowing the smoke in my face. Behind the interrogator and his interpreter were Communist posters and pictures of Communist leaders.

As they were interrogating me, the crusade team was seated in the airport terminal at gunpoint. If they tried to get up from their seats, they were quickly pushed back down by armed guards.

While the interrogation was going on, a few men took the keys to our airplane and began going through it.

As they went through our plane and got the names and addresses of all the Nationals we had registered in morning believers' services through Central America and South America – tens of thousands of names and addresses had fallen into the hands of Communists. They also had taken my Bible, which I had used for years in meetings throughout the nations of the world. They confiscated everything.

When the Communists finished interrogating me, they demanded that we leave Nicaragua immediately – that we all get on the plane and leave right then, without refueling.

We did not know if we would have enough fuel to get to a safe place.

When I got to the plane, my team told me what was missing. I refused to get on the plane.

"I'm not getting on this plane," I said, to the soldiers, "until you return those names and you return my Bible."

The soldiers began pushing and shoving me toward the plane, but I was pushing and shoving right back.

"I'm not getting on this plane," I said.

Hector, our Spanish-speaking pilot spoke to Lowell Warner, our technical director, and said, "You better tell Rev. Cerullo to get on this plane because that guy just said, 'If he doesn't get on the plane, shoot him and leave him there.'"

Lowell grabbed me and pushed me toward the plane, forcing me up into the airplane, and we took off immediately. Right away, Hector noticed that something was wrong; the radar wasn't working, indicating that something might be on the radar dome.

Lowell reached down into the radar dome and found nothing, but the radar still wasn't working so Lowell, who normally is very reserved, hit the radar screen with his hand and said, "In the Name of Jesus!" and the radar blipped on! But we weren't out of danger yet.

The plane was desperately low on fuel. We had to declare an international fuel emergency, and a military airport at Tegucigalpa, Honduras, received our distress call and turned on their runway lights. The airport was cradled in mountains, so it wasn't supposed to be used at night, but we were desperate.

As Hector made the approach to the runway, the lights on the runway went out. He couldn't understand why they would turn the lights out, but he began to lower our landing gear anyway to prepare for a landing – we had no fuel to continue anywhere else.

When the landing gear came down, the landing lights automatically turned on, and the first thing everyone heard was Lowell, shouting, "Those are trees!"

Hector immediately pulled back on the plane's controls, and we veered up over the mountain, which we had somehow managed to nearly fly into. Another fifteen seconds, and we would have plowed into the side of the mountain.

When we landed, Honduran military officers met our plane. Not only had we landed at an unauthorized military airport after the airport hours, we were coming in from Nicaragua, which aggravated suspicions in Honduras.

But as soon as we had deplaned, we noticed the spirit in Honduras was completely different. The soldiers treated us with the utmost respect. We held our meetings in Honduras as scheduled with more than forty-thousand present, and while we were there, I was frantically on the phone to the U.S. Consulates and our people in authority in Nicaragua to get our list of people back. I was trying to call directly to General Ortega, and through some miracle, I did get through directly to the general. I told him what had happened, because I had heard he had some Christian leanings. He told me on the phone not to worry, the whole incident had been a mistake, and he would see that everything taken from me would be sent back to me.

When I got to San Diego after finishing the tour, my Bible and every name and address had been returned.

God used that situation to strengthen our School of Ministry graduates in both Nicaragua and Honduras, and a tremendous wave of God's power still is working in those countries today.

In Bele Horizonte, Brazil, I was scheduled to preach a crusade, and this time, my son, David, had come along to help with some of the arrangements.

While we were in the hotel, a cadre of secret police approached David in the lobby. They knew instantly who he was. The policemen approached David and began demanding his passport and the passports of every person on our ministry team. They also demanded that David tell them where I was.

David bravely refused to give the men any information.

"I'm an American citizen," David told the secret police. "Show me some authorization for what you're demanding. What authority do you have to ask for my passport?"

The men flashed their badges at my son.

"Badges aren't good enough," David said. His face was now less than a foot away from the chief secret police officer's. "I need some paperwork from some authority saying that you can demand our passports."

"I don't have the authorization," the man told David. "But I will get it. You tell your father that if he holds his meeting tonight, he will be arrested and I will put you all in jail. I will be back."

Immediately after he was sure the secret police had left the hotel, David instructed the hotel staff that they were not to divulge any information to the secret police, and then he came quickly to my room.

"Dad," David said, a worried look on his face. "I just had a run-in with the secret police. They said if you hold the meeting tonight, they'll arrest you on the spot, haul you to jail and have us deported."

I looked at David and said, "Okay."

David's mouth dropped open. He was flabbergasted.

"Okay what?" he said. "What do you want us to do?"

"Nothing," I replied. "We're going to do what we came to do."

I understood that we could not fight this natural battle. If the men did indeed come back with authorization, there was nothing in the natural we could do to stop them. If they hauled us off to jail, they could only do to us what God allowed. We were completely in the hands of our Father, and I was not worried. I had faced this many times.

"Dad," David said, concern in his voice and a worried look on his face. "Why don't you pick a National tonight and let him minister. You do it all the time in your Schools of Ministry where you raise Nationals up to train them to minister, and I can't think of a better time to let a National preach than now."

I looked at my son. I am so proud of him; he is the best son a father could ask for. His concern was for me, for my welfare, because he knew the secret police would be back and he didn't want me to be arrested.

"David," I answered, "I'm not going to do that. If I don't go and do what God sent me to do tonight, and if I'm not willing to face whatever might come, how can I expect these Nationals to have any more backbone, or any more faith, or any more courage than what I'm prepared to demonstrate myself? I have to go and do what we came to do. If they arrest me, they'll just have to arrest me. If they want to kill me, I'm consecrated to death."

David's eyes welled up with tears as he agreed, and we began making preparations for that night's meeting.

When we left the hotel and got into the cars on the way to the meetings, David got in the car with me. We prayed on the way there, but we weren't prepared for what we saw when we got to the meetings.

When we arrived, it looked like someone was preparing for a major war.

Hundreds of soldiers were gathered outside the arena, with half-tracks and machine gun nests, complete with sand bags and high-powered automatic weapons.

They literally looked like they expected us to be an armed insurrection force instead of less than a dozen people on a mission to minister the Gospel of Jesus Christ. Every entrance and exit was covered, with weapons everywhere.

And as we approached the gate, the driver turned to me and asked, "Brother Cerullo, what do we do?"

"Drive on," I said. The driver's eyes widened, but he drove forward, and we made it all the way through the gates, soldiers eyeing us as we passed.

That night, the meeting was tremendous. Thousands of people gave their lives to Jesus Christ, and multitudes were healed of all kinds of illnesses and deformities. After the altar call and the closing prayer, I left the platform and soldiers were waiting there to arrest me. But they did not touch me.

The devil's plan had been to intimidate us through the fear of being arrested or deported, but God would not allow the devil victory! We made it through without a scratch, and thousands of people are now part of the Kingdom of God because God's strength was exhibited in us.

In addition, God's providence provided a tremendous lesson for the Nationals who were assembled; Nationals who would doubtlessly face persecution in the future for their Christian faith. God showed them through my trials that they could stand up for Christ without fear.

In free countries, we tend to forget the tremendous sacrifices made in countries that have more oppressive governments than ours. In some countries, it is an outright crime to profess Christ, and through our trials and tribulations, God has taken the opportunity to demonstrate to the Nationals who face such oppression that they need not fear imprisonment or death.

Later that year, we once again found ourselves in peril of life and limb, but this time an ocean away in Poland.

I had been invited to minister in Poland by the newly-elected president of the Evangelical Union of Poland. He and I had spent time communicating, and eventually had settled on a date in the summer of 1982 for me and my ministry team to arrive and conduct our meetings.

But in November of 1981, God spoke to me while I was in deep prayer one day.

"Son," God said to me, "the time is now. I am sending you without delay; go, plant the seed of a new anointing through prayer, intercession and ministry in the souls of Poland."

I began to feel the urgency of God in my spirit, an urgency unlike anything I had ever felt before. The overwhelming feeling all the time, day and night, was "You must go NOW."

I can't describe the feeling fully. The only word I can give to it is unction. An unction of the Holy Spirit was prodding me 24 hours a day to go to Poland. I knew that if I waited until the date we had scheduled, it would be too late to accomplish what God wanted to accomplish.

Immediately, I called my executive assistant, at that time Pat Hulsey, and told her to clear my schedule of all other ministry dates. I also asked her to get in contact with Archie

Dennis, who has now been my crusade singer for more than twenty-five years, and to contact Dr. Alex Ness, who has accompanied me on more overseas crusades through the years than I can count. I sent Argemiro Figuiro to Poland to prepare the meetings.

Now, rearranging my schedule is no small feat. Because of the demands of the ministry, my schedule is regulated by the hour, not by the day. Pat put in a monumental effort to clear the hundreds of items on my schedule and secure visas for me, Archie and Alex to go to Poland and minister.

December 8, 1981, Archie, Alex and I boarded a plane and took off for Poland in a serious, prayerful mood. When we arrived in Warsaw, we stepped off the plane to face the most bitter cold I had ever felt in my life. The chill was so intense that the heaviest coat did nothing to stop it. Even the mildest breeze cut through a heavy coat as if all I was wearing was a T-shirt.

Outside, the sky was dark and dismal. Black clouds hung overhead, and everything was only half-lit, like dusk time.

The Christian brother who met us at the airport invited us to his little home, where he had called a prayer meeting with his friends.

When we got to his home, we were saddened by the situation they faced. Food was so closely rationed that even though the family wanted to feed us, we realized that if they did, the family would have nothing to eat for the rest of the month, so we declined.

We launched immediately into a prayer meeting with this precious Polish brother and his family, and I could immediately feel the Spirit of God move, even in this gathering of less than a dozen people. It was at that moment that I knew God had tremendous things in store for the Polish people.

The anointing is like an electric circuit of sorts. The electricity is always there, always present, but it only starts flowing when something is plugged in, demanding the electricity.

I could feel these people in Poland wanted to be completely plugged into the anointing that God wanted to impart to them – it was like someone just had thrown the switch wide open, and the anointing was rushing in like a flood. I had been in many meetings in my life, but never before the meetings in Poland had I felt such a tremendous receptivity to the anointing as these precious people had.

Our first service in Poland was in a huge Catholic cathedral in the old capital of Krakow. I can't find the words to adequately describe the hunger these people had for anything of God. It was like seeing a cathedral full of men who had just crossed the Sahara desert, and I was holding a large pitcher of water – the thirst for God was that evident in their eyes.

We preached in a Pentecostal church in Warsaw, and everywhere we went, people literally sat on top of one another to get closer to the anointing and to hear the Word of God. The people in Poland were like children; they worshiped the Lord unreservedly. It brings to mind a story I heard that Christians in oppressed countries are praying that American Christians get a taste of persecution so that the sleeping giant American Church will wake up. If American Christians could get a look at the faces of these Polish people as they worshiped in unrestrained freedom – the only freedom they had in their lives – they would begin to look at their freedom to worship God in a different light.

Everywhere I went in Poland, I preached the simple plan of salvation; how sin came into the world, God's plan of redemption and how Christ came to fulfill that plan.

When I asked the congregations for people who wanted to receive the miracle of salvation and have their sins forgiven, more than ninety percent of the people responded and gave their lives to Jesus Christ. Jesus says that angels in heaven rejoice over just one soul who comes to Him; angels must have been throwing a block party those nights in Poland as so many people who lived under Communist oppression found freedom in Jesus.

As we traveled in Poland, the faces of the people told the same story everywhere. As people described their living conditions, they inevitably would break down and cry. Their plight was heart-wrenching, as every aspect of their lives was controlled by the Communist bureaucracy. They could neither eat or drink anything but what they were told. They could not go anywhere they were unauthorized to go. They could not work where they wanted or live where they wanted. Everything was decided for them. In the last service we held in Krakow, a large group of young people fell down on their faces on the floor and wept before God during the sinner's prayer – many of them tasting real freedom for the first time in their short lives.

December 13, the government of Poland declared martial law. Everything was shut down. Telephones were cut off. The media were shut down. Gasoline was forbidden for anyone to buy.

A curfew was imposed, and everyone was essentially under house arrest.

Very soon after the announcement that martial law had been declared, a message was broadcast across the government-controlled radio and television stations: "All public meetings are canceled!"

But I knew God hadn't called me to Poland only to find out we couldn't hold any more meetings. Alex, Archie and I began to earnestly pray that God would open the doors that had just been slammed in our faces.

No sooner had we prayed than another announcement came across the television that said, "We really mean that all public meetings except religious church meetings are canceled."

Because of the providence of the living God, we did not have one meeting stopped or interrupted or impeded in any way! The anointing flowed mightily each night, and the spiritually-starving people of Communist-dominated Poland were energized and born again by the tremendous power of God.

The word in Warsaw was that martial law would not last long, and that we should wait it out and leave after the crackdown was lifted.

But God began to deal with my spirit that we should leave Poland now that our work was done and the seed was planted; we should not wait for martial law to be lifted.

By this time, World Evangelism staff in San Diego were very concerned about us; the lines of communication had been shut off, and they had no way of knowing where we were or even if we were still alive. It was decided that the staff would work for fifty minutes of every hour, and that they would pray ten minutes of each hour until they heard from us; so in an eight-hour day, not including lunchtime prayer, our staff was praying an hour and twenty minutes each day until they heard about our welfare.

Travel was restricted, and everywhere we went tanks and military vehicles blocked the main roads. There seemed to be no conventional way out of Poland. Communication was shut off. Gas was forbidden. Planes were grounded and the airport was closed. In the wee hours of one morning, one of our staff members went down to the hotel lobby and received a tip that possibly one train going to Communist East Germany was still running.

But that didn't sound too promising. We didn't have visas to enter East Germany, and East Germany was at that time controlled by Communists. The Berlin Wall was up.

People spent their entire lives trying to figure out how to get from East Germany into free West Germany. Some went to great lengths, like one man who so desperately wanted to get his fiancee out of East Germany that he carved out a hole in the seat of his car and hid her there like she was just part of the seat so he could smuggle her out. It certainly would be no easy task to get to West Germany, even if by some miracle they let us into East Germany without the proper paperwork.

But as daunting as the task seemed, we knew that God had told us to go, and this seemed to be the only way.

Very early in the morning, at two a.m., we left the hotel, carrying our bags in the freezing wind and snow for several miles until we got to a bus stop and stood in the biting wind. We walked, ducking the militia and the tanks in the street until we got to the train station.

We had no time to buy tickets to the train, and we had no visas or entry permits to go to East Germany, but trusting the Lord, we jumped on the train, believing that He would let us get out of Poland. War and revolution seemed inevitable.

We knew that it was entirely possible that we would be thrown off the train or jailed for trying to get out of the country during war time.

After the train had been moving for several hours, the conductor came by and asked us for our tickets. We explained to him that we didn't have tickets, but we would be glad to buy some.

The conductor frowned.

"That's against railroad policy," he told us.

We negotiated some more, and finally, the conductor's countenance changed. He looked at us, sighed and agreed to sell us the tickets.

When we got into East Germany, we were praying to God that the same favor He had engendered in the train conductor would follow us through this oppressive Communist country.

East Germany was a surveillance state. Everyone was watched, nearly every movement was recorded. Neighbors were paid to inform on neighbors, husbands on wives. Suspicion was the name of the game for the East German government; they were suspicious of everyone – no exceptions.

As we approached the first checkpoint, we were intensely aware of this suspicion. The uniformed guards scrutinized every detail of our party, looking at the luggage, looking at our clothes and our hair. As we got to the checkpoint, the guards demanded our paperwork, but all we had were our U.S. passports. We handed them our passports.

The guard looked at our passports, and then looked at me.

"Where are you going?" he asked.

"We're going back home to the United States."

He looked at me, then at Archie, then at Alex. The guard handed our passports back to us and waved us through – with no visas, no permits, no train tickets.

We could hardly believe the tremendous work of God. Angels went before us and opened the way for us, because it was unheard of for the guards to allow someone with no paperwork to pass through a Communist checkpoint. In fact, the proper procedure for them would have been to put us in jail for trying to pass through their country without the proper paperwork.

If they had thrown us in jail, no one would have known where we were. We simply could have rotted in their jail, and no one would know how to get in contact with us.

Instead, the way opened before us like the Red Sea opened before Moses.

As we approached the Berlin Wall, which was still standing at that time, the Communist military soldiers assisted us, telling us exactly how to get through the wall and to West Germany – these were the same soldiers whose job it was to keep their own people from crossing this wall, and yet they were helping us as if they were tour guides instead of Communist guards.

We went down one set of stairs, through a tunnel, past a checkpoint and up another set of stairs, and we were completely out of Communist Eastern Europe – with absolutely no trouble!

Many times through the years, it has been said that our ministry is a ministry on time, but rarely has it been demonstrated so vividly as God's call to us to minister in Poland six months before we had intended to. We were the last evangelical ministers allowed into the country before martial law was declared, and some of the first people to leave the country after. (And some of the first to return when the doors opened.)

When we arrived home in San Diego, God gave us another chance to turn our hurdle into a ministry opportunity as a bevy of media met us at the airport and interviewed me for a long time, asking the details of our adventure, wanting to know what we were doing in Poland and how we escaped.

God used that opportunity to allow me to minister the Gospel to those reporters, who broadcast the interview on their television stations as a witness, to a huge audience of people!

Another tremendous testimony of God's providence in overcoming hurdles was when we went to Tanzania while the Red Chinese were the governing force there.

The Church in Tanzania was very small and under heavy persecution. We came in to do a crusade and got a very large field in the heart of town that would hold between one-hundred thousand and two-hundred thousand people.

As I was praying in my hotel room and waiting to go to the crusade, the ministry team came by to pick me up to go to the meeting.

Unbeknownst to me, Clair Hutchins and Dr. Ness had been wrangling with police all afternoon, because the police had forbidden us to conduct the meeting under any circumstances.

Dr. Ness and Clair had plenty of time to tell me our lives were in danger, but they were very faithful on following instructions I had given them, one of which was to never tell me anything negative before a meeting; let me find out by the Holy Spirit or after the meetings are over.

So I had no idea that they had been struggling over holding the meetings.

As soon as I got out of the car that was taking me to the crusade, I was surrounded by policemen with rifles, and the whole place was surrounded by trucks, jeeps and hundreds of policemen. There were more than fifty-thousand people on the grounds this first night.

I stood up to straight attention and saluted the police who had gathered around.

The miraculous thing was that when I saluted them, they backed off. I didn't know why, but I later found out that they thought I must have been some sort of dignitary, not the guy they were looking for. They saluted me right back!

I walked right up to the platform and God moved incredibly through the service, as many blind saw, deaf heard and cripples walked. After the service, the policemen knew without a doubt who I was, and they were gathered around to arrest me, but they were afraid for their lives because of miracles God had wrought.

The next day, they came and shut down the platform and the crusade.

We continued the School of Ministry meetings in a large indoor building. The platform in the outdoors area, however, was still up, and hundreds of sick came daily to the platform, even though we weren't holding any meetings there. They would touch the planks of the platform where my posters were up, and God's power would instantly heal them. All around the platform, a pile of crutches, canes, wheelchairs and other discarded signs of sickness began to build up as multitudes were healed simply as they touched the planks of the platform where my posters were.

I returned to Tanzania a few years ago to teach a School of Ministry with twenty-two thousand Nationals from every part of East Africa.

When I arrived, the president of Tanzania, a staunch Muslim, invited me to come meet him in his office. Immediately, God did something between us – we embraced, and God immediately formed a bond of friendship between us. We talked and talked for a long time, and finally I asked to pray for him. I told him about the School of Ministry.

"As president of this nation," I said, "you should be there."

Immediately, his aides – all of whom were Muslim – began to come up with excuses why the president could not go to the School of Ministry. But the president looked at them and said, "I'm going."

When the president came to the School of Ministry, he stepped onto the platform and gave a poignant speech: "I want to thank Father Morris (that's what he called me) for coming to Tanzania. I have been your president for years, but this man has done for Tanzania what I could never do. He's brought us together."

A few months later, he felt the need to resign. The next election, a Christian was elected president over a Muslim country.

God used me in the early 1980s to really penetrate and open Mexico for an explosion of the Gospel.

We began planning a Journey of Power to cover the capital city of every major state in Mexico. I was at home preparing to go, about three or four weeks before the meetings, as my practice is, and on my knees, God said, "Morris, what would you do if I took Theresa home?"

I was startled. I had not been praying for my family at the time, I had been praying for a breakthrough in Mexico.

My heart began to beat faster. Was God trying to tell me He was going to take Theresa from me?

As I thought about God's question, I knew there was only one answer I could give Him.

I said, "God if you want to take her home, I will release her to you."

I did not want to take Theresa to Mexico with me this time because I felt in my spirit that the journey would be too hard for her. I was scheduled to be in every state in a big, mass crusade and daytime National Teaching Seminar.

So I went alone, and in the very first stop on the Journey of Power, my advance people were in jail.

Every place I went during this Journey of Power, we faced tremendous opposition. They took away our stadiums in every place – we had to fight every time to get stadium a back, but we succeeded in every place.

On the third day of the Journey of Power, I got a call from the hospital in San Diego. My son, David, was on the line, telling me his Mom was in the hospital. The doctors were saying they didn't think she would make it. She was seriously ill, and her condition was worsening.

"Dad, you better come home immediately, we don't think Mom's going to make it," David said.

Immediately, I knew what I had to answer, although it would be the most painful words I had ever spoken, especially to my son. God had asked me what I would do if He decided to take Theresa home, and now I was being asked to live up to what I had told Him I would do. I could not tell David or anyone of this personal, sacred experience.

"I can't come home," I told David. Of course, he didn't understand. He got violently upset and I understood everything he said.

"What do you mean you can't come home?" he said. "Its our mother; she's dying."

But all I could remember was that I had promised God I would release her to Him.

Theresa was in a coma. She couldn't hear or see or speak, but she later told me she knew within herself what everyone was feeling. She could feel the pain, resentment and bitterness of the people who didn't understand my reticence to come home. In her unconscious state of coma, Theresa prayed and said, "I don't mind if You take me home, God, but please don't take me home while everyone is feeling this way about Morris."

My entire family was very angry with me, because I hadn't come back to the United States, but I had to put into God's hands what I told Him I would.

I continued to get reports that they didn't expect her to make it.

When I was in prayer at the last place on our Journey of Power, God finally said, "Son, it's all right; now you can go home."

That's all I needed to hear.

I flew up to Mexico City and took the first flight home. I arrived back about midnight and went right to the hospital.

I didn't know it, but the doctors had told our family that if Theresa's condition didn't change, she would die that night.

When I got to my precious wife's room, I just reached over the bed, picked her up and put her in my arms, hugged her, breathed on her and laid her down gently and sat beside her bed all night and held her hand.

God wouldn't let me pray – I simply knew everything was going to be all right, because God had said, "Now you can go home."

In the morning, the doctor walked in and examined Theresa.

"I don't understand it," he said. "you've had a complete, one-hundred percent turnaround."

He called me into the hallway and reiterated his complete surprise.

"I would not have believed she would live throughout the night," he said. "But now we can't find a trace of illness. I want to run a few more tests."

A few hours later, Theresa was sitting up talking to everyone. The doctor told us we could take her home.

Theresa was perfectly healed. I took her home the very next day.

But by far the most difficult and painful hurdle with which I have ever been presented in my life was also a hurdle for my precious wife, Theresa, and the rest of our family. At first, we could not see how any good could come of it, but in the end, we realized that God is faithful, and even when we can't see His plan, He can turn the very worst situation into a lesson that can reap salvation and hope in the hearts of multitudes.

God blessed us with three tremendous children; my son, David; daughter, Susan and our younger son, Mark Stephen.

My toughest hurdle was the tragedy that befell our son, Mark.

When I told God I would serve Him and minister His Gospel, I knew that would mean sacrificing my life completely; giving up everything I had claim to, and allowing Him to take over.

I felt like Paul, who declared: *"Paul, a servant of Jesus Christ, called to be an apostle, separated unto the gospel of God..."* (Romans 1:1)

The literal Greek for that verse says, "Paul, a SLAVE of Jesus Christ..."

A slave does not own any property; it all belongs to the Master.

A slave does not do his own will; he does the will of the Master.

A slave's life is not his own; it is his Master's.

And a slave does not own his family – as soon as the children are born, they belong to the Master.

I knew that as the slave of Christ, I would have to give up everything to serve Him. I would have to dedicate my family to Him and trust Him in every aspect of my life and theirs.

Through the years, it was difficult. I can count the wedding anniversaries, birthdays and holiday celebrations I've spent with Theresa on my hand. Every other wedding anniversary, I have been out in the mission fields of the world, fulfilling the call God has placed on my life. Theresa has been very supportive; she knows the ministry of the Gospel takes precedence over everything in our lives – we are slaves to the Master.

Every time I had to leave my children for the mission fields when they were younger, my eyes would fill with tears as I looked back at their little faces, tears streaming down their cheeks, arms outstretched, begging Daddy to come back and stay with them instead of getting on the airplane or the bus or in the car.

Theresa tells me that when the boys, David and Mark, were younger, they were like any young boys, rambunctious and loud. When they got quiet, Theresa knew it was time to find out what they were up to because with boys, quiet means trouble.

But many times, as Theresa would look through the house to find out what mischief the boys were up to, she would look all over and not find them anywhere, until she heard sobs emanating from my closet.

She would open the doors, and little David and Mark would be clutching my clothes, smelling them and bawling for their Daddy.

I spent as much time as I could at home, and I treasure every second I ever spent with my family – next to Jesus Christ, they're simply the most important thing in my life.

Though we didn't know it at the time, when Mark was in the fourth or fifth grade, some of his peers at school had introduced him to drugs. (Parents who are reading this, take this to heart: if you think your child is too young to be tempted with drugs, think again! The devil's plan is to get your children as early as possible!)

Theresa and I knew something was wrong with Mark, but we did not know what the specifics were. As we prayed over Mark's life, we just knew there was trouble.

Eventually Mark's teachers began approaching Theresa, saying they were concerned about a downturn in Mark's grades. Mark was a brilliant child. We had him tested and his IQ level was in the genius range.

Schoolwork was a breeze for him and he made excellent grades. At school, he would take tests, and every time the tests were returned they would have "100%" written at the top, sometimes with smiley face stickers from the teachers, who were just as proud of Mark as any parent could be.

But Mark's grades didn't just start to decline. Where our son had once scored 100s effortlessly, he was now scoring zeroes. It didn't make sense that a boy so brilliant could fall so far so fast. As we tried to talk to Mark about his grades, he was evasive and we could not get him to divulge what was wrong.

Theresa and I launched into a tremendous bout of prayer. We prayed every day and every night.

One day, Theresa was on her knees in Mark's room, praying by his bedside, asking the Lord to reveal what was going on in Mark's life.

God moved upon Theresa to look on the top shelf of Mark's closet. Up on the shelf, Mark had a metal canister where he kept tennis balls. Theresa got up from her knees and emptied the tennis balls out of the canister, and out came a vial of pills.

She immediately knew what it was God was trying to tell us about Mark. He was involved in drugs.

It was at first nearly impossible to believe. We were ministering overseas in some of the greatest crusades the world had ever seen. Thousands upon thousands of people all over the world were giving their lives to Jesus on a regular basis, and many more were giving up drugs as the Holy Spirit moved upon them, but our own son had fallen into the devil's trap while God was using us to free so many others from it.

On top of that, Mark was so young. It was hard to believe a child so young could have already fallen into the trap of drugs.

I was away ministering, so Theresa confronted the boy, then flushed Mark's pills down the toilet.

As most boys do who are caught with something they know is wrong, Mark made up a story. He told Mama that he was keeping the pills for a friend, because he didn't want the friend to get caught with them and get into trouble. But Theresa knew better. God had been showing her something was wrong, and now He had shown her what it was.

Theresa ministered to Mark and when I came home, I ministered to him as well. We asked Mark why he had started to take the drugs, when he knew they were wrong.

His answer was simple, and a clear outline of the devil's plan to entrap children – "The other kids are doing it. It feels good."

We had raised our son in a Christian, praying, Bible-reading home; a home in which two other children were raised and did not get mixed up in drugs and alcohol. This should serve as a stark warning to Christian parents everywhere – sometimes, even despite the best parenting efforts, you can't control what your children will do. Your best efforts cannot control their lives for them; they will make their own decisions in life, and sometimes they make tragically wrong decisions.

Every day, we had devotional prayer, Bible reading – every day. Our children were reared faithfully in an Assembly of God church pastored by Emil Balliet, with whom we were very close. He shepherded my family and he and I traveled overseas together. He was missions director of the Assemblies of God in Springfield, Missouri.

Though we continually worked with Mark and prayed intensely, he got deeper into drugs for a season. From time to time, Mark would respond, and he would give up the drugs for a while and try to turn his life around; but as the years passed, he got deeper and deeper into the serious drugs, and they got hold of him and took him into bondage.

But Mark was not to be defeated so easily. He knew he was in trouble, and our son came to us and asked for help. Many times, God would deliver Mark, and for a long time, he would be free of the bondage of drugs. Mark checked himself into the Betty Ford clinic for a month, and another time, he went to a Christian recovery center. Many times, after Mark would again fall into trouble, I would pray to God, "Lord, You use me so mightily overseas and in meetings here where You heal so many and You save so many, why is my own son having so much trouble?"

Mark fought valiantly. He would cry and tell us, tears running down his face, "I don't want to do this. You don't understand. I don't want to do it."

We would pray, and Mark would have victory for a season, but inevitably, the drugs would creep back into his life again. It was like a cancer that gnawed away at him – at times in recession and at times coming on full bore.

Mark fought and we fought along with him, tooth and nail. We asked our friends and fellow ministers to pray along with us. Mark had so many people praying for him, but it always seemed that the drugs would come back and drag him back into the miry clay.

In 1993, Mark seemed to have had a breakthrough. He felt as if he had finally won a victory over the drugs. He had enrolled in the Institute of Ministerial Studies at my ministry, and was working toward being ordained to preach the Gospel and share his testimony of God's deliverance after a lifelong struggle with drugs. He was excitedly working full-time in our ministry in the television department. He attended all the crusades with me and he was studying for ministry.

That year, we took the entire family with us to Mission To London, and we had a tremendous time, both in ministry and as a family.

We came home from London and went to Chicago for a ministerial seminar there, where Mark went with us for the seminar. After the seminar, Theresa and I were scheduled to return to London for a meeting, so we left and went to London.

Theresa and I were in bed at 2 a.m. in the morning after the meeting in London. The phone rang beside my head so, groggily, I reached out and picked it up. It was my daughter, Susan, and she was sobbing heavily.

"Dad," Susan sobbed into the phone. "Mark's heart gave out. He's passed away."

Mark who? I wondered. It didn't register with me that Susan could be talking about my son Mark – he was so young, thirty-six, and he had just managed to turn his life around for what seemed to be for good. When it finally hit home that my youngest son had died in the prime of his life, I could feel tears well up within my body. I wanted to cry and cry, but I could not allow myself because I had to tell Theresa, and I knew this would be the most difficult pain she had ever felt. I wanted to be strong for her, to comfort her and help her through this tragedy.

When I told my precious wife what had happened to her son, she cried like I had never seen her cry before. I was heartbroken. I felt helpless. Nothing I could say at that moment would make this pain any easier for her. Nothing I could do would make her feel any better. She and I had lost our son, and nothing would ever change that. It was like a physical piece of my body had been ripped from my chest and had just left an empty, hollow thousand-pound weight there.

I don't think I had ever been as sad in my entire life, but I tried to remain strong for Theresa. I knew if she saw my pain, she would break down even more. So when I was in the shower, with the water up as loud as it would go, I wept before the Lord, trying not to let the sounds of my heartache be heard by Theresa in the other room.

Even today, as I remember the pain of losing my son, I cannot imagine the incredible sacrifice of God, willingly sending His only Son to die for the sins of people, most of whom would never appreciate it and would curse Him for it.

The loss of Mark permeated Theresa's and my entire bodies, we felt actual, physical pain, as our bodies didn't want to believe any more than our minds did that Mark was actually gone.

But even this, the worst of tragedies any parent can face, God was able to use to reach out to people who need His help. A few years later, Theresa felt led of God to minister at a ladies' conference at our annual World Conference we hold every year.

At the ladies' conference, my precious wife tearfully shared the story of Mark, and there wasn't a dry eye in the place – every woman in the building could relate to how much it must have hurt to lose our son. But at the end of the message, Theresa gave the ladies hope – hope that no matter how long you pray for your children (we prayed for years), no matter how hard you fight the devil, and no matter how dismal the situation seems, you can never give up hope.

Mark's tragedy also vividly illustrated a point God has led me to make for more than four decades, exactly as He shared with me in Lima, Ohio – this is not the work of a man, but of the Holy Spirit. Yes, God is in control. Here I learned to share a fundamental lesson with God's people: Satan is not in control of the circumstances of your life. GOD IS IN CONTROL!

# CHRONICLES IN FAITH
## BY ARGEMIRO FIGUEIRO
### (OVERSEAS CRUSADE DIRECTOR FOR MORRIS CERULLO FOR MORE THAN FIFTEEN YEARS, SETTING UP MEETINGS IN BRAZIL, SOUTH AMERICA, CENTRAL AMERICA, MEXICO, SINGAPORE, EUROPE, RUSSIA, POLAND, FROM ONE END OF AFRICA AND INDIA TO ANOTHER.)

Many people do not realize the fruits that have come from the ministry of Morris Cerullo. I am from Brazil, and when I return to the country of my birth, I see a thriving Christian community nearly everywhere I go.

In Belo Horizonte alone, the Assemblies of God have tens of thousands of young people, not to mention the multitudes of adults. Church buildings are everywhere, and where there are no church buildings, new church buildings are under construction. The revival in Brazil is phenomenal.

But what people do not realize is that the evangelists, the pastors and many of the members of those churches were converted to Christ through Morris Cerullo crusades, and many of them were trained during Morris Cerullo Schools of Ministry.

The country is having great benefits today, but the breakthrough was thirty or thirty-five years ago, when Morris Cerullo went and paved the road before them.

All through Central America and South America – not just in Brazil – you find people who are doing the work of the ministry who were converted through the ministry of Morris Cerullo.

It's like a chain that travels through time, like when John the Baptist came to the wilderness, a voice crying in the desert, "repent."

That was a breakthrough. Then a few days later Jesus came. But the real breakthrough in repentance came after four-hundred years when there was no prophet in Israel, then came John the Baptist, breaking through all the dead religious traditions. The Bible says everybody came from everywhere and then Jesus came.

Then when Jesus went through to every town and village, it was a revolution, telling people how to be born again.

It's the same with Morris Cerullo.

For years, the "Christians" in many of these countries were bound up in all kinds of false, dead religious traditions, wrapped up in witchcraft and voodoo.

They were consumed with things that have nothing to do with salvation.

The pastors had never had training. They never went to Bible school or learned the fundamentals of living a life for Christ. Many of them could not even read or write.

But then came Morris Cerullo with nothing but a rude, crude platform. There's no beautiful altar there and things like that – just the anointing, the message.

It revolutionized entire countries where he brought that anointing and message. He just keeps on going to countries and countries and countries, and cities and cities and cities – he seems never to get tired. And it seemed that all the time he's right on time to minister to the needs of whatever area he comes to. As has been said many times in the past, the ministry of Morris Cerullo is a ministry on time.

And he continues until today, that fire, that breakthrough, that spirituality, that power, that anointing, it continues still today.

I am honored to have been able to be a part of the ministry of Morris Cerullo, to have been a part of seeing so many souls added to the Kingdom of God.

# CHRONICLES IN FAITH
## BY LOWELL WARNER
### (CRUSADE TECHNICAL DIRECTOR FOR MORRIS CERULLO)

Morris Cerullo has ministered in some of the most remote places in the world – places where you can't even get running water or electricity. He has preached in some of the most difficult circumstances imaginable.

As technical director, it was my task to find electricity for the meetings, to make sure a platform was built, and that everything was ready to host anywhere from a thousand people to upwards of five-hundred thousand people in a single service.

I always thought I should write a book about my experiences with Brother Cerullo, and I would title it "Lord, are You sure about this?" because it seemed every location presented a new and possibly life-threatening challenge for us.

Many times, when we couldn't get power to a crusade location, we tried anything, including getting permission from the power company to tap into a street pole or from a business to get a source of power.

I remember locations in Africa where I would go to a street vendor and buy a large metal dish pan and knock holes in it and mount light sockets as reflectors to furnish lighting for the meeting.

Power failures were a very common thing. In Korea, we couldn't get enough electricity to even run the public address system, so we ran a battery-operated P.A., and in the middle of everything the lights went out; so I found a man who owned a motorcycle, and he pulled it around and put the headlight on Brother Cerullo for lighting. Brother Cerullo preached the whole crusade service by the light of a motorcycle headlamp.

Power was so hard to come by. There was never enough power, it seemed. Many times when Brother Cerullo would preach hard, the lights would dim, because there wasn't enough power to run both the P.A. and the lights.

Getting a P.A. system to address the huge crowds of hungry people was always a challenge – we even used speakers from a car once because no other materials were available.

I remember once in Indonesia using a huge Russian generator that was ill-suited to our purposes, and every time Brother Cerullo touched the microphone or got close enough, it shocked him – but he kept on preaching.

Once in Brazil, when the lights went out, David Cerullo and I stood on top of a truck and climbed up a power pole where someone had used a piece of wire instead of a fuse; and we managed to get a new piece of wire into the circuit and the lights came back on, and as David and I began to shimmy back down the pole, we realized it was steel – we could have been electrocuted!

I've seen Brother Cerullo face down the military as they pointed .50-caliber machine guns in his face and told him to stop the meetings, but he refused to stop the meetings – he kept right on preaching.

I've seen Brother Cerullo stand in a converted fish market in Brazil in a torrential downpour for eight or nine hours and preach and pray for the sick.

And you never knew what kind of things were waiting for you in your room. One night when we were in Nigeria after a tremendous service, Brother Cerullo came to my room and asked, "Lowell, do bats bite?"

The rooms we were staying in were little more than huts with no running water.

I answered Dr. Cerullo, "Well, it depends on what kind of bat you have."

"I think I've got a bat," he told me.

We got up and went over to his hut, and sure enough, behind a piece of furniture was a huge bat that had gotten in through an opening in the straw roof. I chased the bat around the room, trying to catch it – I'm sure it looked like something out of a slapstick comedy – and Brother Cerullo was encouraging me to "take authority" and get rid of the bat.

We finally got a pail out of the outhouse, placed the pail over the bat, scooted it across the floor and tossed it outside, where it flew away.

Often we would find lizards and all manner of bugs in our rooms, and we just learned to live with them – it was just part of ministering to the nations of the world.

When the full story is finally told in heaven, many people will be amazed at the lengths to which Brother Morris Cerullo has gone throughout the years to reach the nations of the world, never letting any hurdle keep him from fulfilling his vision to see the world reached for Christ.

# CHRONICLES IN FAITH
## BY DET SAYSON
### (GLOBAL SATELLITE NETWORK DIRECTOR, MANILA, PHILIPPINES)

In recent years, many men and women of God have come to our shores, proclaiming that the Philippines will be the launching pad for the Gospel to the nations. Many have spoken and written about this prophetic vision, amazingly using the same words and speaking of the same patterns of God's end-time plans and purposes for the nations, especially in the area that is now called the "10-40 Window." These prophets spoke of an army, an end-time army of God that would march into the "war zone" that is the "10-40 Window," where approximately ninety-seven percent of the unreached people in the world needing to be touched by the power of the Gospel live. "Prophetic seminars" have been held one after the other, stirring the Body of Christ in the Philippines to catch the vision and run with it.

But long before there was any talk about this prophetic vision or any awareness of the nations in the "10-40 Window," Morris Cerullo came to the Philippines with a burden, his heart burning with an intense desire to build God an army that would take the nations for Jesus. He came year after year, his heart full of love, steadfast in his belief that the Philippines with its strategic geographical location, and its people – with their exposure to varied cultures as overseas contract workers and immigrants in various countries of the world, their fluency in the English language and natural ability with languages, their ability to blend in well with other cultures – are a people of destiny, ordained to know the way of Christ and work the works of God, and teach others to do the same – in the harvest fields to the ends of the earth unto the end of time.

311

Morris Cerullo came to build God an army out of the people he found, touching them consistently with revelations and supernatural manifestations, equipping them – reaching out to all, transcending denominational barriers, bringing into fruition and shaping into full bloom the true Body of Christ in our nation.

Thus, when the prophets came to herald the prophetic vision for the Philippines, everything had already been set. Preparations for the battle had been made way ahead. The army had been built strong and is now in full battle gear, standing united, waiting only to be commissioned!

Today, thirteen years after the launching of the first Global Satellite Network training site in Manila, there are more than seventy GSNs all over the country, continuously and consistently training God's Victorious Army. Through these GSNs, the army, which includes believers, pastors and teachers, are trained on a regular basis – in the cities and provinces, even in the hard-to-reach areas over the islands, in the remotest part of the country – partaking of anointing explosions, equipping seminars and School of Ministry training modules through the Victory Miracle Library of Morris Cerullo World Evangelism. At one time or another, roughly ninety percent of all believers and workers have taken part in this training.

It is amazing how God designed everything, using God's servant to prepare in advance God's Victorious Army in the Philippines for such a time as this, for the purposes and plans God had all along, that we might be a people of destiny!

Morris Cerullo first came to the Philippines in 1959. In a crusade at Rizal Park in Manila, more than thirty thousand people attended and witnessed the power of God. Many received salvation and healing, as Morris Cerullo preached and prayed under the powerful anointing of God.

In March of 1970, Morris Cerullo came back to the Philippines and ministered at the Deeper Life Crusade, which was attended by seven-hundred and thirty-five pastors, evangelists and teachers. As in the previous crusade held in 1959, the tremendous power and anointing of God was made manifest in the number of people saved and amazing healings that took place. Rev. Jovie Galaraga, a Baptist pastor and now the editor and publisher of the "National Journal," attended this crusade on the invitation of a friend. He related that he did not witness the actual healings, but his friend who invited him told him about the healing of a woman who had goiter. Pastor Jovie could remember the woman because she sat next to them the previous night he was there. His friend related that as Morris Cerullo prayed for healing, the woman's goiter just popped out of her neck like a cork from a champagne bottle, and she was instantly healed.

With the mandate from the Lord to build God an army, Morris Cerullo returned to the Philippines in May of 1984 to establish the first Morris Cerullo School of Ministry. Seven thousand delegates from almost all denominations and churches including Baptists, Methodists, Catholics, Episcopalians and Anglicans attended the School of Ministry. The manifestation, move and miracles of the glory and power of God – "You will enter into an experience...You will know how to work the works of God. Your life will never be the same again" – were simply amazing.

At that time the Philippines were already undergoing a great political and economic upheaval. The Marcos dictatorship was beginning to take its toll on the nation. Inflation was rising, and poverty, anarchy, violence, mass killings, and mysterious disappearances were fanning the flames of discontent in the hearts of the people. Everybody who had a way and the means wanted to leave the country.

Propelled by a desire to share a fresh revelation from the Lord, Morris Cerullo came back to the Philippines in February 1986 to set up the Second Morris Cerullo School of Ministry. "What Must I Do To Do The Works of God?" – that was the question he wanted to impress upon the hearts of God's people. It was exactly one week before the historic People Power Revolution on February 22, 1986. In a jam-packed crowd at the Araneta Coliseum, Brother Cerullo declared: "Something is going to happen to you, but do not be afraid – Jesus is praying for the Philippines, He is praying for you!" Indeed, the true test of a prophet is that what he says will come to pass. There was no doubt that it was God's time for the Filipino people.

The impact of the ministry is such that there is none like it in the Philippines as of now. The Global Satelite Network has become a special instrument in the hand of the Holy Spirit, and the Victory Miracle Living is the added tool – bringing into fruition and shaping into full bloom – the true Body of Christ in our nation.

Humbly, we can truly say that the glorious vision of God's footprint in heaven revealed to His servant, Morris Cerullo, many, many years ago, is literally covering the entire Philippine archipelago – from Aparri to Jolo. While the teachings are only on the screen and are viewed as a delayed telecast, nevertheless, it amazingly comes out ALIVE and VIBRANT, AND FULL OF THE ANOINTING OF THE HOLY GHOST!

The Global Satelite Network is the only ministry that is able to touch the whole Body of Christ consistently on a continuing basis with REVELATIONS and steadfast SUPERNATURAL MANIFESTATIONS. It is the only Body ministry that reaches out to all islands with the aim of equipping the churches and of fostering unity and harmony among believers of different denominations and persuasions.

# CHRONICLES IN FAITH

## BY CLAIR HUTCHINS
## (CRUSADE DIRECTOR FOR MORRIS CERULLO
## IN THE 1960s)

Morris Cerullo always had imagination, an eye to succeed...and he became one of the greatest successes for the glory of God.

When we get together, we just cry. We had so many experiences together. I used to stand behind him and put my hands on him and pray for him...and weep and cry that God would keep him true. And He has.

Morris never did have a "formula" of faith. It was reality, step-by-step...in faith. It was different. He brought out exactly how to work the steps...the suffering of it...the intensity of it.

He had the ability to speak to almost any audience – no matter what their culture was – and get such a spiritual surge of conviction and repentance; more so than in any other ministry I've ever seen in my life.

Morris is in a very vital place to do a great work in the nations by taking these preachers and bringing them into the first principle of his own success...like the early ministry of Jesus.

Wherever Morris goes, he teaches the pastors how to multiply...fast.

The fruits of the ministry have been the awakening of great sections of the clergy to reach their own people. Spiritually, entire nations have been changed.

Editor's note: Clair Hutchins went on to be with the Lord in 1994. This Chronicle of Faith was taken from an interview Clair Hutchin's gave in 1986.

# CHRONICLES IN FAITH

## BY PATRICIA HULSEY
## (FORMER EXECUTIVE ASSISTANT TO MORRIS CERULLO)

Before I ever came to work at Morris Cerullo World Evangelism, a friend of mine had invited me to attend a Morris Cerullo seminar at the El Cortez convention center before it became the first School of Ministry.

At the time, I didn't know who Morris Cerullo was, but my friend had said good things about his ministry, so I thought I would go. My car had broken down, and I was somewhat lost, so I went all over the place trying to find my way to the center.

Finally, I saw a nice, smartly-dressed couple walking across the street and I stopped them.

"Do you know where the Morris Cerullo meeting is?" I asked the man of the couple.

"Sure," he replied. "Follow me."

So I followed the couple and got to the El Cortez convention center and made it to the large conference room where the meeting was to be held.

When the meeting was about to start, I leaned over to someone and asked, "Do you know which one of these people is Morris Cerullo?"

The lady pointed to a man standing at the center table.

"You've got to be kidding," I said. The lady indicated that she was not kidding.

The man she had pointed out was the man who had said "Follow me" when I asked for directions.

Immediately, I knew this was a humble man.

When I had asked him for directions, he hadn't said, "I'm Morris Cerullo," he simply said, "Follow me."

Morris Cerullo is a completely different minister when he goes overseas.

He's extremely anointed in the United States, but his heart is in reaching the Nationals of the world, and when he goes overseas, that's when the apostolic anointing takes over, and he's in his element.

No matter what direction the ministry has taken through the years, the focus has always been the same: equipping the Nationals to be effective, anointed ministers who can reach the unreached people in their own countries.

Brother Cerullo has always been true to that vision, and his pursuit of that goal has been unwavering throughout the years.

When you see Brother Cerullo ministering to the Nationals, and you see the conviction in his words and his actions, it is then that you truly see where his heart is, where his calling is.

# EPILOGUE: JUST THE BEGINNING

As I finish the writing of this, my life's story, we are just about to start the final year of Mission To All The World – God's call on this ministry to reach the entire world before the end of the year 2000.

The vision is an outgrowth of God's initial call to me in 1962: "Son, Build Me An Army."

As I continue to carry out that call through Mission To All The World, I know one thing for sure – Mission To All The World is the beginning of God's work for me – and for you – in the end times until Jesus returns.

Since the 1950s, wherever I have gone, whether it be to the nations of the world and the most remote location, or whether it be in Chicago, Illinois, right in the center of western civilization, my partners in ministry have always been there with me.

As you have read this book, you have read the exploits of a living God and His ability to move through a simple man, but you also have read of much more...

You have read more than the story of my life, which was dedicated to Christ and the work of the Gospel...

Yes, you have read of much more – you have read of the faithfulness of the widow in Kentucky who faithfully sends what little she can every month to ensure the Gospel is preached to the nations of the world. You have read of the intense battles the National in Nairobi, Kenya, waged as he struggled in intercessory prayer for God to use this ministry to reach his nation. You have read of the faithful prayer and financial support this ministry's partners have given throughout the years.

If partners hadn't been faithful, I never would have been able to go to India to preach to five-hundred thousand people in a single service. If partners hadn't listened to the unction of

319

the Holy Ghost, I would never have been able to preach in Argentina, or Brazil, or Africa or Indonesia, the largest Muslim nation in the world. I never would have been able to distribute millions of copies of evangelistic literature throughout the nation of Israel and to Jews all over the world.

The book you have just read is indeed a story of faithfulness, but it's not just my story – it's YOUR story. When I see the tear-filled eyes of the desperate mother whose deaf daughter has just heard for the first time, I'm seeing the result of your faithfulness – your willingness to send me to the nations of the world.

> *"For whosoever shall call upon the Name of the Lord shall be saved. How then shall they call on him in whom they have not believed? and how shall they believe in him of whom they have not heard? and how shall they hear without a preacher? And how shall they preach, except they be sent?" (Romans 10:13-15)*

You have sent me – through the years – so that millions upon millions could hear, receive, believe and call upon the Name of the Lord.

Only heaven will truly tell of the results that have sprung from the faithfulness of this ministry's partners. Untold millions – even billions – of these souls will rejoice with us as we finally see the true impact of this ministry on the nations of the world as soldiers who have been trained, train others and they others, and they still others. (Yes, there are more than one million Nationals raised up, trained and equipped – truly more than a billion souls have heard of our Savior.) Truly, together we are building God an army, and the army has gotten so large that we can no longer count its strength.

But whoever might think Mission To All The World – our most ambitious calling yet – is the end has another think coming. God commanded us to be faithful until Jesus returns, and only bigger things are ahead of us – you and me.

Who knows what God will call us to do after Mission To All The World? I know one thing: it will be big; it will be ambitious; and most likely, it will seem impossible in the flesh.

But God will never call us to do something that He won't equip us to accomplish. Through your faithfulness and mine, we will continue building this army until Jesus returns.

If you aren't already a partner in this world-changing ministry of Christ, call or write my office in San Diego to find out how you can impact the world.

And until the return of Jesus, let's follow the last advice the Bible gives us on how to pray: *"He which testifieth these things saith, Surely I come quickly. Amen. Even so, come, Lord Jesus"* (Revelation 22:20).